Inimitable Style
George Style

Trooper ~ Man of Letters ~ Lowveld Pioneer

Edited & Compiled by

Alan Stock   John Berry

TSL Publications

The Great War in Africa Association

First published by the British South Africa Police Regimental Association (United Kingdom Branch) 2010

Published in Great Britain in 2024

By Great War in Africa Association, TSL Publications, Rickmansworth

ISBN: 978-1-915660-85-5

Copyright unless otherwise stated, to the United Kingdom Branch of the British South Africa Police Regimental Association (United Kingdom Branch)

All rights reserved. No part of this publication may be reproduced, stored in a retrieval system or transmitted in any form by any means, electronic, mechanical, photocopying, recording or otherwise, except brief extracts for the purpose of review, without written permission of the publisher and copyright holders.

Acknowledgement and thanks go to:

National Archives of Zimbabwe

The Outpost Magazine of the British South Africa Police

Cover Design: Alan Toms (7391)

The History Section Committee, United Kingdom Branch. Regimental Association, (Chairman Alan Toms)

Illustrated Life Rhodesia

Dr Colin Saunders

History Society of Zimbabwe

Alan Stock (6063) was Editor of The Outpost 1966 to 1984

Designed and typeset by John Berry

Apology is made for standard of some photographs. This is caused by scanning from old magazines with poor paper quality.

Contents

Map of Southern Rhodesia	5
Detail Map of Fort Victoria-Bikita Districts	6
Foreword	7
Tribute to Alan Stock	11
PART ONE: Early Life, by George Style	
1925 and all that...	14
Reminiscences of Fort Victoria	30
Reminiscences of Bikita	45
Later Life	
Biography, by Colin Saunders	68
Retirement Years – Farm Guard	88
George Rides Shotgun – at 73	92
PART TWO: Bundu Jottings, by George Style	
Hunting Tales	98
Leopard Hunt	102
Personalities	105
Cape Hunting Dogs	108
A Lesson to All Concerned	114
… Camouflage	118
PART THREE: General Interest Stories, by George Style	
The Crawl	122
Good or Bad? The Story of Scotty Smith	127
Lundi River Rescues	134
I shall never forget those Pointed Shoes	139
The Charge of the Light Brigade	142
When Rhodesia Abandoned the Gold Standard	146
Barnard, the Elephant Poacher	152
A Stolen Person	157
Night Hunt	160
Nda Rashika Torch?	163
When the Lion Walks	167
Tagati?	171

The Marauding Leopards of Bikita   174
Vermin Eradicator Extraordinary   179

PART FOUR: Great Characters of the Lowveld, by George Style
Peter Forrestall   200
Thomas Whitfield-James   205
Thomas Murray MacDougall   216

List of Photographs
Alan Stock
George Style on Buster
Annual Musketry
'Lithium Lodge'
Troopers MacMullen and Style
Bikita Station staff 1938; Morris's quarters; P. Power
Bikita Scenes
'Hunter's Lodge'
George Style, Farm Guard
George Rides Shotgun
Leopard
Victor Rumford-Kennerley
Cape Hunting Dogs
Waterbuck
Lundi River
Inspection by Prince of Wales
Gravel Mining
Zhulamiti ... Taller-than-Trees
L/Corporal Pompey
Yank Allen's Grave
Peter Forrestall
Police Camp, Chibi
Whitfield-James group of photographs
MacDougall group of photographs

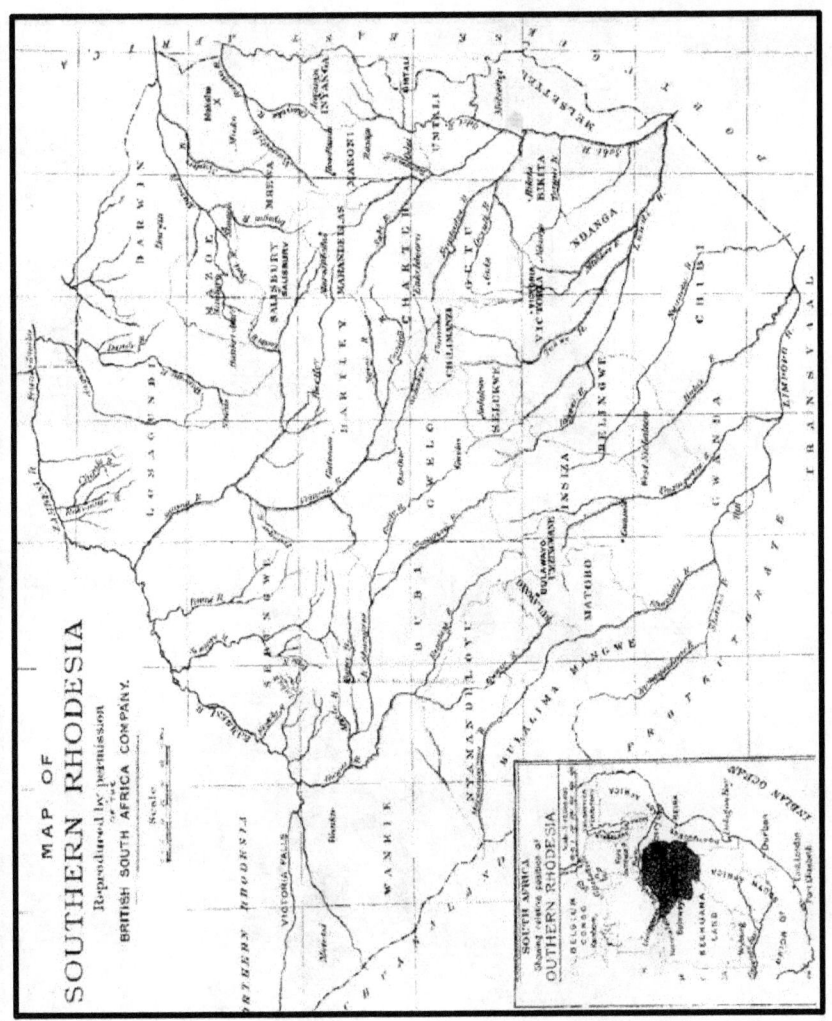

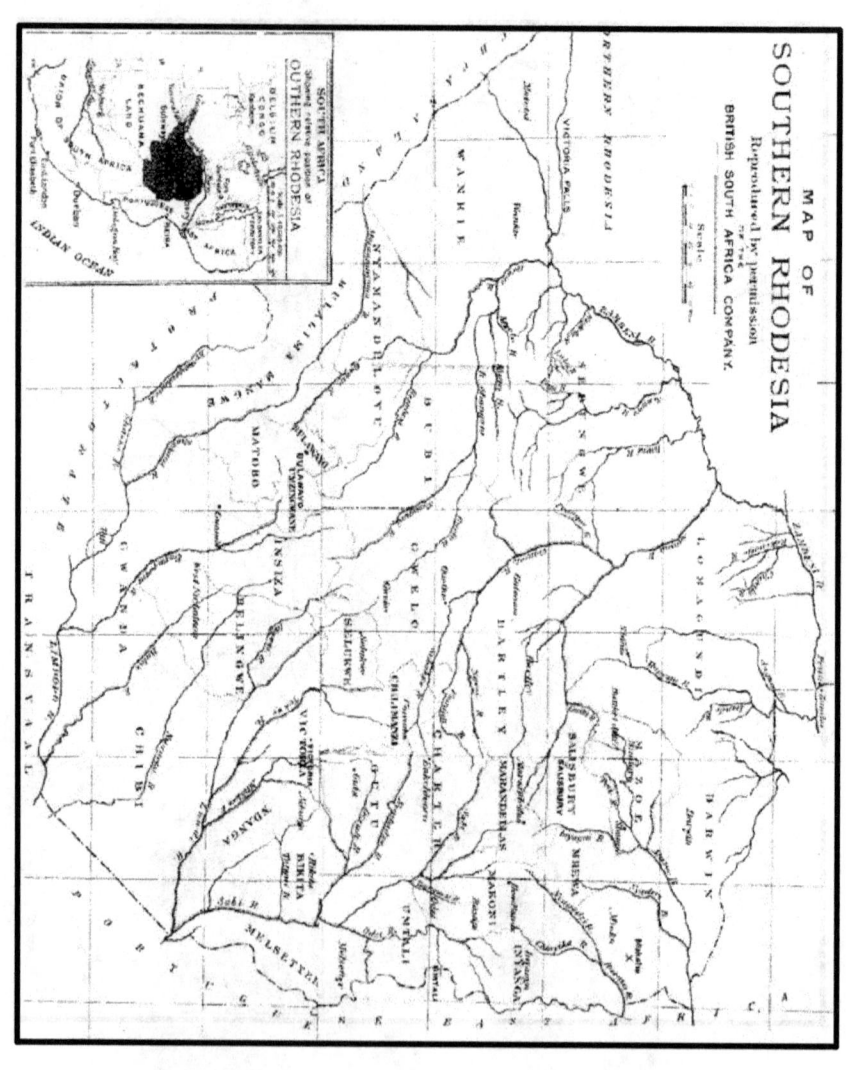

FOREWORD

Dear George,
You can assure Ned Sherlock that I have removed the paper from the typewriter, penned the salutation and am about to pay tribute to Nimrod the Hunter, dogged pursuer of old police colleagues throughout the world, seeker out of forgotten legend, tireless chaser of Lowveld history, man of Inimitable Style...and game for almost anything!
  Rest now,
  Alan

George Style was certainly a man of letters. I have several files full of them. So too, says his GP, Dr Colin Saunders, were there boxes of George's notes and memoirs at Buffalo Range, boxes Colin dredged for the comprehensive and excellent biography he wrote. Strangely, there is hardly a mention of George's formal education. But apart from the narrative talent evident in the many articles republished here which range from turn-of-the-century history to 'modern' emergencies such as flooded rivers, he will be remembered as a time-generous correspondent who constantly supplied *The Outpost* with news of often forgotten ancient troopers and herded them back into the circle of old friends.

A fiction carefully preserved at *The Outpost* office was that *The Chronicler* of the monthly 'Old Comrades' column was none other than the Editor. This sort of ploy allowed the 'two' staff members to have a go at each other should the occasion arise. However, it seemed that the Editor had not signed George up as a contributor in 1962 when *The Chronicler* reintroduced readers to an old hand with the following:

> 'With so much interest throughout the world centring on the possibilities inherent in a new look at land use in Africa, it is good to be able to record that one of our own Old Comrades is in the van of the new movement. I refer to game farming. Authorities overseas have been quoted recently as saying that the whole outlook of African governments towards their wild life was 'too sentimental.' That the natural resources of Africa were being squandered by preserving game in parks, and by handing over land over which game had formerly roamed to cattle which were unsuited by their heredity to make the best use of it. That indigenous game, if properly

cultivated and harvested on the land which had been theirs from time immemorial, would produce a far higher yield of high protein content food than even the best-suited cattle could ever provide.

Well, I'm no farmer, but what they are saying does seem to make sense. Though it should be obvious to any of us that the difficulties involved are tremendous. A United Nations F.A.O. Report speaks of 'mobile abattoirs' for game meat processing and problems concerned with the 'capturing, processing and marketing of hippopotamuses in swampy country.'

A bit high-flown, you may think. But turn to page 1 of the Annual Report for 1960 of the Rhodesian Department of Wild Life Conservation and read there of the permits granted to Messrs Henderson and Sons to crop game on Manyoli and Doddieburn Ranches and read of the 370 impala and 129 zebra, the 25 wildebeeste and many other types of game culled on these ranches during 1960.

Says the report: 'Every confidence is felt in the potential of this type of ranching and numerous enquiries have been received from other land-holders who are interested in the utilisation of this important natural resource. Before this can be achieved on a national scale, however, it is obvious that much research will have to be conducted in regard to not only the scientific culling of animal populations, but also the wider ramifications of economies and marketing.'

Which brings me to the Old Comrades angle. Mr George Style (2696) of Buffalo Range is one of those who took out a permit for game farming during 1961. He was successful in cropping the full 200 impala allotted for the year and in 1962 was granted a permit to crop no less than 800 impala, plus numbers of other game.

As should be obvious from the Wild Life Report and from the observations of the United Nations F.A.O. Committee, this is only a beginning. The implications are tremendous. Under proper control vast regions of S. Rhodesia may become more fruitful than they have ever been before.

And, as I have said before, it is good to see that there, amongst those in the forefront, is an ex-member of the BSA Police.

In June 1962 'Those Pointed Shoes' by George Style appeared in *The Outpost* but it was not until late 1965 that Nimrod's 'Bundu Jottings' emerged from the undergrowth – perhaps indicating that the Hunter was on target with the initial problems of game cropping and had found time for reflection. The blame for revealing Nimrod's identity was never quite allocated but in the March 1965 magazine George had reported 'A Stolen Person' – the most unusual 'kidnapping' in the last century of an orphan who was to become Lance Corporal Pompey with whom George had served at Bikita forty years earlier.

Various other stories by George followed. Then in a November 1965 report by The Chronicler on a Triangle Reunion Dinner it was revealed that George – 'a recent contributor to *The Outpost* of some interesting articles on wild life and life in the Force, has now achieved a new distinction. He is a TV star, having recently appeared in a television feature on game ranching. His Game Section on Buffalo Range is his pride and joy and we know that he would be only too pleased to show visiting Old Comrades his game.'

Many other articles flowed from his pen, making him one of the most prolific BSA Police authors, on a par with, if not surpassing, (1437) Eben Mocke. These not alone dealt with police matters, but also hunting, personalities, wild life matters and, outstandingly, a series on 'Great Characters of the Lowveld', which would be of immense interest to many.

I had the privilege of knowing George Style and of corresponding extensively with him. He was always courteous and anxious to be of assistance, particularly if it involved another Old Comrade. His work to bring (2501) W.E. Poles, MC and Bar, into the author's fold for an account of his adventures in Burma during World War II, is a case in point. Acting on his advice I did write to Eustace Poles, both to introduce myself and, hopefully, have him write an article for *The Outpost* on the exploits of himself and his unit in Burma, unfortunately without success. It is worthwhile quoting part of George's letter, which also throws light on the origin of his use of 'Nimrod' as his nom-deplume.

There are some 29 articles in this book, written over many years, on many topics. So, in what order to publish them here? It was decided the best way was to divide them into four parts by more or less subject matter, although inevitably there was some over-lapping. Therefore Part One covers George's Life, written by George himself and by Colin Saunders, and which also contains many police stories. Part Two consists of the 'Bundu Jottings' series. Hunting, wild-life and general interest stories are in Part Three and, finally, 'Great Characters of the Lowveld' in Part Four. Many photographs and illustrations are included.

I hope the reader takes as much pleasure in reading them as I did in first publishing them.

Alan Stock

June 2010

P.O. BUFFALO RANGE.

26th, February, 1970.

My dear Alan,

        Many thanks for your long and interesting letter of the 21st, received last night, and for the enclosures. I appreciate your effort in writing, knowing how busy you are, and for this reason I usually suggest that you do not bother to acknowledge anything from me. I will now answer your queries.

        I am sure that Bill Poles's adventures in Burma would make most interesting reading, and I think that a request from the Editor himself would have more chance of bearing fruit than a letter from me. The story of Col. Peacock's and Bill Poles' valiant efforts is told in "THE LIFE OF A JUNGLE WALLAH" by G. Peacock (Mrs. Peacock.) They did an amazing job, with a handful of British Officers and the Karen levies they trained. I would be very pleased to lend you the book.

        It was Peacock who put me wise to the poem "Nimrod" (author unknown), and which poem he admired so much, and a copy of which he sent me after spending a spell of nine days here after the war, trying to shoot an impala with a bow and arrow. I wish you could find out who wrote Nimrod. It was not Kipling, and I fancy it was a Canadian. I feel somewhat unworthy of the nom-de-plume I have been using when I see Mrs. Peacock dedicates her book to the "Memory of my husband, Lt.-Col. E.H. Peacock, D.S.O., M.C., Old Nimrod and inciter of this book etc.,"

TRIBUTE TO ALAN PETER STOCK (6063)

Alan was born on 4 June 1937 in Bristol and at one time was accepted for training in the RAF and did some flying on Vampires.

He served in the BSA Police from 1959 to 1984, at first in the Duty Uniform Branch. He became Editor of *The Outpost*, the Police magazine, in 1966 and served as such until he retired in 1984. He must have been the longest-serving Editor and had an unrivalled knowledge of the magazine. I have noticed in the editorial pages of *The Outpost* how he progressed from Staff Section Officer to Staff Chief Inspector over the years. Although in a 'staff' appointment, Alan volunteered for call-ups in PATU, the Police Anti-Terrorist Unit during the Rhodesian bushwar years.

I was very saddened to hear of his death which occurred on 20 June 2010 at Eastbourne in England, after being ill for some time.

I knew Alan quite well in the early sixties when we were both in the BSA Police in the then Salisbury, Southern Rhodesia. I left the Police in 1966 and our paths diverged considerably, both work-wise and country-wise and we were not in touch again until 2007. I was in Ireland and he in England. A shared interest in the history of the Force resulted in him giving me an original typescript of Trooper John Hoddinott's *Zambesi Patrol* diary of 1928 with a view to my typesetting it into a booklet. This eventuated and was published by the United Kingdom Branch of the Regimental Association.

Alan had brought a great deal of written material with him when he returned to England and, working together, we turned this into a total of nine books in the 'Books of the BSAP' series. He was an excellent editor and gave me much information on the finer points of editing and typesetting. These books also raised an appreciable amount of money for Association funds.

This book, *Inimitable Style, the life and stories of Trooper George Style*, was just finished when Alan passed away, and it is fitting that this tribute should be published in this book. Alan, who knew George Style well and called him Inimitable Style, particularly wished the book to bear this name.

As a mark of appreciation for his work on behalf of the BSA Police, Alan was made a Life Member of the Regimental Association, United Kingdom Branch, in 2010.

John Berry
June 2010

Alan (front) in his PATU role

Trooper George Style on Buster

PART ONE

Early Life, as written by George Style
1925 and All That...
Reminiscences of Fort Victoria
Reminiscences of Bikita

Later Life:
Extract from Colin Saunders' biography in *Heritage of Zimbabwe* Journal No. 21, 2002
Farm Guard. *Farmers at War* (Modern Farmer Publications 1979) Trevor Grundy and Bernard Miller
George Rides Shotgun at 73. *Illustrated Life Rhodesia*, Tony Coetzee

1925 and ALL THAT

George Style's previously unpublished account of his early life

On leaving school in 1920, it was my ambition to follow in the Old Man's footsteps and join the army. Not to start at the bottom as he had done when enlisting at the age of 19 in the 17th Lancers, the famous 'Death or Glory Boys', whose famous charge at Balaclava was immortalised by Tennyson, but to go to Sandhurst and start at the top.

The Old Man was justly proud of his Regiment and its feat at Balaclava on 25 October 1854. It will be memorable in all English history as the famous charge of the Light Brigade. Owing to some fatal misconception of the meaning of an order from the Commander-in-Chief, Lord Raglan, to Lord Lucan, the Light Brigade charged what has been rightly described as the Russian army in position. Long, painful and hopeless were the disputes about this fatal order, but all Europe, all the world, rang with wonder and admiration of the futile and splendid charge.

'Some 700 horsemen had charged down the valley, and 195 returned. The 17th Lancers was reduced to 37 troopers, the 13th Light Dragoons could muster only two officers and eight mounted men; 500 horses had been killed.' Lord Cardigan in the lead was completely fearless and unhurried. As well as the two regiments mentioned, the 4th Light Dragoons and the main body of the 8th Hussars, with the 11th, took part in the charge. Lord Lucan refused to sacrifice the Heavy Brigade which was in the rear.

My father had come out to South Africa for the Zulu War in 1879 as a young Corporal, and his regiment went into action for the first time since their famous charge 'into the valley of death', when at Ulundi, Colonel Drury Lowe received the order from Lord Chelmsford, 'Go at them!' and the 17th charged and cut up the remnants of the 20,000 force of impis which had gathered for battle.

This virtually ends the war, and the might of the Zulu nation was broken. The outline of the square where the troops had been drawn up at Ulundi prior to this charge was clearly marked by thick windrows formed by over 35,000 expended cartridges. There was no accurate count of the dead which must have run into many thousands, but over 1,000 Zulu bodies lay in the path of the mounted pursuit.

I had often heard the Old Man talk of Drury Lowe, and many were the tales he told of regimental life, such as the occasion when a trooper was decapitated as his charger bolted for the stables and passed under a small arch, which arch proved to be too low for the trooper's comfort. On another occasion, he had witnessed at Aldershot, a trooper drawing his sword and stabbing his charger to death rather than hand him over to another when ordered to do so, which only goes to show that the oft repeated question put to many of us when being inspected by the Commissioner, Colonel Essex Capell, 'Do you love your horse?' was not so foolish after all.

At the close of the Zulu war, my father seconded to the Cape Mounted Riflemen, being advised that promotion would be quicker, and by the time I had left school he had been retired with the rank of full colonel on a miserably small pension. We were a large family and had grown up in a barrack converted into a house situated at the top of the cantonments, and the military atmosphere had left its mark on me. How well I remember the six trumpeters lining up immediately below our house to sound their calls, from 'Reveille' till 'Lights Out' and is there any call more beautiful than 'Water your horses and give them some corn' sounded on the trumpet? From our back yard as a boy, I daily watched the recruits being taught to ride on the open veld, and never will I forget the late afternoon when, at the age of four, I had wandered out into the veld alone, and suddenly found myself surrounded by 400 galloping chargers, racing from grazing for their evening feed, with some mounted troopers in the rear. Luckily I stood frozen to the ground with fear, as the horses thundered past me, those in whose line of advance I stood moving to the left and right as they reached me. It was many years before I wandered alone again outside the garden fence.

The Act of Union was passed in 1910, and two years later the famous regiment was disbanded as a result. The newly formed South African Mounted Rifles had no tradition behind it, and I had no wish to enlist in this force. The Old Man informed me that, for financial reasons, Sandhurst was out of the question and one morning in 1920 he took me by the scruff of the neck and presented me to the manager of The Standard Bank where I was to spend the next four and a half most miserable and unhappy years of my life.

By 1923 I felt that I could take no more and begged my father to let me join the Rhodesian Police by which name the force was known down south, and where it had a very fine name, but to no avail. A letter I was to find after his death, written to him in 1923 by his greatest friend, Major-General 'Tim' Lukin who commanded the South African troops in the 1st World War, probably had a lot to do with it. Short and to the point, the General wrote:

> Dear............
> I would not advise you to put your son into the Rhodesian Police, it is a small force, promotion is slow, and what is more, you and I both know what life on an outstation is.
> Yours sincerely
> H.T. Lukin.

I was a hopeless Bank Clerk, and hated being shut up all day inside four walls. Thus one day I applied for the job of chauffeur for the Bank's T-Model Ford. This at least allowed me to do two fortnightly trips into the country to Keiskama Hoek and Macleantown accompanied by a senior clerk who did the counter work while I operated in the rear. In addition to these duties, I fetched the manager to and from work daily, when not visiting one of the agencies. He was a jovial Scot called Brown, and I will never forget the morning when, in turning the car in narrow Maclean Street in order to pick him up where he was standing on the steps of the bank, I crashed into an electric light standard and crumpled the offside front mudguard. Brown never turned a hair, but very quietly said, 'You had better take the car to a garage and get that straightened out!' This I did later, after first pulling the mudguard off the tyre and driving him home. The incident caused me to have the greatest respect for Brown. I had greatly feared losing my chauffeur's job. He was later to allow me to keep the car at home instead of in a town garage, and this was extremely helpful, not that the car was ever misused by me, but it saved walking to work and to the garage to pick it up. Another big advantage of my chauffeur's job was that as my girl friend's home, the Methodist Manse, was on the route to Brown's home, I was able to see her daily for three years at lunch time and after work in the afternoon. All went well for some time, with the car being garaged nightly in part of an old fort in our yard, which fort had been used in the Kaffir wars in the middle of the last century.

Unfortunately for me, there was no door to this portion of the fort which had previously housed our carriage and dog-cart. Now some time later Brown was pensioned and a new manager took over. His son was a ledger-clerk on our staff, and incidentally a first class rugger player who represented the Border in Currie Cup matches. Nightly I would hear the car starting up, and off would go 'Tick' Hinds to collect his girl friend from the High School just below us.

In the Bank, we were certainly overworked and underpaid, starting on a salary of £10 per month. In my fifth year, I was drawing £16.13.4d. Very often we worked till after dark, and on balance days often till after midnight.

On the 18 February 1925, my Father died, and having reached the age of 21 I immediately applied for enlistment in the BSA Police.

A few weeks later, a letter arrived from Staff-Captain A.V. Adams to say that, although overheight and underweight, I would be accepted for the Mounted Branch, the elite of the corps, subject to passing the medical and dental tests. The letter was timely for the very next morning while poring over my ledger, with the letter secure in my pocket, the Manager's Confidential Secretary pressed her voluminous bust against my shoulder – a habit of hers – and informed me that the Manager wished to see me. Nervously entering his office, the following conversation ensued, 'Good morning, Nimrod, you made a bit of a blue yesterday!' 'I'm sorry, Sir. What was that.' 'Well, you gave Baker & Co. £800 in excess of their overdraft. Actually it does not mean a thing as their overdraft facilities are for £36,000, but I must teach you a lesson, and am reducing you to Cash Books!' At the speed with which we had to post our ledgers so as to hold no one up, this mistake could have happened to any clerk, but with profuse apologies I left the office. I had always known that there was no future in the Bank for me, and next day I handed in my month's notice in writing. Immediately this was known, my Bank colleagues gathered round to tell me that I should reconsider the matter as I would be giving up a very good pension to go to a wild and woolly land! As if, spending most of my life confined within four walls, I would have lived to enjoy a pension anyway!

A few days later young Charles Rayner, three years my junior, walked into the Bank to make a deposit for a milling company. It was providential that I had been reduced to Cash Books, because my desk was immediately behind No. 1 teller and I distinctly heard Charles say, 'Well, Mr Webber, you will not be seeing me for much longer. I have been accepted by the Rhodesian Police and will be leaving for Rhodesia shortly.' In great excitement I nipped round to the public side of the counter, told Charles of my acceptance, and we decided to leave for Salisbury on 1 May 1925. Before leaving we were given a lecture one evening by Charles' father, Major Rayner, ex-Cape Mounted Police, on the dangers of war, wine and women, with particular reference to the last two, advice which we were both in the course of time to regret not taking.

On the afternoon of 1 May, we entrained in King William's Town for our journey to Salisbury, travelling via Stormberg and De Aar junctions to Kimberley. Here we arrived on a Saturday and broke our journey having been invited to spend the weekend with the Vigne family, he being a well-known auctioneer in the town.

I will always remember this visit as it was my first introduction to the mass slaughter of game. On the Sunday afternoon we were driven out to Vigne's brother's farm, eight miles out, for a bird shoot. The owner of the farm was very incensed because a stranger had asked if he could shoot on the farm the previous weekend. Vigne reluctantly consented, thinking that the man would shoot one or two of his springbok and depart. He did not report to the homestead on arrival on the Saturday, but on the Sunday afternoon he arrived, with a friend, and asked if he might borrow a buckboard to cart their kill to the Kimberley market. On being asked how many he had shot, the unabashed reply was, 'Sixty-four, Mr Vigne!' Apparently, the two hunters had got the springbok up against fences and murdered them. Needless to say, Vigne marketed them himself and no strangers shot on the farm again.

That night we entrained again, and after a long, hot and dusty trip through Bechuanaland (now Botswana), where at every siding hordes of Africans were selling karosses and wooden curios etc., we crossed the border at Plumtree and arrived in Salisbury the following morning to find, most unexpectedly, an officer in the person of Captain 'Cissy' Ross to meet us. We soon mounted the buckboard with its lively team of mules driven by the Coloured driver, William, and proceeded to the Depot.

We arrived there at lunch time to be met outside the mess by the cheerful and very popular Orderly Corporal for the day, Jack Betts, who took us in to lunch. Jack was on his annual posting back to Depot for the rugger season, but he invariably saw little rugger, being crocked half-way through the season, not from rugger but from breaking in remounts, and how well I remember seeing R.H. Long Tom throw Jack one morning, then look round to see where he was lying – a vicious habit of his – then lashing out at Jack and missing his chin by inches. Eventually he did land Jack in hospital and Sergeant Hampton decided that the only thing to do with this incorrigible remount was to inspan him in the buckboard with the mules. The first time this was done Long Tom bolted, taking everything with him, and finishing up in a barbed wire fence so cut to pieces that he had to be destroyed.

On the morning after our arrival, while Charles was being x-rayed for an old hip injury received at school while skylarking in a dormitory, I was summoned to appear before the Staff Officer, Captain A.V. Adams, who greeted me with the words, 'Good morning, Nimrod! Of course you know the pay has been reduced.' 'Yes, Sir,' I replied, 'but I heard this only after my arrival here.' To this day I can see the grin on Captain Adams' face as he looked up and said, 'As a matter of fact, Nimrod, you are alright. You signed on a month ago so are on the old rates of pay.'

How pleased I was that I had not delayed my resignation from the Bank. Charles and I, the latest to attest, were the envy of the rest of the squad, as we drew £16.13.4d monthly, to their £12.10.0d., And that extra £4.3.4d was a lot of money in those days. Mrs Tawse-Jolly, the MP for Umtali was said to be the nigger in the wood pile.

She was said to have raised the question of Police pay in the House, and persuaded the rest of the Members that it was too high. Her popularity in Police circles can be imagined. However, in all fairness, I must say that I can find no reference to this in the Hansards of the day, and Tawse-Jolly was himself an ex-Policeman.

The other members of our squad were Shorty Crossland, a father to the rest of us, who had fought with the French against the Riffs in North Africa, and won a Croix-de-Guerre; Peter Phelps, B.Sc., a teacher from Natal; Webb, whose charming sister was Private Secretary to Sir Charles Coghlan; the baby-faced Lucan-Bull, who had come up with Webb from Natal; 'Buller' Meyer who hailed from East London, returning there after three years to become a wealthy garage owner and pineapple farmer; 'Brusher' Bond of 8 Renfrew Road, Eastlea, Salisbury, who was captured at Crete and as he puts it in a letter to me, 'thus ending a most promising military career!'; 'Morphy' Morris, Brusher's half-section was also a member of our squad.

Our Riding Instructor was an Irishman, Corporal George Sewell, who together with Sergeant 'Hampie' Hampton, wore a Rough Rider's badge. George selected for himself a beautiful remount, which he named Kildare after his home county. As an instance of the love a horse can develop for his master an extraordinary incident happened in Depot one day. George had been away on a six weeks Column, showing the flag, but had had to leave Kildare owing to a leg injury. When he returned, George immediately walked towards the stables to see his horse. As he approached, and when still out of view of the door, Kildare recognised his footsteps, neighed loudly, and snapping his rein, ran through the stable door to meet his much loved master. George took a lot of trouble training Kildare, and eventually he became quite famous for jumping through a hoop of fire at the Annual Shows.

'Brusher' Bond had an annoying habit of calling the South African members of our squad 'a bunch of bloody Colonials'. On occasions, I would have liked to have hit him, but he was a big man, and I thought twice about it! Being in the majority, we Colonials should have chucked him into the horse trough! However, one day I did inform him that he would no doubt be marrying in Rhodesia and rearing a 'bunch of Colonials', which is precisely what happened. In those days, 'Brusher' reminded me of Stanley Portal Hyatt, an English transport rider, who wrote *The Old Transport Road*. Hyatt had a great hate of Colonials and Afrikaners, and mentions in his book that if an Englishman in Rhodesia were married and a child was on the way, a wife was sent back to England so that the infant would not be born a Colonial, and if this could not be managed, he at least sent her to Mozambique for the happy event! My friend 'Brusher' called on me recently but has no recollection of the incidents.

Charles Rayner and I shared one of the old two-bed barrack rooms, and soon settled down to Depot life. In Depot, Reveille was sounded at 5 a.m. when personal servants brought us a mug of coffee, and the first parade every day was for riding instruction. Hastily dressing we were saddled up and on parade by 5.30 a.m. Hard as it is to believe, more than one new recruit fell in with his saddle back to front. Initially all the instruction was done in the Riding-school, which consisted of a fenced oblong of ground with thick grass tied to the inside of the fence.

A few days after our arrival in Depot, we were riding round the school one morning under the instruction of Corporal George Sewell, with our lovable RSM Jock Douglas, mounted on his beautiful, high-stepping horse S.O.B., looking on, when in rode the Commissioner, Colonel A. Essex Capell. He rode up to Jock, and in his rather high-pitched voice said, 'Sergeant-Major, which of these recruits is Nimrod?' Jock then rode alongside me and pointed me out to the Commissioner, who then took Jock's place. Said the Colonel, 'So you are Nimrod, are you? Well, when I was in the C.M.R., your father was a Captain, and taught me to ride, and gave me hell. Now I am going to give you hell. Sergeant-Major, give the order 'Cross stirrups – Trot!'

The order was thereupon given, and round the school we bumped. After we had been round two or three times, came the order 'Halt!', and the Commissioner again rode alongside me and asked how my father was, my reply being that he had died three months previously. Colonel Capell expressed his sorrow at hearing this and departed, while I glowed with pride to think that the rest of the squad had heard that my father had taught him to ride. Dear old Jock did not see it this way, and riding over to me offered his apologies and called the Commissioner by a bad name, finishing with the remark, 'And you have just lost your father, too!'

After leaving the Police in 1930, every time I met Jock in Salisbury he would apologise to me over the incident and slate the Colonel.

After we had been in the School a week or two, we were taken out and trained for a mounted escort for the Prince of Wales, who was due in Bulawayo and Salisbury early in the following month of June. We would ride round the Depot between dozens of Askari and African Police, who together with their wives and children yelled, beat tins, shouted and waved, in order to get our horses used to yelling crowds. By the time we trucked our horses to meet the Prince in Bulawayo, we felt ourselves to be fully trained riders and were quite confident.

When the Prince had departed, we continued our training and would be taken out on to the commonage in the early mornings for gallops up to Gun Kopje, presumably now the suburb named Gun Hill, and for trots through gum plantations. Now these trees were very closely planted and on one of the latter exercises, I well remember my left knee hitting a gum tree with the result that in a flash I found myself on the ground on the off-side of my horse. I got no sympathy from George Sewell and soon caught my horse and remounted. What thrilling mornings they were, how fit we were, and what appetites we worked up on these rides.

On our return to Depot, we would shower and change into khaki slacks and tunic, after which we could not get to the dining room fast enough. We would be absolutely ravenous and used to get very angry with some of the recruits who were in the habit of bribing the African waiters to be served first. These waiters were excellent, carrying as many as six or eight plates of eggs and bacon at a time. What a fool I felt when on one occasion in my eagerness to grab a plate before one of the bribers, the waiter dropped the lot with a tremendous clatter! William Over had the contract for the messing, and the food was excellent, the catering being in charge of Steve Robinson and George Chalmers, who both worked for Over, the former running the bar side of the canteen. I think Over, Robinson – who later managed Meikle's Hotel – and Chalmers were all ex-BSA Police.

At the table just inside the door leading into the Mess sat the Corporals, facing the length of the room. One or two of them would be attached to 'B' Troop which policed Salisbury District. Among them I remember Corporals Seward (later to become Commissioner and now retired at the Vumba), Funnell (later a Captain), Durham, Farrell and Murphin. One member of our squad had taken a dislike to one of these, and one lunch hour, when the sweets arrived, this man rolled his plum-pudding into a ball, and standing up, threw it with considerable force at the particular Corporal. He missed him by inches and the pudding hit the wall at the back with a resounding smack. Of course, none of us recruits witnessed the incident, but others did, and next day our comrade was on a charge and two of us, with side-arms drawn, had to march him before the Commandant Depot. Jock Douglas was the Prosecutor and it was difficult to keep a straight face as he described how 'the pudden' narrowly missed the Corporal and hit the wall. The verdict was that the prisoner was confined to barracks for a week.

During the day our training would continue, with the very gentlemanly, meek and mild Sergeant 'Tickey' Brighton, at one time a school master, taking us for foot drill. How we sweated on a hot day on the square in front of the memorial to that outstanding character, Sergeant-Major Blatherwick who was for over twenty years RSM of the BSA Police.

Our Musketry Instructor was Sergeant-Major Walker, while Sergeant Paddy Graham, who is still going strong in Salisbury, instructed other squads. Sergeant Hughes Halls, always immaculately turned out, took us for Law and Police. 'H.H.' is now enjoying much-earned retirement at 44 Argyle Drive, Highlands, Salisbury. One of our most popular instructors was Farrier Sergeant-Major Henry Ashwin, who, wearing a snow-white moustache, taught about the veterinary side of horses. He and Jock Douglas did not get on at all well. Veterinary classes were held after lunch and we would lie on the dry bedding behind the stables and doze, it being an effort after a heavy lunch to keep awake. Often Henry would say to us 'Hi don't give a b- - - - -r for the RSM, laddies' and virtually invited us to mutiny. More than once, however, after such an utterance, he would get a shock as he spotted Jock coming along on his tour of inspection when he would rather nervously exclaim, "Ere 'e comes, lads, sit hup hand pay hattention!' As Jock joined us, Henry would be most deferential and proper in the extreme. They were both lovable characters.

We had arrived in Depot in winter and rugger was in vogue. I had played for my home town – something that had appeared in one of my recommendations – and was well received by the other players, Edward Rowley escorting me to the police 'field' one afternoon a day or two after I had arrived. There was not a blade of grass on our rugger ground, as I will have to call it, and it consisted of hard, red earth. It was often impossible to see the scrum from the touch-line owing to the red dust that was churned up around it, and being one of the forwards, with Jack Betts as hooker, I found that I was on the Monday morning after a Saturday home match, still blowing red dust from my nose and spitting it. Why we forwards did not all contract phthisis, I cannot imagine. The ground was hard too, and it was a treat to play away-matches on the turfed Salisbury Club ground.

One Saturday we motored out to play against a Sinoia team, visiting the Mazoe Citrus Estate and the Sinoia Caves en route. From photographs taken at both places, I can recognise Jack Betts, Bill Boyce, Walters, Jack Collard, Jerry Marshall, L.V. Quinn, Corporal Farrell, 'Chick' Fowler, Peter Phelps, F.A. Allcock, Schultz from Enkeldoorn who later joined the N.R. Police, and Ritton.

Like Jack Betts, I was always put on remount riding, and I well remember the day in June 1926 when I was instructed by Jock Douglas to take out in the afternoon R.H. No. 434. The horse had very recently arrived with a bunch of remounts from de Beers, Kimberley, and was a very lively and intractable animal wearing three socks. I saddled up at about 4.30 p.m. and set off at a walk through the Depot buildings. Eventually I reached the golf course, when, without any warning, up flew the hind legs of No. 434 – yet unnamed – and over his head I flew, landing on the base of my spine. I thought my back had been broken as the pain was intense and I found that I could not get up. I turned and started crawling towards Depot where I shared a room in the Sick Lines behind the stables, with Farrier/Corporal Murphin. By the time I got to the barrack-room it was quite dark. Most recruits were in the canteen and as it so happened I reached Murphin's room without a soul seeing me crawling. I pulled myself up on to my bed and a little later 'Murph' arrived, gave me the use of an empty rifle oil can, and went off to make a report to Jock Douglas.

Presently, old Jock arrived, looking somewhat alarmed, and with his huge frame filling the doorway, he addressed me in his husky voice, as follows, 'Nimrod! Who told you to take out Horse No. 434? Get up now, and I will give you a nice soft job! Go up to the Mess, and take over the duties of Mess Orderly! Just see that all the tables are in order!'

Jock was obviously worried and did not want to believe me when I told him that I could not move, so I reassured him that I would get up as soon as possible and go up to the Mess.

That night I was taken by ambulance to the General Hospital and was x-rayed next day, when it appeared that only bruising had taken place. I spent six happy days recovering and being nursed by two most beautiful girls, both I think, from the Shamva district – Sister Lilian Frith (later to become Mrs Jack Higginson) and Sister Lorna du Preez. They were kindness itself and I was sorry when the day came a week later to be passed fit for duty.

Several of the remounts brought up from the De Beers farm at Kimberley were found to be vicious and intractable, as in the case of Long Tom. I well remember holding the lunging rope in the middle of the riding school one morning while Corporal Sewell was lunging a small pony. This pony had caused a lot of trouble and was now the last on the list for breaking in. Kindness had been tried without effect, and he had a nasty habit of coming for you with jaws open and legs pawing. Suddenly he came straight for me and throwing down the rope I made for the fence, mounting it in the nick of time, the deep sand in the school making the escape difficult. After this incident he was shot. Ex-Sergeant-Major 'Hampie' Hampton, now living in Salisbury, will remember how this vicious animal got him into a corner of the school some time before when, with the pony pawing at him, he narrowly escaped with his life.

We recruits were often put on to breaking-in remounts in the school, and Jock would get a lot of fun out of this. He would assist in holding some intractable animal, in the meantime talking in his husky voice to the recruit thus, 'Now jump on his back, Raynor! He is a nice quiet animal and won't give you any trouble at all!'

Next minute Raynor would be flat on his back in the sand, while the RSM, who had moved away a few yards, would be facing the other way with his shoulders heaving while he had a good old giggle to himself! This was a regular occurrence. Who could blame him, though recruits were sometimes seriously hurt, and we felt we had a right to Extra Duty Pay. Barrett received a compound fracture of his arm, and had to have it re-broken and set eight times before it was satisfactory. We had heard that a fellow called Bam had been thrown onto his head and rendered insane for life.

There was not much social life in Salisbury in 1925, and one event we recruits looked forward to was the weekly Friday social evening arranged for us by dear Matron of the Hospital, Sister Christian. We spent many happy evenings with the nurses who dispensed tea and coffee and cake, before we left. Alas, these evenings were soon to come to an end, with a certain member of our squad getting a little too amorous on the lawn with one of the nurses. Whether the evenings were ever renewed, I do not know, but how we cursed our amorous comrade.

Before leaving home, my mother had asked me to call on a cousin of hers, Mr Tom Law, who lived in Montague Avenue. Shortly after arriving, Charles Rayner and I made our first call, and were lucky to meet his daughter Molly, who later was to marry the late Colonel Rolfe, with her friend, Molly Atherstone, whose father was the Surveyor-General. As a result of meeting these two girls, we received much appreciated hospitality in their homes. To take the latter girl to the weekly dance held at the old Grand Hotel one Saturday night, I had to nip smartly down to the store of Wm. Over and Co. in Manica Road, and buy a dress suit off the peg and on credit.

One afternoon after parade hours I was approaching that famous and extremely well-run institution in Stanley Avenue, Pocket's tearoom, when I saw Molly A. walking towards me. Wishing to return, although inadequately, some of the wonderful hospitality I had received in her home, I invited her in for tea. The tea duly arrived served by an immaculately dressed African waiter, while a very smart and well-dressed woman wandered among the tables supervising operations.

Now I felt obliged to offer my guest something to eat, the cakes, scones and sandwiches etc. being always superb. Probably seeing a look of apprehension on my face she refused, much to my relief. I had exactly sixpence in my pocket, the price of tea in those days being only threepence a cup!

Another gracious home with its beautiful garden I visited on occasions was that of Sir Percy and Lady Fynn, also situated, I think, in Montague Avenue. My mother had known Sir Percy when he was a student at Dale College in King William's Town.

Another old family friend, the lawyer Fred Howe-Ely, was very good to me in Salisbury, and on occasions he and Mrs Ely invited me to dinner on Sundays. Fred was a great supporter of the Police rugger team, and often I heard him egging me on from the touch line. Many years later I was to serve as Dip Supervisor under his brother 'Toots', when he was Native Commissioner at Bikita.

Although Charles and I knelt at our beds nightly, and said our prayers – as we had been brought up to do – we were nevertheless very naughty young men, and despite the good social contacts we had in Salisbury – Charles' uncle, Taberer, was then Superintendent of Natives in the old Native Department – we drank far too much. When the evenings were spent in Depot, a couple of beers in the canteen, while munching chunks of bread and cheese, sufficed, and the only man who came to any harm nightly when in the canteen, was 'Chick' Fowler who played for our rugger team, and was a first class wing. Chick drank rum, and when the Orderly Corporal came round to close the bar at about 1900 hours and Chick walked outside into the cold air, he always dropped unconscious and had to be carried to bed.

We frequently got late passes to go into town on a pub crawl, and it was then that we got into trouble. If we had not obtained a pass and suddenly decided that we would like to go out, we would wait until we estimated Jock Douglas had had two sundowners, and then went to his house which is still standing at the entrance road to the Officers' Mess, and Jock always cheerily obliged. I often think of the story told by old 'H.H.' of his Depot days under the very austere Sergeant-Major Blatherwick. Hughes Halls decided that one night he would like to go into town for a binge, and having no money, confided his wish to Corporal Patten, probably hoping for a loan from him. However, the Corporal, deciding to have his bit of fun, informed H.H. that all he had to do was to go to the house of the RSM and ask for the loan of half-a-crown, as the RSM regularly made loans to the troops. H.H. duly presented himself to Blatherwick and made his request for half-a-crown. Blatherwick apparently saw the funny side of things, despite the shock he must have got, and made the loan, but first made sure of finding out the name of the instigator who, no doubt, received a rocket next day.

Now in 1925, the European population of Salisbury was only 5,000 and to walk into town from Depot one crossed open blocks of ground all the way down to the Palace Bar and Theatre. (The Roman Catholic Cathedral was built that year, on one of these blocks, and I well remember the red bricks which lie behind the façade of stone.) Thus it did not take long to get into town, and on a binge night we often had our first beer at the Palace. Then the bar crawl would start and we would wend our way over to the Empire Bar, a lively spot, situated on the corner diagonally across Second Street from Meikles Hotel where until recently, Kingston's stood.

From the Empire we would wend our way down Manica Road, visiting in turn the Posada, the Castle, the Queen's, and perhaps on into Pioneer Street to the Masonic. In those days, taxis were virtually unheard of, and the rickshas were in vogue, plying their trade. We always hired one and were pulled back to Depot for the sum of about 1/6d at the most. It was not uncommon to see the ricksha boy sitting in the back and the trooper doing the pulling. In the pubs one certainly got to know one's fellowmen and a lot about human nature.

As the evening wore on and the liquor took effect, men told you things that they would never mention in cold blood. We used to say that you never got to know a man until you got drunk with him, and this was borne out by a much decorated Danish friend of mine recently, who told me that during the last war he was appointed a submarine commander at the age of 25 and told to select his crew from a body of men. He did this very satisfactorily by taking them all out on a binge. He was sure he could judge the man who would panic by watching them when they were 'in their cups'.

Writing about rickshas brings to mind an incident we heard of while in Depot. Our Commissioner, the aforementioned Colonel A. Essex Capell, had a really beautiful daughter, and one night one of the troopers – an exceptionally decent and gentlemanly type, and now a retired Colonel – invited her out to a dance. Apparently, much to the Colonel's horror, he found that the method of conveyance was to be a ricksha. Some time later, a lawyer brother of mine wrote home to say that he was taking the same lady to a dance – 'the most beautiful girl in Salisbury', as he put it in his letter. I hope that in this case a taxi was hired. In 1925 Salisbury, being thecCapital, was a town of – we thought – rather snobbish Civil Servants, there being then no industries in the town. With a population of only 5,000, all those of any consequence knew each other. When we took our Mounted Escort down to Bulawayo to meet the Prince of Wales in June, we found the Bulawayo people much friendlier. We thought it was, perhaps, a case of 'no man being a prophet in his own country' with our Escort much more admired in Bulawayo than in our home town.

The African was very primitive 48 years ago, and it was illegal for him – presumably by town by-laws – to walk on the pavements, and nor did he expect to do so. As for entering European shops, this was unheard of until several years after the last war. His dress was primitive in the extreme and a suit was never seen. At the same time, the European farmer of those times virtually lived in khaki shirt and shorts and this dress was accepted in any hotel at all times. Of European crime there was very little owing to the strict immigration laws of those times and, apart from a few alcoholics and a few naughty women, the Europeans behaved themselves, though at times not to the letter. We recruits were not fond of the CID whom we felt spent much of their time watching us during our pub crawls and I have no doubt this was the case and necessary. I remember the night that I was talking to a very attractive bar-maid at the Palace, when I was called aside by some completely strange and middle-aged man and reminded who my father was!

I knew of one Salisbury man who was prosecuted some time later, and he happened to be my lawyer brother, who had served in the R.F.C. in the First War. He had kept up his flying in between wars by taking refresher courses every year at Roberts Heights, now Voortrekkerhoogte, and was mad on flying. By this time, Jock Douglas had retired, and the huge ex-Guardsman 'Tiny' Tantum had taken over as RSM. One afternoon, 'Tiny' was invited by my brother to accompany him on a flip, and spotting three men on the Golf Course, the pilot dived extremely low over them – so low in fact that they sought refuge under a bush, and after the incident, being extremely annoyed, they reported the matter to the Police and a prosecution ensued. The pilot-lawyer who had been a great friend of the three complainants, decided to defend himself, and in the course of the trial the magistrate asked if the complainants were friends of his. Looking sideways at the three, there was some amusement in the Court when he replied, 'Well! They were, Your Worship!'

The accused was discharged, the magistrate deciding that he was sufficiently experienced to know what he was doing. At the time he was the O.C. of our first Air Wing, when it was a part-time show before Squadron-Leader Powell took over and it became a regular Force, and Chairman of the Flying Club in Salisbury.

With crime affecting so few Europeans, we were all very distressed one morning to hear that the father of Trooper Hamilton of 'B' Troop had been murdered the night before on his farm in the district. He was a man of over 80 years of age. His son was a very keen and plucky boxer, and very popular in the Depot. I have no doubt that the accused was brought to justice.

All too soon our training came to an end, and in September 1925 I was drafted to Fort Victoria. I am sure that all those who knew him would like to see a memorial erected in Depot to that lovable character RSM Jock Douglas, who had deserted during the First World War to join his old regiment, The Scots Greys, been extradited from Britain, and brought back to serve a six months sentence in the Guard Room, during which time he planted most of the trees in Depot.

NOTE: For the August, 1974 issue of Outpost, *George Style wrote an article entitled* 'WITH NO REGRETS' *which was practically word for word the same as the first few pages of '1925 and all that...', up to where he and Charles Rayner entrained at King William's Town for Salisbury.*

On this account 'WITH NO REGRETS' is not included in this book.

REMINISCENCES of FORT VICTORIA

It was a beautiful morning in September 1925, when William, the Depot driver, took me down to the station in the buckboard to catch the train for Fort Victoria. I had been in Depot for five months and, having been disappointed earlier at losing a transfer to the Umtali District through hospitalisation, I was thrilled to be leaving for outstation life at last. I felt like a prisoner being let out of jail or a bird released from a cage. I celebrated my freedom before the train was many miles from Salisbury by ordering myself a beer.

A little later I invited a lone female traveller who had been gazing wistfully from the open balcony of the coach to join me. One thing led to another and we were soon chatting gaily at one end of the dining saloon. My companion was perhaps a little on the old side but European ladies were in those days few and far between – it was said that we males outnumbered them ten to one.

At the other end of the car sat a corporal of the BSA Police enjoying a solitary beer and winking good-naturedly when he caught my eye from time to time. He turned out to be Cedric Gibbs, later to rise to sergeant-major at Fort Victoria and much much later to become Wing Commander Gibbs when he escorted some of our airmen to Britain at the beginning of World War II. After the war the popular 'Gibbo' became Town Clerk at Gatooma before moving to Triangle where he eventually became Managing Director and Vice-Chairman of the Company. That wordless introduction on the Salisbury/Fort Victoria train was the beginning of a long friendship and many happy parties shared over the years. It was inevitable that my lady companion on that long ago journey would be recalled on every occasion. In June 1968, at Gibbo's Induction Dinner as President of the Chiredzi Rotary Club, I was fined five shillings by the Rotarian Sergeant-at-Arms, Bobby Stirrup, for 'travelling on the Salisbury/Fort Victoria train in 1925 while wearing '"rose-coloured glasses".'

We changed trains at Gwelo (a minor point which I did not think worth challenging when fined 43 years later) and approached Fort Victoria shortly before 5 p.m. When I spotted the little shanty town my earlier mood of happiness changed to one of deep depression. My first look at the place might well have been improved by 'rose-coloured glasses'. The total European population was only three hundred and it did not take very long to get to know every man, woman and child living there.

Trooper Perkins and a driver met me with buckboard and mules. Minutes after unloading my kit from the train, we arrived at the camp. We pulled up close to a group of men sitting 'sun-downing'. Trooper Richens, who had just taken over the station from Corporal Cazalet, came forward with glass in hand to give me a most hearty welcome. As I was to discover, he was a very efficient policeman who spoke Chikaranga like a native. Unfortunately he had missed the only two promotion examinations held in seven years.

'Richie' then introduced me to his companions. There was the very gentlemanly Farrier Corporal Noakes, shortly to take his discharge and return to England, and his tradesman-mate Saddler 'Waxie' Makins. Corporal 'Johnnie' Johnson was in from Chibi where he was Member-in-Charge. 'Perky', who had greeted me at the railway station, handed down to me the title of most junior recruit and told me he hailed from Cape Town.

After depositing my kit in the barrack room to which I was shown by Perky, I was invited to join the company for a drink and was made to feel at home right away. This atmosphere of friendship and total acceptance was only the beginning. For the next five years and nine days I was one of the happiest men in Rhodesia.

We retired early and the next morning I was allocated my mount – Buster, a quiet bay with a white blaze. No time was wasted on getting to know each other; I was sent out almost immediately on my first patrol.

There was a distinct shortage of policemen in Rhodesia in 1925 and Fort Victoria was no better off than other stations. Because of this a grass fire, reported earlier at a farm some four miles out, had remained uninvestigated. This was my first assignment. Accompanied by Native Constable Mondiwa, I arrived at the farm which belonged to a retired native commissioner, 'Jakata' Williams. As I was tying Buster to a tree just outside the front gate, feeling extremely nervous at the weight of responsibility lying on my shoulders, a very loud and angry female voice greeted me from a front window. 'And about time too!'

This was the signal for a charge by a pack of 14 fully-grown Alsatians. I stood rooted to the spot, expecting to be torn limb from limb at any minute. The hounds were called off before they had inflicted any physical damage although the charge had done nothing for my already shaky morale. (On a subsequent visit to the farm I was not sorry when told that Williams had shot the whole pack after the dogs had killed eight heifers in one fell swoop.) More nervous now than ever, I crept up to the front door which was promptly opened by a large buxom woman who repeated her opening volley. 'Yes, it's about time the police arrived. The fire happened ten days ago!' 'I'm sorry Madam,' I replied meekly. 'I arrived from Salisbury only last night.' Madam thawed, and after a cup of tea I drew my map, completed enquiries and thankfully returned to camp.

On my second day of duty I was sent out to Glyn Tor Farm on the Mashaba road, again about four miles from the station. It was a case of assault and after I had warned and cautioned Hutchons, the farm manager, he admitted that he had thumped a herd boy for 'throwing a cow with a stone' and breaking off a horn. I hadn't been well briefed and had no idea who actually owned the farm. When the case went to court a few days later, the Chief Magistrate, Mr C.W. Cary, was on the Bench and, with the case proven, he had little option but to fine his own farm manager five pounds for the offence.

My first tour of duty at District Headquarters was for six months and initially I patrolled the eastern part of the area. Visiting farms in those days was comparatively quick and easy as the only farm in the district which was fenced was Eythorne Estate, bordering the Umtali road some twenty miles from Fort Victoria. Farm patrol was simply a case of riding across country from homestead to homestead. Usually it took three weeks to cover the area, first visiting the farms to the west of the Beza Range, travelling as far as the Bikita and Ndanga borders and then back to camp through the farms to the east of the Range.

We were encouraged to shoot for the pot where this was permitted and we always took our rifles with us. Ammunition for our .303's then cost ten shillings per hundred rounds and although I had always been keen on shooting, up to the time of my enlistment I had shot only one animal – a hare which I had poached on the King William's Town commonage at the age of twelve with a borrowed 0.22. While stationed at Fort Victoria I quickly added to my score, often shooting duiker and steenbuck within a mile of the camp in the area where the suburbs have now been built.

One morning when I was riding through the hills on the Bikita border, my native constable drew my attention to a herd of eight reedbuck. Thinking I was well within the Reserve, where shooting was permitted, I quickly dismounted and opened up – ten rounds rapid to no effect. Much to my embarrassment, a farmer came over the rise within a few minutes. 'What's going on here? I thought the war had started up again.' It was Jock Patterson, the Scottish owner of Shalloch Park Farm. He accepted my profuse apologies and laughed off my attempted poaching but I had my leg pulled about the incident for years afterwards.

All the farms to the east were on a party-line to Bikita and Zaka. Whenever one phoned there was click after click as other receivers were lifted, I once had occasion to phone a beautiful girl who was staying at George Brunette's farm, Msali, to accept an invitation to tennis. On the morning of the appointed day I had to call officially at Shalloch Park. Jock's dear old mother, then 84, greeted me with the jibe, 'I know where you're going, George! You're off to Brunette's farm to see Miss… and play tennis.'

She then informed me that she listened in to all calls on the line and had even moved the telephone alongside her bed in order not to miss a thing. The party-line was her source of entertainment. When the Van Aarde family listened in one could always hear the clucking of hens and the crowing of cocks from their run by the back door. We soon learned to be very discreet on the phone!

I enjoyed my weekend at the Brunette's farm and found the family most hospitable. The police generally however, were not very popular at the farm after the visit of one District Superintendent, a predecessor of Captain Mickey Hamilton. Having been pressed to stay for a meal the DSP had tried a little *voetje-voetje* (footplay) for which the officer was noted with an unresponsive Mrs Brunette during lunch. He left without commenting on the meat which he had enjoyed or remarking on the leg of kudu hanging on the back veranda. The next day a trooper arrived with a summons for George — for shooting kudu without a licence!

There was a sequel to this tale of ingratitude which I heard only after leaving the Force. Troopers on patrol rarely accepted overnight hospitality and having spent the night camped on the banks of the Msali River, only a mile from the Brunette homestead, I saddled up after a cup of coffee at daybreak. George was already up and about and I was guided to him by the sound of voices as he conversed with his neighbour, Japie Potgieter of Bon Air Farm on the other side of the river. They were both extremely civil to me as I came up out of the dawn and George was most insistent with an invitation to coffee back at the house. Some years later they told me of the fright I had given them as I appeared over the rise. Japie had just shot a large kudu bull and the carcass was lying close by. Needless to say, he had no licence.

In similar vein was the tale of a hunter of some note in the district. Oom Gert Bezuidenhout had just taken up a farm on the Ndanga border when I first visited him in the early days of my service. His new pole-and-dagga house was nearing completion and on the morning I called a native woman was smearing the floor of the *zitkamer* with fresh cow-dung. This didn't worry Gert however as he led me to a dry corner of the room where we sat drinking our coffee. In those days Gert would make frequent trips to the Lowveld to hunt on both sides of the Chiredzi River in an area which abounded with buffalo. He always shot from the saddle and it was well known that he would ride down and shoot a dozen buffalo — fourteen on one occasion — before breakfast.

A few years later I was a patient in the Fort Victoria hospital (built at the end of 1925 with the charming and immaculately dressed Dr Henson as GMO) and Oom Gert was in the bed opposite mine. He was down with double pneumonia and in a bad way but late one afternoon, after expectorating noisily into his spittoon, he looked across at me and chuckled, 'You police chaps think you're smart, eh? Well, the other day I played a nice trick on a trooper from Zaka. I was travelling through the Ndanga hills with my wagon loaded with thirty buffalo skins I'm allowed on my two licences, when I spotted this large kudu bull on the side of a hill. I shot him, but having no licence and not wanting to take any chances, I tied the carcass well up under my wagon. No sooner had I done this when up came Trooper

Jefferies. He counted my skins, rode round the wagon and took a good look at my two licences. Then he rode happily away. Jong! That kudu made good biltong!'

With another chuckle Oom Gert passed into an even happier hunting ground where no licences are required and there are no patrolling policemen. His son Willie was stockman on Triangle Ranch for many years and was a good second to his father when it came to hunting.

Another pair of characters were the Scottish brothers, Bill and Andrew Erskine, who lived on Townlands Farm a few miles from the station at the Flesk Plots. They built themselves a very nice house, one of the best in the district at the time. Only one thing was missing from the completed homestead – a bathroom. Over the siting of this necessity the brothers just couldn't agree. Neither would give in and the large bath lay outside the house for years. Until they died the brothers heated hot water in a paraffin drum and scrubbed in a small tin bath.

Andrew looked after the farm while Bill ran the trading store, a wood and iron building situated where Barclay's Bank now stands. The storekeeper was the living image of Popeye-the-Sailorman, as he always dressed in white shirt and ducks, white shoes and a cap pulled down over his forehead. He had a moustache and a small beard. A pipe was always in his mouth. Mrs Strover, the wife of Dr Minto Strover who was GMO in Fort Victoria during the 'thirties, tells me that Andrew died first. Bill died some time afterwards, was wrapped in a blanket, placed in the coffin and buried. Only then was it discovered that he had been interred with his keys – from which he could never be parted – on his belt. His safe had to be blown open to wind up the estate.

I am recalling – with fingers crossed against a possible libel suit – some of the characters who lived in and around Fort Victoria in the 1920s. Perhaps it is only advancing years which create the impression that there were in those days a much larger number of farmers, miners, tradesmen and officials with their own very individual peculiarities. Perhaps today's authors of 'Station Notes' can prove me wrong – and they of course run a much greater risk of retribution from their victims.

A prominent farmer to the south of Fort Victoria was the late J.A.H. He had an unpleasant manner, was always rude to the police and eventually refused to allow them on his farm. Local members of the Force retaliated by taking him to Court on every possible occasion, no dog licence, an unlicensed scotch cart and so on. It got so bad that eventually J. A. broke down before the magistrate and complained that he was being persecuted, not prosecuted. He may have been right, but he asked for all he got with his rude and uncompromising attitude.

After 47 years it is difficult to remember all the farmers in the district but among the leading lights were Joe Rademeyer, after whom the Farmers' Hall was named; Bob and Norman Richards; Dick Rennie, whose father spent his time prospecting and mining and who discovered the famous Renco gold mine; Jock Paterson, who has been mentioned already, and his brother McDonald; old 'Father' Readman who helped many who were in financial straits and Kennedy-Bayne of Chevedene, a very sound Scots farmer who, being related to the owners of Teacher's Whisky, made it his business to ensure that Meikles introduced the brand to Rhodesia through their store at Fort Victoria.

Then there was Franklin who hailed from Grahamstown and who farmed on the other side of the Beza Mountains near Chevedene; Pepler, a skilled fruit farmer originally from the Cape; Japie Potgieter, a noted stockman who moved his cattle down to the Crown land which now comprises the Hippo Valley/Buffalo Range area on the Chiredzi when his original pastures suffered in the severe drought of 1946-47 and, of course, there was George Brunette who has already been mentioned.

George was always something of an anarchist, threatening to get the farmers to take up arms, motor to Salisbury, and surround the House of Assembly until such time as the Government righted his particular grievances. But despite this – or because of it – George was still very popular. So much so, in fact, that a few years later he decided to stand for Parliament himself. Wearing his best suit he canvassed the district and his chances of election seemed good. Then funds gave out and George had to pack up his campaign before polling day.

He didn't get on so well with the local Africans though and was hauled up on a charge of assault on one memorable occasion. He was duly fined five pounds and, as he left the dock, was heard to remark in a very cutting tone, 'Some bloody court this is!' He was promptly called back by the magistrate and fined one pound for each word of contempt – another five pounds.

Another well respected farmer was L.R. Hartley who farmed Wondedzo which is now run by our local MP, Colonel G.H. Hartley, whose uncle he was. And on a farm nearby, Riverdene North, lived perhaps the most eccentric character in the district, one Captain Reginald Herbert Joyce, Master Mariner and former Lieutenant Commander, RNR Reginald led the life of a hermit and did not appreciate visitors in any shape or form. His house was encircled by a barbed-wire entanglement intended to keep out friend and foe alike. However, the Captain deigned to see me in the course of patrols and, as with so many others of those days, never had a complaint. He took the law into his own hands. Colonel Hartley tells me of the time when Reginald's boys went on strike. When our sailor discovered the mutiny he loaded his .303 with ten rounds and launched a foray on the compound. He advanced from cover to cover and then, from behind the last bush, fired all ten rounds rapid. Then he fixed his bayonet and charged – to find that every living soul had long since disappeared from the scene of the engagement.

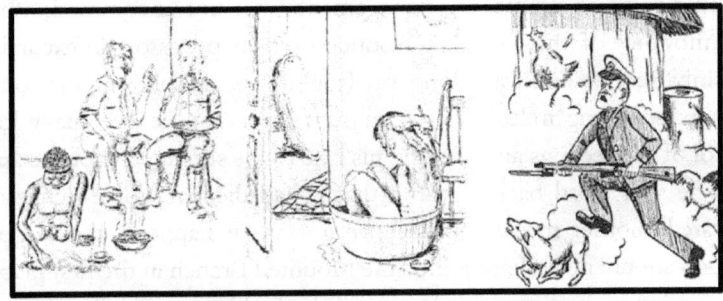

One late afternoon, riding Buster and followed at a distance by my entourage of African police, Sixpence and a pack mule, I approached the Popotekwe Drift on the Umtali road. There I found the river running a banker from a storm higher up in the catchment area. As I got closer I recognised Polly Hughes of Nyika Store, Bikita, and Charlie Osborne of the Bikita Tin-fields. The couple were sitting patiently on the river bank at the water's edge, passing a long object between them and alternately raising it to their lips. Great was the welcome when they spotted me. Beside them was a bottle of Scotch. Polly and Charlie had been on the usual binge in town but the swollen river had interrupted their unsteady return to Bikita. A terrible thirst had caught up with them and in the absence of glasses, Polly had produced a pair of new shoes bought that morning at Meikle's Store. One shoe provided a shared glass while the other served as a water jug.

The river dropped sufficiently before nightfall to allow Polly and Charlie to continue on their way in very good spirits. With my entourage, I camped on the riverbank.

I'll never forget the morning I set off on patrol towards my first port of call, Brown's Farm, about four miles out at the Flesk Plots. I arrived at the farm, tied Buster to a peach tree near the veranda and made my presence known. The front door burst open, out flew Mrs Brown and off flew Buster. I swore and, whistling enticingly, took off after my mount. To no avail. As soon as I got within ten yards of dear old Buster, up would come his head and he'd gallop fifty yards away at which point he would resume his innocent grazing. The comedy went on all the way back to camp where, at Richie's suggestion, I abandoned the day's outing and continued the patrol the next morning.

Similar cases of 'animal mismanagement' were not uncommon, much to the annoyance of the patrolling trooper. One chap was on an excursion in the Chibi Reserve and was a long way from camp. He followed his horse for many exasperating miles trying to mount the beast, he eventually lost all control of his feelings and, putting his rifle to his shoulder, shot the animal. Then he sent word back to camp that it had died of horse-sickness and requested another mount – which he got. As it happens, the trooper in question should never have joined the Mounted Branch in the first place. He was terrified of horses. Added to which he had been given the largest and most intractable mount in the whole police district. The Commissioner, Colonel A. Essex Capell, was in the habit of popping the question of whether a man 'loved his horse' and I hate to think of the honest reply he would have received from the trooper at Chibi. And I must say that after my own experience at Brown's farm, I sympathised to some extent with my comrade.

The only hotel in town in 1925 was the 'Victoria', one in the Meikle's chain and the same building (apart from the annexe added in 1934) which is in use today. Managed by George Shepherd, a former sergeant of the CID, the Hotel Victoria kept an excellent table. With due respect, it has never been bettered to this day. All kinds of meat and poultry were on the table d'hote menu each night, thanks to the popular local butcher, an ex-Bishop's boy called Elliott, or the farmer contractors to the hotel.

The hotel pub was the nightly rendezvous for townsmen and policemen alike. Tot measures were almost unheard of then and if your tipple was hard liquor, you were passed the bottle to help yourself. Even a shortage of cash meant no shortage of drink as the iniquitous card system was the vogue – a 'courtesy' which was to get a lot of us into trouble as time went on. Later, at Bikita, where I was stationed with Frank Blake as Trooper-in-Charge, I recall the well-known trader, Gordon Hughes, calling at the camp one evening to tell us that a 'blacklist' had been posted up in the pub. Those named would be given no more credit. Frank and I both appeared for six and eight pounds respectively but the generous Gordon, not wanting to see us embarrassed, had paid our accounts. We were invited to settle up with him at our convenience. Avoiding the stigma wasn't that serious. The Chief Magistrate was also on the list and Gordon had treated him as understandingly as he had the police. Shades of Omar Khayyam and Abou Ben Adhem!

Rejoining the clientele of the Hotel Victoria, one regular incumbent – if not recumbent – was Farrier Corporal Tiney, a very diminutive Cockney in whose presence one often heard the expression 'Tiney by name and tiny by nature!' He was generous to a fault while his pay lasted but that was never for long. The card system was an irresistible temptation to an invitation 'drinks all round', a custom which was infrequently abused.

Corporal Tiney had his own system however. When broke and blacklisted, he would get spruced up at 5 p.m. and then confront me with the plea, 'George, could you lend me my entrance fee.' The entrance fee, as Tiney called it, was sixpence with which to buy himself a small beer. With this in hand he would then take up his stance nightly behind the half-circle of townsmen at the bar counter. The usual composition of this group would be J.K. McGhie, chemist and chairman of the T.M.B.; Elliott the butcher; Thornton, bookkeeper for the Bechuanaland Trading Co. where virtually all the local policemen ran liquor accounts; Ted Gourley, the stone-mason who built Fort Victoria's War Memorial; William Paley, a general agent; 'One-Eye' Scott, who was the local manager for Zeederberg's Transport and who permanently wore a white shield over his left eye and a Standard Bank cash bag at his belt; and perhaps E.M. Baden, the auctioneer and estate agent,

Deputy Sheriff and farmer; ex-policeman John Moore Fitzgerald, and finally 'Daddy' Hayles, the market-master and general agent.

Near this august company Tiney would stand sipping his small beer and before long someone would notice him and invite him to have a drink. 'Don't mind if I do,' was the standard reply and night after night, Tiney would reel back to camp, his investment of the sixpence entrance fee showing remarkable profit. One thing I remember about Tiney was his habit of opening soda-water bottles with his teeth. The last time I saw him he was selling vegetables from a barrow in London.

Out at Zimbabwe an equally well-run hostelry was managed by another former policeman, ex-Sergeant Stappard and his wife. Mrs Stappard's brother, Marmaduke Mundell, was the owner of the Great Zimbabwe Ruins Hotel and lived with them. On many occasions, the troops would motor out to Zimbabwe after hours to continue drinking with Stappard behind closed doors.

More than once I was dragged out of bed to join them. Captain Willis. with his Model T Ford, was usually engaged for the journey. When the number of travellers reached double figures, Reichert's taxi would join the procession. In this way I visited Zimbabwe a dozen times before I ever saw the Ruins.

We called our usual driver 'Uncle' Willis and many were the riotous nights he enjoyed with us. If Uncle happened to be tired, he would take no chances but would pull up at the side of the road and take a nap. His Model T was fitted with a special speedy 'Rucksdell' gear of which he was very proud. He certainly drove extremely fast. One night we nearly came to grief en route to our midnight revelry. Rounding a corner of the narrow road, we were confronted by an oxwagon travelling in the same direction. Uncle swerved to the left and actually brushed the horns of several oxen as we passed by in a flash – at probably the only spot on the whole road where there were no trees on the verge.

In 1927 Corporal 'Cracker' Cross, MM, was transferred to Chibi after being at Nuanetsi for some time. Cracker was a strict disciplinarian and a first-class policeman but he had never gotten over being jilted during the war. Periodically he suffered from attacks of depression and consequent 'taking to the bottle'. When Cracker felt a fit of depression coming on – perhaps once in six weeks – he would telephone the District Superintendent and get a week's leave. Then it was a case of drinks on Cracker for a week, not that anyone wished to take advantage of him, but he simply would not take no for an answer. All day, and for a large part of the evening, Cracker drank – without leaving District Headquarters. Apart from this one vice, his behaviour was exemplary and he was greatly respected by the different officers under whom he served and who were fully aware of and sympathetic to his periodical lapses.

At the end of one such bout of indulgence, Cracker returned to Chibi allowing himself a couple of bottles of Scotch with which to taper off. Trooper Frank Blake was with him and did his best to help Cracker to recover from the spree. With one bottle almost gone, Frank hid the other. During the night Cracker hunted high and low for the second bottle and, in desperation, picked up the lamp, drank the paraffin out of it and walked outside into a cold 'guti' night. Frank, meanwhile, slept on unknowingly. The next morning he was shocked to find Cracker lying unconscious outside. Pneumonia developed and it was said that poor old Cracker, knowing that he would lose his stripes because of the incident, turned his face to the wall. He, who had served with such distinction in the 1914-18 War, was buried with full military honours.

Life in Fort Victoria was very free and easy in the 1920s. Everyone knew everyone and there was almost no crime at all – among the Europeans at any rate. This was the case throughout the country and was helped by the strict immigration laws. Much skylarking was done by policemen but without endangering the respect of the community who took it all in good part.

I remember the evening when Trooper Jefferies rode his horse, a beautiful grey, into the bar at the Hotel Victoria. Without any fuss, George Shepherd came quietly forward and led horse and rider out. On another occasion a trooper rode his horse into the lounge of a private house. It belonged to a man named Whitaker who worked at the Power Station and the fact that he had three attractive daughters no doubt motivated the intrusion.

When coming off patrol from No. 3 Area it was customary to ride our horses in and out of the pillars of the hotel. On early morning exercise rides we invariably lined up in the main street at Traicos Corner and raced past the hotel down to the Macheke River. We were a happy crowd and the civilians shared this happy relationship. Our sergeant-major was Bill Hewlett. Bill was a strict disciplinarian and could be rather snotty on occasions. I well remember the time I was sent down into the heart of No. 3 Area to investigate a suicide case. A crippled native had murdered his wife and then disappeared. Six weeks later he had been found in dense bush hanging from a tree alongside a large sloping rock. The cripple had scrambled up the rock, attached the end of a riem to the tree, slipped a loop around his neck and stepped off into limbo – literally. What hell I got from Bill for not untying the knot embedded under the decomposing skin of the neck to prove that it was a slip-knot. It might have been a case of murder, he admonished, and he might have been right.

After six months my patrol area was taken over by Trooper Knowles from Cape Town, an excellent dancer who spent much of his time practising in the barracks, with a broom as his partner. For some unaccountable reason the new District Superintendent, Captain Lawrence, allowed Knowles to do the patrol on a bicycle accompanied by a native constable similarly mounted. Having no packmule or supplies Knowles was dependent on hospitality and once again the reputation of the Force suffered. The only advantage was a saving of time, the patrol taking only one week instead of three, and the saving on Knowles' pocket. I strongly suspect the latter was the main reason for his request to the District Superintendent. One day I was in the process of investigating a case at James' Matabele Mine on Bob Richards' farm a few miles from town. Knowles was camped in the area and invited me to lunch with him. Much to my disappointment I discovered that Knowles' commissariat for his week's patrol consisted of four Hot Cross buns (this was on Good Friday) and a tin of jam. It did not take us long to polish off the lot, after which I returned to camp and a more substantial lunch.

Having handed over the eastern patrol area to Knowles, I became responsible for the No. 3 Area which continued below Zimbabwe to the Lundi River and was bordered on the west by the Chibi Reserve and on the east by the Mtilikwe River and Triangle Ranch. In February 1926 1 set out on my first patrol of the district and, at Morgenster Mission, just beyond Zimbabwe, I met the Rev. and Mrs Louw who had founded the settlement. Mrs Louw was a sister of Dr Malan, onetime Prime Minister of the Union of South Africa. Dr Steyn was the mission doctor, an eye specialist and a very charming man. He is still alive, in retirement in the Gutu District.

On that particular patrol it seems that it rained every day or every night for a solid month. I camped in native huts which made things only slightly more bearable. Richie had asked me to call on Tom MacDougall when opposite Triangle, pay my respects and enquire if there was anything I could do for him. There were no bridges in the country at the time and the Mtilikwe was in high flood. So it was that my native constable and I were ferried across nearly half-a-mile of rushing water by a Shangaan in a frail dug-out. When I think of that passage through tree-tops and rocks I don't think it's a trip I would undertake today.

On the Tokwe I met a farmer called Martin who, surprisingly for those days, was running a herd of pedigree Sussex cattle. On my way home at the end of the month I called in at the leper settlement situated below Morgenster Mission and managed by No. 1518, former policeman Horatio Lewis (Horace, who came from London originally, is now living in Salisbury at Carly's Hotel.) It rained day and night for the three happy days I spent with Horace waiting for a river which cut us off from Zimbabwe to subside. On the fourth day I felt that I was outstaying my welcome and could no longer put off my return to camp. So, with the aid of pack-mule and horse, we crossed what had become a raging torrent. I hung on to one of the stirrup leathers of my horse while the native constable and Sixpence clung for dear life to the mule.

Mrs Carbutt, wife of Colonel C.L. Carbutt, Superintendent of Natives, decided about this time to organise a dance band – and did so very successfully. She held a meeting with the troops at the hotel and it was decided that Corporal Tiney should take over the drums while she herself played the piano and yours truly joined in on a swanee-whistle. Someone else played a violin and many enjoyable dances were held to the music of our rather original pop-group. Six happy months came to an end all too soon. In March 1926 I was transferred to Bikita.

Circa 1926. Travelling out to the Rifle Range to fire Annual Musketry Course. Tprs Stan Perkins, Frank Blake and George Style on muledrawn buckboard. Cases of beer invisible behind George.

REMINISCENCES of BIKITA

The Bikita area formerly constituted part of the Ndanga District where the first Native Commissioner was Alfred Drew. In 1907 the Clerk at Ndanga found himself appointed Clerk-in-Charge of Bikita. Mr E.G. Lenthall opened a sub-station at a place called Guramusana in 1908 and he remained there until 1912 having been elevated from Clerk-in-Charge to Assistant Native Commissioner. Cyril Blackwell followed him and in 1913 moved the station to Denga (Heaven), the highest point in the district on Hanyanya Hill.

The view from Denga is magnificent. The Mashaba hills, more than a hundred miles away, can be seen clearly on a fine day. In 1915 Mr H.N. Watters took over from Blackwell and stayed there until 1920. I well remember Mrs Watters telling me about the 1917/18 summer when record rains were experienced – 132 inches being measured at Denga. In NADA No. 40 (1963) there was a short article by *'Murombo'* – my old friend Leslie Ball – in which he wrote, 'in February 1917 we had over six inches of rain on each of three successive days.'

According to Mrs Watters, Denga was completely isolated for six weeks because of flooded rivers and supplies were eventually coming from Fort Victoria only by way of Gutu. There had been a serious famine in 1916 and as a result of the relief organised by Mr Watters, he was accorded the native name of 'Muponese' – the Saviour.

J.B. Henry took over as the first full Native Commissioner in 1920, followed by Willie Coates-Palgrave – Mrs Watters' brother – a year later. In 1923 Willie moved the station to its present site because '132 inches of rain in one season was too much!' I'm told that in those days Denga was forever shrouded in *guti* and everything turned mouldy. Palgrave remained at Bikita until 1925 when Watters returned to reign for a decade. Successive Native Commissioners thereafter, not necessarily in chronological order, were Fred Lemon; Aylward, the popular ex-policeman; R.M. Kelly, a really loveable character, and Toots Howe-Ely. Senior clerks on the station during my time were Turton, Clarence Sissing, Phil Braybrooke, Fred Champion (ex-police) and Walker. Junior officials were Frank McCabe, ex-Trooper C.D. McCallum. Stan Morris, ex-Trooper Tubby Colyer – whose cousin was the famous woman tennis champion in England, Jack Nesbitt, Noel Hunt – a prolific reader – and Alick Durham.

Tubby Colyer managed to sprain his ankle on one occasion and commuted to his office daily in a wheel barrow. One Sunday afternoon he returned unexpectedly from Fort Victoria – to find his cookboy wearing his best suit.

Members-in-Charge at Bikita at different times were Busky Knight, Frank Blake, Bob Elliott, Wright and Mervyn Harries, Troopers stationed there included Mac Mullin, Henry Freese, Charles William Howe Thatcher, Jack Frost, Tubby Giles and Ned Sherlock – the latter, who went on to become Native Commissioner, Melsetter, is now in sunny retirement in Portugal. Ned had a great sense of humour and was a frequent contributor to *Outpost* under the nom-de-plume 'Quien Sabe'.

From my mother's diary, into which she used to copy my letters virtually verbatim, I am able to date exactly the first of my three transfers to Bikita, On May 7 1926, she wrote:

> Cecil wrote on April 24. He had arrived at Bikita on April 22. He says it is a posh little camp situated on a kopje among the mountains. It is about 65 miles east of Fort Victoria and the village is composed of the police camp, the Native Commissioner, a couple of Native Department clerks and two pole-and-dagga stores. A second Paris in fact! That is Cecil's remark. Took him three days to ride out. They were starting on the Census on the 28th and will be out for two weeks – a week delivering and a week collecting the forms – for which they get an extra 10/- a day. Some time he will be patrolling the ranch where a boy named Wilson was killed by a lion. He says a lot of recruits are coming out from England again – ten arrived the other day.

The lion business happened on Angus Ranch. Wilson had wounded the lion and in following it up, climbed on a large antheap to look around. The lion happened to be lying behind the antheap, attacked Wilson and dealt him a blow on the neck, knocking him to the ground. I believe an African who was with Wilson finished the lion off, and then helped Wilson to the river after he had complained of thirst. As he leaned forward to drink, he collapsed and died. Presumably his jugular vein had been severed.

On the evening of my arrival at Bikita, Busky Knight – Trooper-in-Charge

– produced a bottle of Chateau brandy and insisted that we kill the bottle before dinner. It was a common saying in the Victoria Circle that you never got to know a man until you'd got drunk with him. True enough – and Busky was determined not to waste time. He was an old hand who had dug himself in at Bikita and would like to have ended his days there. He was moved to Zaka before his retirement.

The Native Commissioner was Henry Nash Watters, an Irishman and an ex-trooper in the BSA Police; the senior clerk was Turton, destined to reach the top of the ladder, and the junior clerk was Frank McCabe. One store was run by a recluse – old 'Timber' Wood – and the other must have been managed by an African for a European – probably Gordon Hughes.

My predecessor was Trooper Richards who had gone on leave to England where he eventually decided to take his discharge. Richards was something of a poultry fancier and, like Busky, had dug himself in at Bikita. He had built up a magnificent flock of White Leghorns headed by an imported cock, complete with leg ring, price six guineas. I was most impressed when I heard the price as a trooper's starting rate of pay had been reduced from £16.13.4 to only £12.10.0 per month just before I enlisted. The Bikita hills abounded in leopards in those days. their sawing grunt being heard often and it was a sad night when a pair of mating leopards came into the camp and killed 22 of the fowls, including the imported cock, and a turkey. I bagged the male leopard the following night and the story has been related elsewhere.

Busky and Richards both ran herds of cattle, as did so many Native Commissioners and Members-in-Charge of stations in those days. Grazing was no problem as the Reserves were then usually understocked, but the practice was frowned upon by the authorities about this time and came to an abrupt end. Could the officials be blamed for trying to augment their meagre salaries?

Eggs were still plentiful in those days and as there was not much of a market for them, Busky would walk behind his barrack-room nightly and throw away a basketful. After one enterprising gentleman had purchased a clutch of eggs for eating, and then surreptitiously placed them under a hen with the intention of competing with Busky's prize flock, the latter carefully pricked with a needle all eggs subsequently sold for eating. The flock was a valuable one and the breed jealously guarded.

Lance Corporal Inkosana Pompey was in charge of the African Police when I first joined Busky Knight. He had been taken over to England as a small boy by Captain Vearey, and had spent a few years there. He spoke with a very cultured English accent, so much so, that if out of view, anyone hearing him talk could easily mistake him for someone just down from Oxford. It was interesting to find that he and Gordon Hughes had met as boys and wrestled on the lawn at a garden party in Norfolk. Pompey died last year at the age of about 88 at the Tinfields, where he was being looked after by George Nolan.

I did not visit the three large ranches, Devuli, Angus and Humani Estate, on the census patrol which was confined to the north-western part of the district. One of the first people I called on was Don Cameron who then had a farm on the Turgwe River. He was growing cotton but was much hampered by the depredations of kudu. Don had come up from Bedford in the Eastern Cape, and I found him a most pleasant personality. After a chat over a cup of tea he walked with me to meet Gordon Hughes, who was living, and had started trading, a few hundred yards away. The ever-cheerful and hospitable Gordon came out to meet us. His buildings consisted of two pole-and-dagga huts – built Makaranga style, with no plaster on the outside – the one being his residence and the other his store.

Gordon had served with the Artillery in France in the 1914-18 war – with distinction – and won a Military Medal, but was badly gassed, and suffered as a result for the rest of his life. He had just given up gold mining on the Walsingham and Leicester mines, Bikita, and had taken to trading. His brother Polly had followed him out from Norfolk and opened up the Nyika

Trading Store. Gordon's and Polly's small set-up of those days was the origin of the large and thriving chain of stores he later handed over to his niece, Mrs White and her family, who came out from England to take over. Donald Cameron, with his charming wife Ruth, have for many years been living on their farm Lochiel, south of Fort Victoria. I later called on Polly Hughes at his Nyika Store on the Fort Victoria-Umtali road, and found him and his friend Charlie Osborne, from the Tinfields, very affable. My next port of call was Pamushana Mission, run by the Rev. and Mrs Botha of the Dutch Reformed Church. On the staff were three lady teachers, two of whom were Miss Heymann and Miss Coetzee, the latter now being Mrs Pienaar of the Makorsi River Ranch. On the Tinfields I met George Nolan battling to make a living and I wrote and told my mother – 'these are the only tin mines in the country. At present they are purely alluvial, no one having any money to sink shafts'. A far cry from the day, when, after the discovery of several other minerals, George was to build himself the truly palatial £404,040 Lithium Lodge on the Tinfields, where he now resides. In my mother's diary under May 21 1926, I read:

> He had returned from his Census Patrol and glad to get back as he had run out of skoff. He had a very interesting patrol and the few people in the area were very hospitable.

Apart from acting as census officers, the police, who were then still the first line of defence, performed many extraneous duties. We acted as pass officers, immigration officers, prosecutors and gaolers, and vaccinated the Africans in the Reserves, the latter duty bringing us in some most welcome E.D.P. I shudder when I think of the large wounds and subsequent scars we caused on the Africans' arms as a result of the method then in vogue. Two needles were pushed through a cork about ¼ in. apart and the left arm scratched for about an inch across and then down across the middle for the same length, as in a game of 'noughts and crosses', until blood was drawn. Onto the blood was blown the vaccine. No wonder the children yelled! How different is today's technique of a tiny mark with no blood drawn.

Front Entrance of George Nolan's 'Lithium Lodge'

I read in the diary the following, the result of a patrol from Nuanetsi in December, 1927: 'He got back from patrol on December 6. Was away for a month during which he vaccinated 1,909 Africans for which he received £9.4.1d. He struck a pack of wild dogs but only managed to get one – for which he got 10/-. They are the only vermin on which the Rhodesian Government pays a bounty.' We were paid 3d. each for the first hundred Africans vaccinated, 2d. each for the second and 1d. each thereafter. The extra revenue was much appreciated. I had been transferred to Nuanetsi after returning to Depot from Bikita for the rugger season and had been relieved at Bikita by Trooper Mac Mullin, keen physical culturist and ex-woods man from the Pirie Forests near King Williamstown. Mac is now resident on Faversham Estate near Triangle. During this break from Bikita I had spells at Chibi, Mashaba and again at Fort Victoria before returning to the station, and, after illness, eight months at Gutu before my final return, to spend eleven long years on end at Bikita.

In June 1926 I undertook my first patrol to Devuli Ranch which had been started in 1919-20 by Lucas Bridges and his two brothers, William and Despard. They had big interests in South and South West Africa as well and Despard was in charge of the Rhodesian operation. The diary records that I had lunch with the Bridges family at Ranch HQ after the patrol. The manager was Don Somerville who was married to Tonita, the elder daughter of Despard Bridges. The younger daughter, Violet, was to marry Ian de la Rue many years later. Don was at one time MP for Fort Victoria.

Long since forgotten by me but recalled by the diary was the following:

Somerville and young Bridges shot two lions when driving the motor car the other night. They at first mistook them for oxen – they were so big. In the leg of one they found an iron pot leg which had evidently been there for years. Cecil says he struck bags of lion spoor on patrol.

Lions were indeed very plentiful in those days. While at Davel's section at the Sabi, a very distressed Shangaan arrived to report that lions had killed eight of his cattle the previous night. He asked Davel to do something about it. The mule cart was duly inspanned, our food and blankets loaded, and off we set for the kraal. All the carcasses were removed except one on which the pride had partly fed. We laid our beds on the grass in the open approximately 100 yards away.

Soon after dark, with Davel wearing the carbide shooting lamp of those days (this was just before the introduction of the electric lamp), we circled around for an hour looking for the lions. It was my first lion hunt, and though clutching my service rifle loaded with ten rounds, I did not feel very happy behind the weak light. Davel then complained of a headache and we retired to bed intending to get up when they returned to the kill. Imagine our chagrin when next morning we discovered that a pride of eight had returned and silently polished off the whole carcass, leaving only a skeleton. We packed up and returned to the homestead.

An interesting character on Devuli was old Ali Hamman, the official vermin destroyer, who is reputed to have shot 66 lions, mostly along the Sabi, and to have trapped over 300. Ali was a second Jim Corbett, in that where Jim could call up tigers, he could call up lions. This he did most successfully by grunting loudly into a calabash.

He was quite fearless when it came to lion hunting at night and his advice, as practised by himself, to anyone wounding a lion, was to dash in close with the light and give it the coup-de-grace before it could get away. His theory that a lion would never charge a night lamp was nearly to cost me my life some years later when I met a pride of nine on the Sabi, shot one and was charged by a second which I luckily hit in the head as it sprang. The exception to the rule.

Ex-Trooper Herriot-Hill was employed at Devuli in the late 1920s, and lost his life through an unfortunate accident. He was filling a truck with petrol for ex-Trooper C.D. McCallum, a fine allround sportsman, when the petrol from the hose caught alight from a hurricane lamp and Herriot-Hill was badly burnt on the leg, dying later in the Fort Victoria hospital. 'C.D.' was in the Native Department at Bikita after leaving the Police, then went trading for a time and later helped Mercer open the first Birchenough Bridge Hotel, about 1936, when the bridge was being built by the Dorman-Long Company.

Ex-Trooper Paddy Power from Waterford with Dick Dott from Kimberley, opened up Angus Ranch in 1919 and built up a fine herd of Aberdeen-Angus cattle. Paddy had served three years in the police, during which time he managed to open a couple of trading stores in the Bikita or Zaka area. He was on leave pending discharge when the Great War broke out. He was recalled, much to his annoyance. I got to know Paddy, a fine type of Irishman and the handsomest man I ever met, extremely well, as we lived in close proximity at Bikita for ten years after I took my discharge in April 1930. Many were the yarns recounted to me by him over sundowners. He had set up his chief trading store at the station where he brought up his family.

Paddy had told me that he did not have a single case during his few years of police-cum-trading service, but Mrs Power tells me that there was a case where he had to give evidence against the accused so he donned his uniform. The tunic collar was too tight for him, and when he stood up to give evidence he fainted!

On another occasion he was brought up on some minor charge and on being sentenced refused to pay the fine, electing to go to gaol instead. While he was being stubborn, our popular Deputy Sheriff of the time, Fitzgerald, of Desmondale Farm, and an ex-Sergeant of the BSA Police, paid his fine.

Paddy had quarrelled with Dott in 1929 and the partnership broke up. He had the Irish trait of not forgiving very readily, and a few years later, when Dott asked me to ask Paddy to go and see him and 'bury the hatchet' Paddy replied in a flash, 'You go back and tell Dott that the only place I will bury the hatchet is in the back of his skull!'

His green-ribboned shillelagh hung outside the bedroom door, and many were the nights he sang 'For the Wearing of the Green' after a few sundowners. Paddy used to trek cattle all the way to the Johannesburg market on the hoof, a distance of about 600 miles. He rode on horseback with the drovers on foot.

On one occasion some Shangaan men came to the Ranch headquarters to make a report and ask Paddy's advice. It appeared that on the previous very hot evening, a man and his wife were sleeping out of doors. A hyena had dashed in and torn away the mask of the woman's face, leaving virtually nothing. Their proposition was to knock the woman on the head with a knobkerrie and put her out of her misery and Paddy concurred. There was no alternative. They had a famous lion on Angus, called by the Shangaans *Mangwana-mangwana* (tomorrow-tomorrow) who through vomiting must have got over strychnine poisoning early in his career or broken out of a trap, for he never returned to a kill. In all this lion killed over 400 cattle without once returning to feed a second time. Then one night – probably through old age – he did return, and died of strychnine poisoning at the carcass. He presumably got his name because he so often killed afresh on the morrow.

An interesting character, of whom I have written before, and who shared a rondavel with Paddy on Angus Ranch was Victor Kennerley-Rumford, the son of the famous contralto, Dame Clara Butt. Victor, a wonderful specimen of humanity standing 6 ft. 4 in. in his socks and built in proportion, had been living a fast life in London and his physical and mental health had seriously declined. Dott, for a certain figure, had agreed to restore him to health.

One hot summer afternoon, Dott, who was inclined to bully Victor, sent him out to shoot some meat for the boys against his will. Eight shots were heard, and a little later Victor came back and announced to Dott, while holding up some tails as evidence, that he had shot eight. To Dott's horror he found that the tails were from eight of his best Aberdeen-Angus oxen. Victor was cute enough to know that owing to his past mental illness he would 'get away with it' and confided to Paddy that night that he had shot the oxen deliberately as he was tired of being bullied. His father had to foot the bill in full, however, £30 per head!

When Coates-Palgrave was Native Commissioner at Bikita he had occasion to visit Angus Ranch with his family and, with Dott and Paddy, the party continued on to the Sabi where they camped for the night. Now the Sabi in those days was infested with lions, and probably for safety's sake Palgrave's little daughter, only a few years old, slept between Paddy and Dott. Paddy was much embarrassed when at a party many years later, the now adult young woman turned to him, and in a very audible voice remarked, 'Do you remember the night we slept together at the Sabi?'

Jimmy Whittall was on Humani Estate, which had been opened up on the Sabi by Somerville in the late 1920s. Jim had immigrated from Turkey. I had occasion to send Trooper Mac Mullen down to investigate a nasty accident on the ranch. A lorry, piled high with bags of maize on which Africans were sitting, passed between two tall gate posts held together at the top by a strand of wire. The wire caught one of the boys on the neck completely decapitating him, throwing his head back on to the road.

Talking of necks reminds me of the prevalence of suicide by hanging among the Makaranga, and I had five such cases during my brief service. One morning I sent Native Constable Taruwinga off on a general patrol of the southern area. He had not been gone long when he returned to make a report. It appeared that while following a footpath through a *Mashuku* (Wild Loquat) forest he heard a baby crying in the treetops. Looking up he saw a woman hanging by her neck with a baby strapped to her back in an *mbereko* (skin-shawl). He obtained help from the nearby Chipkanya Kraal, removed the child and then cut down the body. The motive for suicide appeared to be a scolding from her husband the night before for a bad brew of beer.

On another occasion a very determined suicide was investigated on one of the ranches by Dr Williams, of Ndanga, and myself. A cattle herd-boy had strangled himself while lying on the ground and straining on a riem tied to a post of his temporary shelter. The motive in this case appeared to be the unfaithfulness of his girlfriend. I noticed that the old doctor could not keep his eyes off the beautiful figures of the young Shangaan girls in their topless attire and wearing only their much pleated Salempore skirts, the national dress of the Shangaan women. Quite unnecessarily he drew my attention to the girls.

The mention of girls reminds me of the time in 1929 when, with marriage in view, I went up to Salisbury on a promotion examination. No trooper of under ten years' service was then allowed to marry. No wonder so many of the older hands like Busky Knight were single. However, before the examination, I had never drilled a man in my life, unlike others seeking promotion who had had instruction on outstations or at District H.Q. With the Commissioner of the day, Colonel 'Georgie' Stops, sitting on his charger a few yards away, I was instructed to march out and get the Askari Platoon, who were on parade for us, to 'Present Arms'. Marching nervously forward, I halted and yelled 'Present Arms!' Nothing happened, the squad remained in the 'Stand Easy' position. Now, more nervous than ever I was called over by the Commissioner who addressed me thus, 'Nimrod, you lack character and personality! Do you read much? You should read more.'

How often had this advice been given to me by my mother! However, had the platoon been properly trained, they would have automatically come to attention, sloped and presented arms! That was that, and I returned to Bikita under Frank Blake, who was later seconded to the Town Police. Shortly afterwards I took over the station with Trooper Mac Mullin relieving me as patrolling trooper.

In a recent issue of *Outpost* the Editor writes, inter alia, 'this issue takes a rather penetrating look at interrogation techniques' and goes on to say 'wouldn't polygraphy, narco-analysis, hypnotic questioning (and even a few old-fashioned witchdoctors) speed up the course of justice in these parts?' With respect, but with the knowledge of how difficult it is to bring so many African cases to a satisfactory conclusion and thus to court, I have always felt that members of the Judiciary should have spent at least three years in the police before sitting on the Bench. It was only after I took my discharge and read in the press of young policemen being discharged for minor cases of 'third degree', that I realised the seriousness with which this method was viewed. I am not now talking of such stringent methods as hanging Africans in trees by their toes, etc., etc. but merely mild chastisement.

I would like to cite a case I investigated at Bikita. One morning a very distressed African, Amon, arrived in camp to make his report. Amon had just returned from a spell on the mines in Johannesburg and had been to recover his cattle which had been left with a friend, only to find the biggest and best ox was missing. The friend, Takawira, claimed that the ox had died from natural causes, but something had made Amon strongly suspicious.

Accordingly I detailed Native Constable Gondokindo to proceed to Takawira's kraal with Amon to investigate. He returned to camp in the evening with Takawira and his family, Amon, and the skull of the ox, which had died 'from natural causes'. On the top of the skull, immediately behind the horns, was a small cleft about 2 in. long, obviously made by a tribal axe. Next morning I settled down to investigate but knew nothing about 'polygraphy, narco-analysis and hypnotic questioning', and had no witchdoctor handy. Nor had we a Forensic Laboratory in those days. Takawira could not account for the cleft in the skull and was adamant that the ox had died a natural death. As was our custom we seated the family at 50-yard intervals so that they could not communicate, with a constable watching them.

I spent the day interrogating Takawira, his wife, son and daughter, and got nowhere. As each member of the family left the office, I tried to bluff the incoming member that 'the beans had been spilt' and get confirmation, but to no avail. They were blindly loyal and stuck to their story. They just would not talk. It had been a long, weary day of continuous interrogation when, at dusk, while questioning the son of about 12 years of age, I spotted a *sjambok* (hippo-hide whip) hanging behind the door of the office. Merely taking it down had the desired effect – and I would not have used it anyway – and Gamuchira admitted that his father had killed the ox, giving full details. The case went to High Court and Takawira was sentenced to nine months I.H.L.

One day in 1927 I entered a hut in the village of David Masuka, a younger brother of the Chief I think, and found some long robes, drums and a long hooked type of bishop's staff. On my return to camp I reported the matter to Busky who told me to submit a report to Mr Watters. Apparently David Masuka had introduced a new sect, based on the Old Testament, from Johannesburg. The followers were known as Zionists. Mr Watters informed me that he knew of the matter and three years later the Government, fearing subversion, banned the movement and burnt down the village. However, the movement spread like lightening and the ban was eventually withdrawn. Today there are many thousands of followers of the sect in the country. They wear the most colourful long robes bearing crosses of different colours, and at their gatherings dance themselves into a frenzy and 'speak with tongues'.

I had first endeavoured to enlist in the BSA Police in 1923, but my father had consulted his greatest friend, General Henry Timson Lukin, who commanded the South African troops in the Great War and who had been O.C. of the Cape Mounted Riflemen. The following was the text of a very brief letter passed to me by my father one day: –

> 'Dear...
> I would not advise you to put your son into the Rhodesian Police, it is a small Force, promotion is slow, and what is more you and I

know what life on an outstation is.
Yours sincerely,
H.T. Lukin.'

I think today, I am as qualified as the two old friends were to talk about life on an outstation. After serving my last year in the police at Bikita, latterly as Trooper-in-Charge, I took my discharge and not wanting an indoor sedentary life, as I had endured in a bank for four and a half years, I rejected an offer of employment in the Native Department and in April 1930 took over the Dip Supervisor's job at Bikita from ex-Trooper Paddy Hodgins, who had also been Trooper-in-Charge for a time. With eleven years in succession at Bikita, I was to learn much about outstation life – spells of great happiness interspersed with some very unhappy periods.

Troopers Mullin and Style (r) with Native Constables at Bikita

It was my experience that if there were no wives on the station the men got on like a house on fire. If there was one wife, everything in the garden was lovely and she was 'Queen of the May'. If there were two wives there was perfect harmony. But if there were three or more, the petty squabbling started and social life was seriously disrupted. Horses and turkeys would get into flower gardens and bitter quarrels would ensue. Husbands took the side of their wives and the pettiness was unbelievable. Once, as I entered the Native Commissioner's office to make a report, I was greeted with – 'Nimrod, how dare your wife remain friendly with Mrs – when my wife has quarrelled with her!'

One bitter quarrel resulted in the closing down of tennis, our only recreation. Orders were given to this effect and for three long years the dispute went on and the weeds grew on the tennis court. I suppose these things happen on outstations the world over, and I would like to pay a tribute to all wives compelled to live an outstation life.

However, there were some very good times. Mr Watters was never as happy as when he had the whole station sun-downing with him and Mrs Watters on his veranda, where we often danced.

Clarence Sissing, with the aid of others, had composed a ditty which, with Mrs Watters accompanying on the piano, we frequently sang. These were the words – sung with much gusto:

> How can Bikita lads show they're pleased
> If they haven't got a girl to rag.
> All other gay lads so they say,
> Have got little girls with whom to play.
> If they'd only send some girls to Bikita
> And finish off a decent job;
> Well, the price of lobola would go right up
> From a *huku* (fowl) up to fifteen bob.

Government were not very generous to outstations in those days and Frank McCabe had had to build his own quarters. When C.D. McCallum took over from Frank he bought the quarters, and when McCallum, ever a lover of sport, left to go trading he passed the quarters on to Stan Morris for a tennis racquet.

Troopers Paddy Power and Batterzat built the first police camp at Denga. I remember the latter well for, on returning from the Zambesi patrol of several months, during which he had found excellent shooting, he hawked around Depot postcard-size photographs of the big game he had shot. We recruits bought these eagerly to send home.

In 1934 the popular Sergeant 'Tommy' Thompson (later to retire as Colonel to Newcastle), a great soccer player, arrived at Bikita with his pioneers to build the new camp. Among the men I well remember were Wally Walshaw (now a Major living in Salisbury) Browell who was later to become a successful tobacco farmer, and George Watt, but have forgotten the others.

Eventually the beautiful camp was completed, and Corporal Mervyn Harries (the station must have been upgraded) decided to throw a house-

At Bikita in 1938 - Mervyn Harries, Henry Roper-Cooke Sergeant Turner (from Zaka), Jack Frost and C.W.H. Thatcher

The quarters which Stan Morris bought with a tennis racket

Paddy Power - photo taken just after World War II

warming party. We were all enjoying our sundowners on the veranda when we saw a car approaching at speed. It failed to take the corner in front of the building and hit one of the main pillars with a resounding smack, knocking it over on to the veranda, narrowly missing Mervyn, and smothering him in dust. The latest caller was Jack Tarr, our popular Cattle Inspector and a notoriously fast driver, who came forward unhurt with profuse apologies. We all enjoyed a laugh except the pioneers, who were held up another day or two effecting repairs.

George Style notes:

Mervyn Harries, who kindly sent me the photo of the five policemen on the verandah of the Bikita Police Station, says he thinks that the snap was taken the morning after Jack Tarr tried to knock the office down.

'... As Corporal-in-Charge, I was deep in thought as to how we could rebuild the pillar that had been demolished. Eventually Gordon Hughes sent his builder down to make good the damage – but he did it so badly that I decided to lay my cards on the table and report the incident to the District Superintendent, Monty Surgey. His reply was: 'I understand Inspector Tarr was reversing his car when his foot slipped off the clutch and he ran into the pillar!' Monty then sent Pioneer Jansen out to rebuild the pillar completely.'

Mervyn's photo also adds a little confusion to the date of the incident but as he has marked the reverse of the snap as being 1938, I'll take his word for it.

Two ex-troopers served as Cattle Inspectors for a time, the handsome Doug Forrester, with his snow-white hair and dark eyebrows, and 'Brusher' Bond. Doug and I spent many hours together at Dip Tanks in the depressed days of the 1930s, when the ruling price for cattle was £1 for the biggest and fattest ox, 15/- for the best cows including fat Queen slaughter cows, and 7/6d. for the best heifers. In 1931 we had the first outbreak of Foot and Mouth disease in the country and were kept very busy, creating cattle-free belts, inspecting and inoculating.

Times were hard, and initially I had to run my own transport out of my salary of £25 per month. After paying car instalments, petrol and car repairs, I had approximately £4 per month to live on. However, I had an excellent vegetable garden, and was asked to kill cattle and supply meat to all on the station in return for which I was to get my meat for nothing, thus saving 1/- for all my hard work! John Crawford, a son of the old pioneer, ran a butchery at Penhalonga, was a pal of Jack Nesbitt's and used to come over cattle buying. John taught me how to butcher and each household received weekly a large tray of choice meat for the price of 1/-. Usually the meat was from a Queen cow bought for 15/-. There were six households to supply, including mine, so that left 10/- to find. The forequarters were snapped up by the messengers for this amount.

On one occasion the Native Commissioner, whose knowledge of cattle was not very great, sent me out to buy 62 oxen for the Roads Department: 'Look, Nimrod, go out and buy these oxen. As you know the ruling price is £1 for the biggest and best oxen, but if they have extra long horns you may pay up to 25/-!'

Five shillings was a lot of money to pay in those days for an extra length of horn! It was actually half a farm labourer's wages.

Despite the depression, with all of us being so hard up, we managed to buy the odd bottle of liquor and throw an occasional sundowner party. The Silveira Mission was founded by the Revd. Father Ferguson S.J. in the 1930s. He was the youngest of a family of 14 and came from the West Indies. The Father was a wonderful and lovable character, enjoyed his drinks, told the naughtiest stories, and was the life and soul of every party. His presence was always in great demand. Whenever I called at the Mission, near which we built a Dip Tank, I was ushered into the dining room and asked to sit down and excuse him for a minute. Soon afterwards he would appear with a bottle of brandy in his hand, and I could never break away until that bottle was finished. When some nuns were drafted to the Mission he spent much time gambling for matches with them.

The Trooper-in-Charge of the station, being also the Gaoler, had to find work daily for the 'bandits' (the name by which the hard labour prisoners were known). The hard labour consisted chiefly of working in someone's garden, and I was lucky enough to get help now and again in keeping up a very beautiful flower garden. So much so that one Native Commissioner was heard to remark, 'By what right has the Dip Supervisor the best flower-garden on the Station?' Perhaps the reason was that the Dip Supervisor had more time to devote to his garden than anyone else!

One morning the Gaol Guard – Mahash, a second General Amin – had his gang of prisoners working away happily in the garden when one of the gang came running up to the house to ask my wife to come and shoot a large snake. We were infested with snakes and her father had presented her with a 0.410 shotgun for the purpose. She said to the prisoner, 'Why doesn't Mahash shoot the snake with his gun?' 'Because he has no bullets!' replied the prisoner. Despite this fact, Mahash was never parted from his showpiece, an old carbine that must have gone back to Pioneer days.

On another occasion, with a hue and cry, the whole gang of about thirty prisoners took off and ran into the bundu, the stout Mahash well in the rear. It appeared that one of their number, doing time for something more serious than tax-defaulting, had taken to his heels in a bid to escape. With much spurring on by Mahash the bandit was recaptured by his fellow prisoners and handed over with great glee to the perspiring Mahash.

Gaol really meant nothing to the outstation bandit and this is brought to light in a story told of Lobengula, who was asked on one occasion by one of the early missionaries why he did not build gaols and incarcerate his wrong-doers instead of cracking their skulls.

'What!' replied Lobengula, 'Give them a roof over their heads, blankets to sleep in, and plenty of food to eat! Why! I would have the whole Matabele nation in gaol within a week!'

The roads in Rhodesia were in a shocking condition and it was only in the latter part of 1927 that work started on the low-level Beit Bridges, and in the depression of the 1930s that the first strips were laid by the unemployed Europeans. We all used chains on our wheels in the rainy season, but despite this invariably stuck in the mud in the hills near the Tinfields and had to be pushed out by gangs of boys. Cars were far from numerous in the early days, and even as late as 1920 Mr and Mrs Henry, apparently noted for a love of their sundowners, travelled to Fort Victoria on the water-cart. But only literally so!

As far as I know, the late Chief Ziki, formerly Head Messenger Rusakaniko, was the first African in Rhodesia to buy a car. The Bikita roads were some of the worst in the country and the car was always breaking down and Ziki would have to be towed home by a span of oxen. Car dealers were pretty unscrupulous in those days too, and running back the mileage of a car and then selling worn out vehicles was common practice.

One day Stan Morris and Clarence Sissing climbed to the top of a very high hill called Gurundema situated west of the Rozwa river. It was on this hill that Chief Mukanganwe had his kraal, and nearby was an exceptionally tall dead tree, considered to be virtually unclimbable. Apparently the old Chief had a very pretty daughter much sought after by the young men. The Chief had stipulated that whoever could climb the tree could claim his daughter in marriage. One day a young blood succeeded and claimed his bride and from then onwards the tree was known as '*Muda-wa-Moyo*' (I want your heart). After many years the tree fell down but no one was allowed to use the wood.

The whole of the Bikita district, both the Native Reserve and the ranches, abounded with game of all descriptions in those days, and there being very little other recreation, especially during the three years the tennis-court remained grass, I enjoyed much hunting. By 1930 Gordon Hughes was well established as a trader with his main store at Huzi near the Turgwe River. Here he had improved on his original 1925 home of a pole-and-dagga hut and built himself a comfortable brick under thatch cottage where he loved to entertain. One weekend in December 1930, with the concurrence of Mr Watters and the police (Frank Blake being again temporarily in charge with Ned Sherlock as patrolling trooper), Gordon gave a hunting party for nine of us. Those in the party that I remember apart from Frank, Ned and myself, were 'one-eyed' Scott, manager of Zeederberg's transport in Fort Victoria, and O.C. of the Rifle Platoon, 'Mealie' McLeod of Meikles Store, and McLeod of the Standard Bank who later joined Mazoe Citrus Estate.

Most of us met for dinner on the Saturday night, when the liquor flowed freely. It was about 9 p.m. when we eventually sat down to a sumptuous meal, the main course of which was roast chicken. Everyone was in good spirits, both literally and figuratively. Eventually, after soup, the chickens were carved by Gordon and served. Now Frank Blake and Ned Sherlock were seated opposite each other at the ends of the table. All of a sudden, I noticed Ned, with a mischievous grin on his face, throw a chicken bone the length of the table onto his superior's plate. His aim was perfect and it landed right in the middle. I will never forget the look of amazement with which Frank looked at Ned, who, eyes now downcast, was tackling another leg. Frank said nothing. Ned picked his bone clean and it followed the course of the first bone, landing squarely on target. This was too much for Frank, who promptly invited Ned outside. We all trooped out, and after a little preliminary sparring, during which no blood was shed, we separated the two and pacified Frank. We then finished our dinner and retired for the night, most of us dossing down on the hard cement veranda.

We set out in two cars next morning travelling down the old Turgwe Drift road. At a spot just 19 miles from Bikita and about seven from Huzi, we saw a very large herd of sable antelope grazing on the left side. We all debussed, and as the sable crossed the road, those with rifles dropped five. As the herd was very spread out we were able to get a fairly accurate count, and were all in agreement that the total number exceeded 200. It was a magnificent sight. In those days sable were very plentiful indeed along the Turgwe, as were Lichstenstein Hartebeest, the latter especially around Nyarunwe kopje and on both sides of the river. Having now obtained sufficient meat, although it was still early in the morning we returned to Huzi to enjoy a day of drinking and feasting.

One morning in the early 1930s I found Sergeant Jock Harvey camped on the borders of the Sangwe Reserve where he was in charge of a Foot and Mouth disease cattle-cordon. The jovial Jock informed me that he had met a herd of over 400 buffalo grazing in the area. I was told by the local Shangaans later that these buffalo drank in a pan about half-a-mile from the Sabi. I had a large *dare* (platform) built in a tall tree near the pan and, with my family, spent the next night of full moon in the *dare*. Much to my disappointment only eight buffalo arrived that night, and on upbraiding the Shangaans next morning for lying, they assured me that the buffalo drank in the pan only every second night. This turned out to be the case, and on the second night four herds arrived. After drinking they joined up and stood in the moonlight under our platform. As the day broke they trailed off into the bush towards the Mkwasine, where presumably they drank on alternate days. There were at least 400 in the herd.

I will always remember my first buffalo hunt. In September 1930, Bob Elliot and I motored down to the Mkwasine and camped on the banks of the river. At the crack of dawn we set off in different directions, Bob travelling upstream while, with my two guides, local Shangaans, I went downstream. Game was exceedingly plentiful in the area in those days and was concentrated within a few miles of the river, which, although not running, held large pools of water.

I was using a beautiful rifle, a new 9.3 mm with a white bead foresight. It proved to be a most accurate weapon. We had been walking only a few minutes when a bushpig got up and ran along the top of the opposite river bank. A lucky shot bowled him over. We hunted all morning with a brief half-hour's rest, and I dropped, with a shot each, an exceptionally large eland bull, a lone sable bull, and a zebra stallion grazing on its own. This was not considered as slaughter in those days, nor was a scrap of the meat wasted, every morsel being carried away by meat-hungry natives, however far they had to walk.

At about 3 p.m. we met a herd of about 60 buffalo standing in a large open vlei. They were very tame, and my guides had apparently been quite impressed with my marksmanship. They led me to within about eighty yards of the herd. I was terrified, but felt obliged to follow. I didn't like the way the buffalo put their heads back and looked at us down their noses. I aimed at the head of the nearest and fired, whereupon the herd turned and bolted. We saw the one I had hit drop a hundred yards off but there being no cover, decided that discretion was the better part of valour and that we would return to camp.

Now the long trek back to camp started. We had been walking since daybreak with only two stops of about half-an-hour each. My legs felt as though they were in irons, and we didn't arrive in camp until 9.30 p.m. to find that Bob had had exceptionally bad luck and shot nothing. Next morning we returned to the vlei and collected a buffalo cow, the bullet having travelled through one cheek and entered the heart.

One afternoon Doug Forrester and I were driving through Crown Land below Angus Ranch on the way to inspect cattle at Gudo Dip Tank in the Sangwe Reserve, when we spotted a herd of about sixty buffalo grazing among mopani trees to the left of the road. Doug had, up to that time, not shot a buffalo and was very anxious to bag one. So we got out of the car, and keeping downwind, stalked the herd. We climbed a tree in order to look for a large bull among the thick undergrowth. Eventually Doug grew impatient and asked if he should shoot a smallish animal clearly visible. He dropped the animal with a shot through the shoulder, then the herd came together and stampeded.

Dropping to the ground I gave chase and noticed one enormous animal. It was head and shoulders above the others and running on the left flank. I got in a raking heart shot and it dropped to the ground 100 yards ahead. I was most surprised to find that I had not shot a bull, but an old cow. The horns were so large that a shovel fitted in between the tips, and it could well have been a record for a Rhodesian cow, but 'The Book' (Rowland Ward's) was something we never thought of in those days. However I wish I had the horns today, but being very hard up when I enlisted during the war, I put them on Knight's Auction Market in Bulawayo together with a lot of other junk. I hope they are gracing someone's veranda today.

I was relaxing on the banks of the Sabi late one afternoon, with my hunting-boy, Johnny Bandura, after a tiring day's hunting. As we sat dangling our legs over the embankment we saw a Shangaan approaching. After greeting us he sat down next to Johnny and was soon in earnest conversation with him. Although not a very good linguist I was able to pick up the gist of the conversation.

It appeared that our visitor resided on the other side of the Mkwasine in the Zaka district. The story he told was interesting. A fellow Shangaan called Smoke had stolen some arsenical dip from one of the Zaka dip tanks, put it into beer, and poisoned another man. On the death of the man, Smoke had buried the corpse in his hut. Although Trooper Jack Frost, then at Zaka, had just been on patrol in the area, our informant had been afraid to make a report.

We returned to Bikita that evening and next morning I telephoned all particulars through to the Member-in-Charge Zaka, who sent Trooper Lanning down to investigate. Sure enough, the body was found buried in Smoke's hut and he was arrested, admitting the charge. One night on the trek back to camp the prisoner was put in a hut after being handcuffed and leg-ironed. Lanning laid his bedding across the doorway and settled down for the night. To Lanning's horror he woke up to find that the bird had flown, having quietly stepped over him despite the leg-irons. Smoke was never arrested and it was thought he had escaped into Portuguese territory.

On the night of September 2 1939 – a Sunday – I was camped at Maziwa Dip Tank in the Matsai Reserve with 'Brusher' Bond, awaiting a cattle sale due next morning. We switched on the radio at 8 p.m. and heard that war had been declared.

'Nimrod,' shouted Brusher, 'I'm off to enlist first thing in the morning! To hell with the cattle!'

His resignation was accepted – there was no alternative – and he was soon overseas. Captured at Crete, he spent three miserable years behind the wire, perhaps pondering at times over our Bikita patrol and his eagerness to enlist. We had served in the same recruit squad in Depot in 1925 and I must say I shared his enthusiasm and was in the army as soon as possible myself.

Brusher is now with the Postal Headquarters in Salisbury.

Clockwise from top left:
Trooper-in-Charge George Style at Bikita, 1929
George and family at Bikita
George's Bikita homestead with his two-seater Ford parked outside, 1931
George with the old 'Chev' at Kufa Tank

On previous pages George Style brought his life story up until the time he left the Police (in 1930), got married and got a new job, still at Bikita. The story is now carried on from that period by a long extract from Dr Colin Saunders' article, 'Great Characters of the Lowveld, George Style of Buffalo Range', as published in Heritage of Zimbabwe *No. 21, 2002. Of necessity there may be some small duplication of events in both accounts. The story here is taken up from when George returned from meeting Bvekenya Barnard, a full account of which is in George's 'Barnard the Elephant Poacher' at page 158.*

Next morning George returned with Eric Chapman in his new vehicle to Crook's Corner, there to resume his patrol. It was not until forty years later that George Style revealed the facts of his meeting with Bvekenya Barnard. Shortly after this excursion George was smitten by severe malaria, verging on the dreaded complication 'blackwater fever'. On medical advice he was transferred from Nuanetsi back to Fort Victoria. Thereafter, being a young man and therefore liable to frequent transfer, he served successively at Chibi (Chivi), Mashaba (Mashava), and Gutu, before being sent back to Bikita, this time as Trooper-in-Charge.

Policemen stationed in the outposts of that era had responsibility for many extraneous duties, among which were those of immigration officer, prosecutor, gaoler, vermin control officer (meaning the person charged with responsibility for hunting carnivores which preyed on livestock in the district), and vaccination officer. While no additional income was derived from the first three duties, a bounty was payable for each lion, leopard, or wild dog killed by the policeman, the last-named fetching top bounty of ten shillings each, and therefore much sought after and persecuted. He was also paid a fee for vaccinating local residents against smallpox – the medical staff of the district having no itinerant personnel who could perform this function. George's memoirs record that during a month-long patrol in 1927 he vaccinated 1909 tribespeople, for which he received the very welcome sum of nine pounds, four shillings, and one penny – the rate being threepence each for the first 100, twopence each for the second 100, and one penny each for the remainder.

Late in 1929 he went to the capital for a promotion examination, which he failed – a common experience for first time applicants in a service where maintenance of high standards was rigidly enforced. He had by that time fallen in love with a young lady whom he had met while on a previous visit to Salisbury, and George had located his desired partner for life in the form of Miss Ethne Pilkington. In those days there was an inviolate rule of service in the police, according to which marriage was forbidden to any policeman in his first ten years of service.

The couple desired to be married, and being unwilling to wait all those years, there was no option open to George other than to resign from the BSA Police. He duly resigned, on 30 April 1930, after more than five years of most enjoyable service, during which he made a host of friends.

AT HOME AT BIKITA

He had found life at Bikita much to his liking, and decided that he would stay on there in some other job. As soon as he heard that young Style was leaving the police force the District Commissioner (then known as 'Native Commissioner') at Bikita offered George the post of District Clerk. However, he had decided that his four years in the bank in South Africa was more than enough time working in a space enclosed by four walls. So instead he accepted an offer to take over the post of Cattle Dip Superintendent from an incumbent who was also an ex-BSA Police Trooper. A condition of appointment was that he had to purchase his predecessor's motor car – a very smart blue Chev tourer – without which he would not be able to carry out his duties in the district

He and Ethne were duly married, and settled down to a very happy life together in the small community of civil servants who lived and worked at Bikita. Life was pleasant, but very necessarily rather humble in view of the meagre monthly salary paid; he records that his salary was £25 per month, of which payments for his car (instalments, repairs, and petrol) took £21, leaving the couple only £4 with which to pay all their household expenses. They were fortunate in being able to augment their income through Ethne's skill in growing and selling vegetables, and also through selling fresh milk from the eleven Jersey cows which George had gradually acquired. In addition, he was the unofficial butcher and distributor of fresh meat, for which service he received no wage, but instead was entitled to a very welcome supply of fresh meat, free of charge.

Although Bikita was generally a very happy outstation, it was inevitable that there should occur from time to time the eccentricities and interpersonal feuds which characterised life in such small closed and isolated communities. George's opinion was that any such problems invariably arose because of actions and attitudes on the part of the wives. He records rather wryly the following conclusion: no women present, and everyone gets on like a house on fire; one wife on the station is adored by all – 'the queen of the May'; with two wives the community lives in happy harmony; but when there are three or more wives, there is constant friction! He recalled that on one occasion, when entering the office of the Native Commissioner, he was startled to be castigated because Ethne had befriended the wife of another official! On another memorable occasion, the wives of two local luminaries fell out over a trivial issue, and the resulting rift resulted in the closure of the tennis court (the only recreational sports facility on station, patronised by most of the civil service community) for a period of three years.

The Bikita district was extraordinarily rich in wild life of all kinds, and opportunities for sport hunting abounded, with the added bonus of augmenting the meat supply. When the tennis court was closed for a prolonged period, hunting became an even more popular outdoor pastime at weekends. The most famous and popular area of all for hunting was down to the south on the Mkwasine River, a very sparsely populated area holding amazing numbers of game animals of great diversity. There were also great numbers of animals along the Save' in those days. George recorded 300 buffalo in Gudo's Pool on one occasion, while on another he watched spellbound during a drought when a massive herd of buffalo, crazed by thirst, stampeded down to the pool, resulting in 25 of them being drowned by the pressure from those in the rear, providing a huge feast for gargantuan crocodiles.

Leopards were particularly plentiful in the hills surrounding Bikita. On one occasion Jock Ferrie, a notable local store keeper, had 72 of his prized sheep killed in their kraal by a single marauding leopard in one night. George had plenty of opportunities to hone his 'vermin' hunting skills. However, his first attempt had an embarrassing tragic ending: hunting a problem leopard with the aid of a hunting lamp, he shot a creature whose eyes reflected the telltale green glow back at him, only to find that he had killed his friend's sheep dog 'Jock'. He later became a proficient hunter of leopards. It was at this time that he engaged the services of a renowned local hunter named Johnny Bandura.

On the surrounding large-scale cattle ranches lions were even more of a problem than the leopards in the hills. On Angus Ranch a wily lion known as *mangwana-mangwana* to the local people (because, unlike most of its kind, it never returned to its kill, striking elsewhere the next day) killed in excess of 400 cattle during its reign of terror. It survived all attempts to get rid of it, until it made its first and last error and returned one night to feed on the carcass it had left the previous day, which had in the meantime been poisoned with strychnine. On Devuli Ranch to the east of Bikita lived a renowned lion hunter named Ali Hamman, who had shot 66 stock-raiding lions, and poisoned in excess of three hundred others. From Hamman the young ex-policeman learnt many tricks of the trade in hunting lions.

Besides Jock Ferrie, two other interesting characters – Paddy Power and Gordon Hughes – made their living from trading in the district. Ethne from time to time assisted one or other of them during their absence or when they were particularly busy. She at once demonstrated a considerable flair for trading, an interest which was to be of great benefit to the family in later years.

It was while they were at Bikita that the couple's two sons, Rodney and Clive were born to Ethne in 1931 and 1933 respectively. They enjoyed an idyllic close-knit family life in a warm and loving home, probably the more so because of George's determination that his children should not endure the austere fatherhood which had caused him so much unhappiness in his own childhood. They spent a great deal of time out in the open air, the little boys accompanying their father as often as possible on his trips around the district, where he was responsible for the health of thirty thousand cattle. They often swam in the shallow waters of the broad Sabi (Save') River, watching, with great interest the construction of the massive bridge, the Birchenough Bridge, which was to provide a more comfortable and dependable method of crossing the river than being hauled through the great expanse of water and sand by Jimmy Whittall's trek oxen – the only method of crossing, prior to construction of the gracefully arched bridge.

In later years, when the boys were of school-going age, they were sent off to boarding school at REPS in the Matopos, and then on to the high school at Plumtree.

George was in his element in his bush life, building on his love of wild things and wide open spaces which had started during his spell at Nuanetsi.

Creatures great and small fascinated him. Apart from the tales of lions and leopards which he wrote, and with which he regaled his little boys, he recorded such things as the fascinating phenomenon of the annual swarming of dense clouds of a green shield bug known as *Harurwa* (*Haplosterna delegorguei*) which gathered in dense swarms on Rumedzo hill in Chief Mazungunye's area of Bikita. Countless millions of these insects arrive in April each year; they are then collected in an orderly process under the jurisdiction of the local headman, and shared out amongst the tribesmen, to be dried and fried as a greatly relished delicacy.

He travelled widely in the district to carry out his allocated task of supervising the health of the cattle which were so valuable to rancher and tribesman alike. In 1931 he recorded the first ever case of foot and mouth disease ('FMD') in the country, a disease which was later to occupy much of his time as the eyes and ears of the Veterinary Department. The efficient control methods of regular close inspection, inoculation and strictly enforced cattle cordons which the vets devised were the responsibility of himself and his subordinate cattle inspectors. Also in 1931 the country was hit by the devastating depression which affected the whole world. The value of cattle plummeted, fat oxen fetching only one pound at the periodic cattle sales, while quality heifers went for seven shillings and sixpence.

During the depression the popular local Chief Ziki became the first African gentleman in the country to own his own motor vehicle, presumably acquiring it from some unfortunate individual who had been hard hit by the depressed state of the economy. It was also at about this time that George on patrol recorded that one David Masuka had started a new religious sect known as the Zionists. At first the authorities were concerned that the movement might be quasi-political and therefore troublesome, but their fears were unfounded, and the sect attracted great numbers of members of sincere religious conviction.

THE ARMY CALLS

While camping out with a colleague named 'Brusher' Bond prior to a cattle sale at Maziwa Dip Tank deep in the heart of the Matsai communal land on 3 September 1939, they switched on their radio to listen to the 8 p.m. news broadcast, and heard the grim news that war had been declared against Germany.

George now had the opportunity to follow the example of many of his ancestors who had joined the army and followed a military career. On their return to base they both hurriedly made arrangements to enlist in the armed forces. After initial training in the capital, George was posted to the Infantry Training Centre at Zomba in Malawi, and enrolled in the King's African Rifles, where he was engaged in training army recruits. During his time in what was then Nyasaland, still a remote and comparatively sparsely populated country, he made something of a name for himself as a lion hunter of note, killing three man-eaters which had been terrorising the local peasant folks.

Demonstrating great leadership skills and excellent race relations, he was commissioned and sent with his men to fight in the East African campaign. They were posted to the Headquarters of 25th Brigade in the Northern Frontier District of Kenya, where they saw active service. Style survived the war without any mishaps, but his friend Bond was not so lucky – he was captured on the island of Crete, and spent three miserable years 'behind the wire' as a prisoner of war.

While still in East Africa towards the end of the Second World War, George heard that the government at home had formed a Land Settlement Board to enable suitable returning servicemen, many of them now without a job, to embark on a farming career. Government were convinced that expansion of the post-war economy of the country would be based on organised agriculture. In addition, there was obviously a need to expand food production after the hardships which had prevailed during the war, and besides, they wanted to reward those who had risked their lives in the interests of the country. Before returning to the country, George applied for a farm under the ex-serviceman's settlement scheme.

On cessation of hostilities in 1945, full of excited expectations, he hurried back to what was then Salisbury, only to be bitterly disappointed. His application had been rejected, the reason given being that the scheme was for men under the age of 40, and he had just turned 41. In vain did he appeal against the decision.

GEORGE STYLE, TOBACCO FARMER

There were then no prospects of meaningful employment at his old home of Bikita with good prospects for a wife and two growing boys, so he applied for employment as a farm assistant. In November 1945 he was engaged as a tobacco assistant to a farmer at Mvurwi, for a salary of £25 per month, and a bonus of 10% of nett profit. He did very well that year, and in the following season he agreed to join his brother-in-law on a half-share tobacco farming venture, also in the Mvurwi district. He borrowed from his previous employer the sum of £1000, being his half-share of the input expenses in his new partnership. Again he did very well, and grew an excellent tobacco crop. After the tobacco had been sold at auction, he set his mind on obtaining a farm of his own.

In July 1947 he heard that a neighbour called Page had subdivided his property at Umsengezi River Ranch, and two subdivisions were for sale. George was successful in securing one of the properties, 2,500 acres in extent, which he named Chidziwa after a waterhole of that name on the farm. He had saved £4000, from which he had to repay the loan of £1000 and pay a deposit of £1500 to Page for the farm, leaving him very little money for the many expenses of growing a crop. He borrowed £2000 from the Land Bank, and was favoured with a credit facility of a further £2000 from the local Farmers' Co-op. Life was very tough that year, with two boys at boarding school at Plumtree, and he and Ethne could afford little for their own comfort. They built a small mud hut as their first home, with a slit trench as a latrine, and a bucket in which to perform the ablutions. A dilapidated borrowed tent served as their general storeroom for all the farm's requirements. As it had been a poor rainy season, there was a severe shortage of thatching grass, and they could see the stars through the roof of their hut at night.

Ethne was very keen to commence trading in order to provide an income. George started making bricks from ant-heap, and the first building that he constructed was a little trading store for her. The profits from Ethne's trading enterprise paid for the wages. With Ethne demonstrating rare flair and commitment, the trading venture prospered and expanded, until within two years she had a chain of six local stores. The income thus generated was an absolutely vital factor in providing for their farming expenses!

George purchased an old ox-wagon for his transport requirements, and from the Cold Storage Commission he bought two spans of oxen to pull the wagon and his plough. Construction of tobacco barns and sheds soon followed, and as they were so far from the shops in Harare, they also had to buy an old 'jalopy' for their periodic trips to town. His neighbours were generous in sharing their experience and providing advice on the intricacies of growing tobacco successfully, particularly H.J. Quinton. One of the country's most successful farmers, he was later to be appointed Chairman of The Sabi-Limpopo Authority, which was constituted in the early 1960s to co-ordinate the great development programme in the lowveld.

The Styles' first crop on their own farm was a record one for the district, fetching the highest price on the auction floors. They had engaged an excellent farm builder from Malawi, and they soon moved into a little three-roomed cottage which he built to be followed by accommodation for their workers, and then, a year later, a farm clinic. By this time George had established 140 acres of tobacco. Two more good productive years followed. They purchased a new car, and a new truck to transport their crop to the auction floors.

In January 1950 they proudly sent their elder son Rodney off to the University of Cape Town to study for his life-long wish to be a chemical engineer, and in the same year Clive, who had always wanted to be a farmer, was enrolled in the first year's intake at the new Gwebi College of Agriculture. In June of that year, during their younger son's half-year break from studies at Gwebi, George, Ethne, and Clive set off to Cape Town to join the budding engineer on the family's first seaside holiday. By this time Rod had decided that university life was not for him, and at the end of that month he returned to Chidziwa to help his father with the farming venture. He became a very enthusiastic and successful tobacco farmer.

At the end of 1951, having acquired his Diploma in Agriculture from Gwebi, Clive joined the family venture, George having in the meantime established a mixed farming operation, as his younger son had made it quite clear that he was not interested in tobacco. He took over and expanded an enterprise which included pigs, sheep, poultry, and 80 acres of maize. They built three dams, and established a fish farming project with the advice of Dr Maar, the government's fishery specialist.

The Style family thrived in the Mvurwi farming community, becoming very active members of the Umvukwes Country Club, where the three men, being competent horsemen, all played polo with great gusto on the ponies George had purchased for them. In time they established their own polo field on Chidziwa. All the while Ethne's trading business continued to prosper, paying the whole wage bill – a much appreciated contribution to the family's farming fortunes.

BACK TO THE LOWVELD

In June 1952 a Government Gazette arrived on George's desk, and he noted with a sense of excitement that applications were invited for the lease, with the option of purchase, of three proposed Crown Land Ranches in the District of Ndanga near the lower Chiredzi River, not far from the areas where he had spent many happy days while stationed some way to the north at Bikita. He had begun to feel 'crowded out' by the feverish development of tobacco farms in northern Mashonaland, and the thought of the possibility of establishing a ranch in the Ndanga district rekindled for him that old lowveld magic which he had first experienced when stationed at Nuanetsi. He and Ethne at once travelled down to the area, where they were met by Jock Murray, the local Lands Inspector, who drove them around the three ranches. There were particularly large numbers of impala on Ranch No 2, as well as good populations of kudu, eland, sable, and zebra. To settle in this area was all that he could have desired at that stage, and even in those early days George dreamt of creating a private game reserve if he was successful in his quest to secure the land.

Immediately on his return to Mashonaland he submitted his application for Ranch No 2, a property of 54,448 acres. His application was accompanied by a strong recommendation by Stanley Morris, District Commissioner at Umvukwes station, who stressed the success that George had made of his farming venture.

Then followed several months of impatience and frustration while the Style family waited for a response. Eventually, in September of that year, George could bear the suspense no longer, and he decided that he and Ethne would go off on a long holiday. Accordingly, leaving the boys in charge of the farm at Chidziwa, the two of them went to Malawi in a brand-new Plymouth 2-seater sedan which he had purchased with part of the profits from the previous very successful season. In Blantyre he looked up an old friend from his army days, Bert Smith, who was now in charge of the charge office at the local police station. Recalling George's prowess as a lion hunter in days long before, Smith told him that he had just received a report of a lion killing livestock on a nearby farm, and asked him to go after it.

Leaving Ethne at Ryall's Hotel, George wasted no time in travelling out to the farm, to find that a lion had the previous night killed three cattle. He arranged for the construction of a platform in a tree overlooking one of the carcases, and that night sat up for the lion, which he managed to shoot by the light of a hunting torch. This did his reputation as a mighty hunter no harm at all!

Continuing on their tour, they travelled throughout Malawi and on into Mozambique down to the coast, and then to Gorongosa Game Reserve. From there they returned via Mutare to Chidziwa early in November, refreshed after a very enjoyable holiday. Going to fetch their mail bag at Concession next morning, George was thrilled to find a letter advising him that his application for a lease on Ndanga Crown Ranch No 2 had been successful, and instructing him to make arrangements to take up the land. In order to become eligible for the right of purchase, he was required to carry out certain improvements and to establish a herd of a minimum of 800 cattle.

The family wasted no time in making plans for the move. It was decided that Rodney would continue farming at Chidziwa to continue bringing in an income during the time that the new ranching venture was being developed, Clive would assist his father with the cattle ranching operation, and Ethne would accompany them to set up home and, inevitably, to start a trading enterprise. They held a very successful dispersal sale to get rid of their livestock and certain other items which they would no longer require.

George's memoirs record:
> I immediately made a few preliminary trips down to the ranch with furniture, etc, and, on each visit, nailed notices made out of planks from paraffin-boxes on trees all over the ranch. I had burned on the planks with a hot poker 'SHOOTING PROHIBITED', but all this seemed to do was increase the poaching!

Having settled their affairs on the farm at Chidziwa and enjoyed a number of farewell parties hosted by their friends in the district, George, Ethne and Clive set off in February 1953 in a brand new International ¾ ton truck to take up occupation of the ranch, with Ethne doing most of the driving. She had loaded up the truck with chickens, ducks, and turkeys, as well as all their personal effects. It was a particularly wet rainy season, and when they reached the old low level bridge across the Tokwe River between Masvingo and Beit Bridge they found that the river was in high flood, and the bridge several metres under water.

They turned back and booked in to the hotel at Great Zimbabwe, where they had to stay for ten impatient days while they waited for reports that the flood was subsiding, Ethne turned all her poultry out into the hotel garden, where the management for a few days tolerated their noisy messy presence, before politely asking George to make alternative arrangements. Fortunately he was able to arrange accommodation for the flock of birds at the nearby Morgenster Mission.

Tiring of life at the hotel, they eventually decided to cross the Tokwe River on the road to Shabani (Zvishavane) and then to travel down through the Chivi communal area to rejoin the Beitbridge Road, and on through Ngundu and Triangle to their new home. They duly arrived at their new lowveld property after a long, wet and very wearisome trip.

BUFFALO RANGE

The family were required to submit to the Registrar of Deeds three possible names for the ranch, in order of preference. Their list was 1) Buffalo Range, 2) King Ranch, and 3) Horse-shoe Ranch (after two horse-shoe bends in the Chiredzi River on the ranch).

They first built a simple 'pole and dagga' cottage on a chosen site near the Chiredzi River, and then the infrastructure such as dip tanks, fences, water supplies, and cattle kraals for the ranching business. Clive set about building up a herd of cattle, commencing a life-long passion as a rancher – 'I'm not a sod-buster' he would say. The first permanent brick building they erected was a trading store for Ethne, in which she rapidly established a thriving business. When later they moved the family headquarters to its present site eight kilometres east of Triangle, on the road to Chiredzi, the old store down by the river became George's store room for the game-ranching enterprise which he was in the process of establishing. It was agreed that a separate game section of 12,000 acres would be established along the Chiredzi River frontage, with cattle excluded from this section, and the majority of the ranch given over to cattle ranching under Clive's control (but game was free to move in and out of the cattle section).

George recorded his feelings very early on in the family's new lowveld enterprise: 'It is really only the game, and the game section, which interests me'. Ethne was responsible for the trading function, which grew rapidly, and she was later assisted by Clive, who had the same flair as his mother for this branch of commerce. George later referred thus to his wife's flair and passion as a merchandise trader:

> Ethne's old store was the first building on the ranch, where she worked so hard to establish the ranch, and with her flair for buying, and the 'basella' system (10% in gifts, returned for each pound spent) attracted buyers from as far away as Zaka and Ngundu, over 60 miles away. I will always remember the cash given to me for paying the labour force, both on the ranch and on Chidziwa, and what she wrote at the bottom of the pay sheets: 'NOT RETURNABLE!' At times the whole family served behind the counter.

Later on, in 1959, the family sold Chidziwa, and Rod moved down to the lowveld, there to assume an increasingly important role in the family's business interests. George was happy to confine his interests to the wildlife, though remaining as Chairman of the Board of Directors of Buffalo Range (Pty) Ltd.

THE BEGINNING OF GAME RANCHING IN THE LOWVELD

I think that it was Tommy Orford, a National Parks Ranger stationed on the Mkwasine, who first suggested that George should crop the impala as a source of revenue from the sale of meat and hides. There was at the time an awakening interest in the sustained commercial exploitation of wildlife. Dr Reay Smithers, Director of National Museums, had arranged for two Fulbright Scholars from the USA, Drs Ray Dasman and Archie Mossman, to research the subject on Doddieburn Ranch, owned by Alan and Ian Henderson in the West Nicholson area. Smithers was interested in what his old friend Style was doing on Buffalo Range, and he arranged for Dr Archie Mossman to go there to advise George on latest developments and ideas in this field. The Henderson brothers had already commenced commercial game ranching on Doddieburn, and it took little persuasion for George Style to follow suit.

The legendary game ranger Rupert Fothergill ('Roop' to George) was a frequent and very welcome guest. On his first visit in the mid-1950s he said that one herd of impala, estimated to be more than 200 strong, was the largest he had ever seen.

At first it was the culling of impala, with the aid of a spotlight at night, which was the mainstay of the initiative, there being an almost insatiable market for fresh meat for employees of the burgeoning lowveld sugar estates. At this point I must recount an amusing incident which occurred in 1963, when George invited me to accompany him on a nocturnal outing to crop impala.

After a quick light supper, we set off in an open Land Rover, without windscreen or doors, to harvest the night's crop. Three of us sat in the front seat. George, armed with a 30.06 rifle with telescopic sight, sat in the middle, between me and the driver. My job was to hold the spotlight. We soon came upon a herd of impala, which stood, dazzled by the spotlight. George whispered to me to hold the beam steady on a large ram, while he took aim. 'George!' I whispered urgently to him. 'Shhh! I'm aiming.' 'George!' again, louder and more urgently, drew the same impatient response from my companion. 'George, for goodness' sake!' and I grabbed his arm. Shaking me off, he pulled the trigger, with (to him) a most unexpected result: the loud crack of the rifle was followed immediately by a louder bang, and the whining sound of the ricocheting bullet disappearing into the night, while the targeted ram cantered safely off into the distance.

Peering as he was, through the elevated telescopic sight, my mighty hunter companion could not see that the business end of the barrel of the rifle was firmly bedded against the spare wheel, which was in usual Land Rover style carried on the bonnet of the engine. Ignoring my attempts to warn him, George had demolished a brand new tyre and wheel rim. When he saw what he had done, George shook with laughter for several minutes. Our first night-shooting trip together was memorable for the wrong reason!

An adviser on policy in the early days was Allan Savory, who had a short time previously been appointed to head a Game Ranching Unit in the Department of National Parks and Wild Life Management. There were approximately 5,000 impala on Buffalo Range, and the conventional wisdom of the day demanded that for sustainable cropping of this species, 20% (1,000) should be taken off annually. As time went on, other species were utilised as well, particularly kudu, zebra, and eland. An interesting feature of those days was the arrival of a herd of wildebeest. When George told Murray MacDougall of this, Triangle's pioneer refused to believe it, stating categorically that no wildebeest had ever occurred in the lowveld north of the Lundi (Runde).

Salted hides became a valuable side-line, especially those of zebra and impala, and as time went by more and more wildlife products from the ranch were sold. Successive National Parks Provincial Wardens in the Victoria Province, among whom Bruce Austen stood out, were keen spectators and strong supporters of the game-ranching experiment, and the Parks staff from Chipinda Pools were frequent visitors during their infrequent trips to town, always willing to give advice and assistance. On the other hand, the ranchers on the boundaries of Buffalo Range, and beyond in the wider lowveld, were virtually unanimously not at all pleased with the game ranching business. Game animals were little valued by cattlemen; they competed for grazing, broke fences (zebra were particularly culpable), were host to tsetse flies which carried Trypanosomiasis, and also to two other serious cattle diseases, (FMD and Theileriosis), and they were thought to attract predators.

At the same time as an increasing stream of wild life conservationists and interested National Parks staff were making tracks for Buffalo Range to see what George was doing, a vociferous body of members of the Chiredzi Cattleman's Association were setting up a powerful counter-current of opposition, strongly supported by more conservative vets, especially successive Directors of the Government Veterinary Service.

One of them, Dr T. Lees-May, uttered the much-quoted opinion, 'You can't farm in a zoo, man!' at a crowded meeting called to discuss this departure from conventional land use in the lowveld. Another Director, Dr McKinnon, visited Buffalo Range with the Government's Chief Conservation Officer, later Secretary for Agriculture, C.A. Murray. They added their voices to those of the doubters, though it was significant that Charles Murray, following a change of heart when he was later appointed a Director of the giant Nuanetsi Ranch, actually revisited Buffalo Range to get some ideas on the introduction of game ranching on the extensive property for which he had assumed responsibility, and which harboured an immense population of game animals. Interestingly enough, George Style was contracted to harvest game animals on this huge property.

The game section went from strength to strength, and kept George very busy. Not long after his arrival he was joined by Johnny Bandura, the skilled hunter who had worked with him at Bikita, and from Chidziwa came Saizi Ndawana, who had served with George in the KAR during the war, and who was appointed Senior Game Scout on Buffalo Range.

George Style loved dogs, and his unquestionable favourite was an Alsatian called Rin-Tin-Tin, a most energetic and plucky animal. He averred that Rin, always his companion on hunts for dangerous game animals, had many times saved him from wounded lions and buffalo in thick bush on Buffalo Range. Rin was a battle-scarred warrior, always in the thick of things. Among other mishaps, he had been kicked by a zebra, and mauled by a crocodile which caught him in the Chiredzi River, and from which he was very fortunate to escape. He eventually died as the result of wounds inflicted by a sable bull, which gored him in the chest. George was heart-broken. He buried his friend near the game section homestead, and erected a statue in his memory with the legend:

'In memory of Rin-Tin-Tin, 1951-1957, who many times saved his master's life from wounded lion and buffalo. Gored by a sable, he has gone to happier hunting grounds.'

There were great numbers of lions in the area, and they caused severe losses from the cattle herd in early days. George spent much of his time hunting them, and as they became more wary and difficult to hunt, he imported several bear traps from Canada, with which he trapped a fair number of lions which returned at night to feed on the cattle they had killed, only to be caught in the powerful jaws of the traps set around the kill, and to be dispatched by being shot next morning. In later years George expressed his shame and regret for using this inhumane technique, and also for his ardent persecution of the nomadic packs of wild dogs which intermittently visited the property and preyed on the family's prize heifers. In my view this behaviour was at that time in no way reprehensible. Eliminating 'vermin' was a mind-set of the day in an attempt to protect valuable livestock from stock-killers and enlightened attitudes to the value and interests of wild animals were in the very early days of development.

George Style was a very keen observer of natural history, interested in everything going on around him. He corresponded regularly with his friend Dr Reay Smithers who had got him started by sending Archie Mossman to see him. The Chiredzi game rancher recorded a number of aberrations amongst the animals he encountered, including a black impala, and albino bushbuck and porcupine.

As activity on the game section of the ranch intensified, it became obvious that George was in need of assistance. A number of competent young wildlife enthusiasts worked for him over the years that followed, each bringing new ideas or skills to the fledgling industry. Notable among them was Brian Marsh, whose wife Jill was a niece of the Style family. Marsh went on to establish his own game-cropping and safari business, and subsequently became a well-known author of wild life novels.

GUESTS AT HUNTER'S LODGE

In addition to the wildlife enthusiasts and vets, the family's visitors' book records a very large number of guests visiting George and Ethne in the attractive and comfortable 'Hunter's Lodge' which they established down near the Chiredzi River on Buffalo Range Game Ranch. The Styles were very generous and welcoming hosts, and the numbers of guests increased dramatically once the enterprise had become established, the sugar estates developed apace, and the town of Chiredzi was established in the early 1960s. Many visitors came out to the ranch specifically to see the Carmine Bee Eater colony which bred annually in a cliff on the Chiredzi River. The site of between one and two thousand of these most beautiful of birds was an unforgettable spectacle, drawing visitors from far and wide in September, October and November each year.

George entertained politicians, policemen and priests; merchandise salesmen selling their wares to Ethne and taking time off for a game drive; school-children and fellow ranchers – even those who were opposed to this nonsense of running wild animals with domestic stock; and even waifs and strays. All were welcomed, fed hearty teas or drinks and snacks, even lunch, and proudly shown around by the lowveld's pioneer game rancher. As the fame of the Buffalo Range wildlife enterprise spread, a number of very well known public figures were hosted at 'Hunter's Lodge' which was filled with fascinating memorabilia and collectables with a wildlife theme. Hollywood star Stewart Granger and internationally renowned author Stuart Cloete were among the most interesting and appreciative guests hosted by George and Ethne.

A very generous host he was certainly, but it was Ethne who had to bear the brunt of the ceaseless entertaining. Her husband even brought in itinerant nobodies that he met, people who in truth were unemployed or of no fixed abode. They happily parasitised their generous host, often to the chagrin of poor Ethne, until they eventually responded to a gentle hint that they should move on.

My father and I became very friendly with George. When my parents visited us at Triangle, we were invited to come out to the ranch early in the morning over weekends to shoot game birds, which abounded on Buffalo Range, especially near the river. After an excellent morning of wing shooting, we would return ravenously to the homestead for breakfast, there to enjoy a memorable feast and to swap yarns. One morning we were shooting at the far southern end of the ranch near a large and famous pool called Chidlai. After bagging a few guineafowl, and driving a short way in George's Land Rover, we came across a sable bull which had broken its leg in a snare and was unable to walk. I dispatched the poor beast, and our accompanying game scouts loaded it onto the vehicle.

Just then we heard the noise of a vehicle racing through the bush, and around the corner came a police vehicle which skidded to a stop alongside. Out jumped a Patrol Officer, who at once stated triumphantly that we were under arrest for illegally hunting on Buffalo Range, and, even worse, hunting a sable without the necessary permit. He was a little nonplussed when we pointed out that we could not be poaching in a Buffalo Range vehicle, with ranch staff with us. When we stated that we were on our way to breakfast with the owner, he left to return to the police station at Chiredzi, after taking our names and personal details and stating that we would be hearing from his member-in-charge.

On our return to the homestead, we told George what had happened. He laughed, and apologised for the embarrassment we must have endured, stating that it was entirely his fault. What had happened was that a number of citizens of Chiredzi had taken to poaching on the southern section of the game ranch, far from head quarters, where gunshots could not be heard, and in a situation where they could quickly leave the ranch if anybody approached. George had offered a bounty of £100 to anybody who apprehended the culprits. He had also concluded an arrangement with the caretaker of a guest lodge across the river from Chidlai, through which he would notify her by telephone if anybody was hunting or cropping in that area. If she heard gunshots in the absence of such notification, she was to phone the police in Chiredzi, who had promised a rapid response. George had forgotten to call her concerning that morning's hunt – and what made the matter worse was that she had reported to the police that she was under fire, apparently pellets from one of our shotguns had rattled on her roof, presumably when firing at a guinea fowl winging across the river. We all had a good laugh about the incident.

In August 1971 the Chairman of Triangle Limited telephoned me and asked me at very short notice to arrange a hunting trip for two distinguished Americans who would be visiting the country within the next week. It was not possible at that late stage to secure a formal reservation at a hunting camp, nor in fact to hire the services of a professional hunter, so in desperation I contacted George and his son Clive. As always they readily agreed to assist. The nett result was that we welcomed Harry Tennison, President of Game Conservation International, and Walter Schirra, hero of the Gemini space exploration venture and doyen of the US astronauts. With no other alternative available, I took time off from the hospital to accompany them on a most enjoyable hunting trip on Buffalo Range, with Clive acting as the guide/professional hunter for Harry, and myself doing the same for Walter.

Our friends from the USA enjoyed the experience immensely. Fortunately Walter did not have great expectations concerning record trophy sizes for 'The Book' (*Rowland Ward's Records of Big Game*), unlike many visiting hunters who judge the success of the hunt by the size of the trophy and its acceptance for publication in the said volume. This was extremely fortunate for me, as the trophy kudu bull which my client managed to bag had horns measuring a mere 26 inches (an acceptable trophy being in the region of 54 inches and upwards). Neither George nor Clive allowed me to forget this episode. For some reason, after being probably the first hunter/guide for a foreign client on Buffalo Range, I was never again invited to assist.

The founder of Buffalo Range celebrated his 70th birthday with a party at Buffalo Range, attended by a large body of family, friends, and admirers, many of them from wildlife circles. George was a celebrity.

During the previous few years, with more time on his hands, he had written a large number of articles for the BSA Police magazine *Outpost*, recording with splendid literary talent a most readable series of very interesting experiences during his service in the BSA Police and thereafter. Some of them were published under the pseudonym *Nimrod*, others in a section of the magazine entitled *Bundu Jottings*.

With the passing of time George Style began to do less and less of the actual work on the game section, relying instead more and more on his assistant of the day. Ever a man with a strong sense of community, he became increasingly involved in activities in the Chiredzi area. He was a committed member of the Rotary Club of Chiredzi, and was Chairman of the Lowveld Anglican Church Council.

He somewhat unwisely accepted the Chairmanship of Impala Ranching Company, the ill-fated private organisation which was set up by the government to spearhead the game-ranching industry – a disastrously planned and executed response to a national call for an organisation to pioneer the necessary research and operational experimentation for what appeared to be a very promising industry. With the responsible Minister having made the choice of operator, there was no way that George or anybody else could make a success of this venture, which had been given perhaps the country's best tract of wild life land in the country (on the Mkwasine), but that is another story.

SADNESS IN THE TWILIGHT YEARS

With the way that things had been going for George Cecil Style, the success he had enjoyed, and the admiration he had earned, he should have been the happiest man on earth. I never did understand the basis for the deep depression and feeling of inadequacy and dejection which enveloped him at this stage. He and Ethne, having endured increasing friction between them, tragically fell out at that late stage in their lives, and he left her. His sons, who were by that time controlling the rapidly expanding Buffalo Range enterprise, agreed to purchase a house for him in Harare, and he moved to a beautiful home in Highlands. He was unable to settle, and was very miserable most of the time.

A very sympathetic and caring female companion moved in with him for a while, but he remained unsettled and uncertain. He moved back to the lowveld, and he and Ethne were apparently happily reunited for a while, but it did not last. Another house was purchased for him in Harare, and again he moved away from the lowveld which he loved.

His twilight years should have been blissful. He had everything, and had achieved everything, that ever he could have wished for. Instead, he was a somewhat tragic figure.

George Style, pioneer of Buffalo Range and of the game-ranching industry in Zimbabwe, died in Harare on 7 January 1987, another of the Great Characters of The Lowveld who had led an eventful life and shown the way for those who followed. George, we salute you.

Hunter's Lodge, Buffalo Range

RETIREMENT YEARS – FARM GUARD

George Style is a tall, rangy, active ex-farmer, hunter and policeman, who has packed a lot of experience into his 75 years – experience he's now willing to put to good use, helping farmers in the operational areas who need to get away for a break.

'I'm just a house guard, really,' he says deprecatingly. In fact, he does a lot more than guard houses; he runs farms in the absence of their owners, supervises the labour and pays them, and generally keeps a watchful eye on all that is going on.

Not surprisingly, he's in great demand; during a recent five-week stint he had seven telephone calls and six letters asking him to come to other farms. One man booked him a year in advance! He goes mostly to the Eastern Districts, like Penhalonga, the Vumba, Melsetter, Cashel and Chipinga, which he says is like a second home, he's made so many friends there.

He has plenty of anecdotes about his experiences, like the story of the terrorists who were taking R & R in the compound when he was looking after a farm over Christmas. Then there's the African baby, Georgina, who was named after him because he got her mother to hospital just in time. There's the lunch parties he'll be giving on his next stint; 'I've been to this farm before, and they've got a marvellous cook,' he says. 'I buy mostly all my own food, though. I don't want people coming back from holiday to enormous food bills, and saying that old George has been living well.'

Not all his anecdotes are funny: he tells the story of a young coffee farmer near Chipinga, who, although badly wounded, routed a gang of 30 terrorists singlehanded. He was ambushed, and his companion also badly wounded, but, with his right arm smashed, he loaded his rifle with his left hand, propped it in a tree, and wounded one terrorist who dropped his rifle before the rest ran away. If that wasn't enough, he also managed to administer first aid to his companion. Though he lives constantly with danger, George Style wouldn't have it otherwise for anything – he's enormously grateful for the chance to do his bit. Retired, and living in Chisipite, Salisbury, while his two sons run his Buffalo Range ranch, he tried, three years ago, to join the Police Specials, those older men who do invaluable duties in the suburbs. They wouldn't have him, regretting that he was 'too old' – they just don't know what they missed!

So he put an advertisement in the local newspaper, and a few replies resulted. Once he started, though, the word went round and the whole thing snowballed. 'It's been so rewarding,' he said. 'I've regained my health, and I've got an interest in life. I could have been six feet underground by now.'

Though nervous about publicity, because he is basically a modest man, he insists that there's nothing special about his work, and says that there are plenty of men of his age who could do the same. 'They sit around in old people's homes, waiting to die,' he said. 'They might just as well get out there and do something useful.'

But before anyone starts up a Grandad's Army, it's only fair to say that not many septuagenarians have George Style's energy, ability, and, bluntly, money. He says it is really all thanks to his sons, who support him. In fact, he built up a fantastic ranching and hunting business from practically nothing. There were many times in the early days when it was a real battle; his wife, Ethne, a true partner who still backs him all the way, ran trading stores to help the farming operations, and to help keep the boys at school. He takes her along on his stints very occasionally, but mostly she's like any other war wife, left in Salisbury, with the widow of a Police comrade of 53 years ago, Mary Perkins, to help and keep her company.

All George's stints are done at his own expense, and he uses his own car. 'I live pretty rough sometimes, too,' he says. 'Some of these so-called cooks can't even make tea, and lots of them are busy pinching food – I catch them at it sometimes.' Not all cooks, obviously, are of the luncheon party variety.

Because of his experiences in the operational areas, especially on border farms, he has plenty of tips for farmers. He suggests that many are 'underdogged' – a word he has invented. 'All very well having these little yappy things underfoot,' he says. 'True, they make a noise, but what is needed is big, fierce, Alsatian or Labrador-type dogs – I've often known terrorists running from dogs like that. And they must sleep outside, it's no good having them indoors.'

Just the same, he has a small, adorable white Maltese terrier, Kachito, named by her first owner, a Spaniard. Her mistress was killed in an ambush, and her farmer husband couldn't bear to keep her dog, the memories were too much. So George asked if he could take her to Salisbury, where she is now very happily at home.

He's also horrified at the number of farmers who keep fire-arms locked up during the day. 'You've got to have them right beside you, readily available, at all times.'

And, while he sympathises tremendously with wives in the sensitive security areas he'd destroy the trees and large shrubs in their carefully tended gardens if he had half a chance. He points out that the value of a security fence is diminished if you have lots of cover within the fence. When there's a shoot-out, it is all too easy for terrorists to reach the house, through garden vegetation.

He's now worked on farms a total of 21 years, and says he can still run a farm efficiently, provided there are good foremen. 'Age doesn't matter – one just has to supervise, and maybe drive trucks into town for supplies. Many of these farms have first class foremen, but no drivers.'

It isn't easy to get George Style talking about himself; he'd rather talk about his family, of which he is very proud. His father, an ex-colonel who served originally in the 17th Lancers,(the Death or Glory Boys of Balaclava fame), was mayor of King William's Town, in the Cape, for 10 years. George's brother, Claude, nicknamed 'Stylo', was officer in charge of the first air unit formed in Rhodesia, and chairman of the first flying club in Salisbury, during the Thirties – he'd joined the Royal Flying Corps at 16, and won the DFC in the First World War. Claude's son Colin has recently won a poetry award in South Africa.

Of George's own sons, Clive, now managing director of Buffalo Range Safaris, was on the first Gwebi College of Agriculture course while Rodney gave up university to return to farming.

Reluctantly, George is persuaded to talk about his current activities again, but he swiftly turns the conversation to the farmers themselves – about the tension they all live under in border areas, how they have no social life, and can't travel at nights. And how sometimes, terrorists who shoot up homes, leave notes advising the owners to 'get out now.'

George Style Photo: Alan Stock

And finally, he gets on to the subject of compensation, something he sees, or rather, doesn't see, at first hand. He mentions a farmer who has lost everything, and has waited months for compensation of any kind. George is angry; the people he has helped have become his friends, and he waxes eloquent about politicians who ignore their needs.

George Style has kept letters sent to him by farmers and their wives. They paint a picture of life in the frontline of the terrorist war, bringing home more clearly than any official communiqué, what it is like to live with danger, every day. Below are just a few extracts.

'Labour driven away, and their huts burned, tobacco barns burned, and house attacked.'

'The terrorists called all the labour to come close so they could show them what power was. Then they opened fire at point blank range, killing 13 and injuring 16.'

'You never know if your labour will be there in the morning, and we dread dipping day in case the cattle have been stolen.'

'Our friends have vacated their farm after being ambushed in daylight, at 5 p.m. at the security fence.'

'Our neighbours leave for good next month.'

'Two ponies were shot in the stables on the next farm.'

GEORGE RIDES SHOTGUN – AT 73

Sixty in Rhodesia usually means retiral: too old for anything more strenuous than pruning the roses or planting the odd garden shrub. As for one's seventieth birthday, this conjures up visions of a very senior citizen indeed, fit only to sit in the sun with one's memories.

George Style of Salisbury is the living refutation of these concepts. At 73, he has just completed his fifth stint in Rhodesia's operational area. All told so far, he has completed 14 weeks guarding fences on the country's border with Mozambique.

A former rancher and policeman, George is one of a group of older and dedicated men who are increasingly playing a vital role in Rhodesia's anti-terrorist war by standing in as locum for farmers in the rural 'hot spots'.

Many farmers feel they cannot take a much-needed holiday for fear of a terrorist attack on their unoccupied property; others are being called up as much as three times a year, or have commitments with PATU or the Police Reserve. As far as the latter section are concerned, there is the perpetual worry of leaving wives and children alone on unguarded farms. If the families are sent to safety in the nearest city, farms could become neglected, or suffer plundering and ravaging at the hands of vandals or terrorists.

This latter possibility was illustrated by the Matabeleland Branch chairman of the Cattle Producers' Association, Mr Stanley Nicholle, when he said that 1,000 head of cattle have been stolen from ranchers on the border with Botswana in the past five years. When older men, like George Style, heard of these problems, it occurred to them that they could help out, and thus play a useful part in the war effort. It is nearly four months since George started guarding farms. He says now, 'I feel so much better. It's given me a new purpose in life – I'm no longer just an old man sitting back and doing blow-all. My blood pressure has righted itself and my "ticker" is vastly improved.'

George (who is known by Africans as *'Mafura Nunzi'*, the man who can shoot a fly) spent five years apiece in the Army and the police during the Second World War. His African nickname refers to his prowess with a gun – he was a crack shot during his 47 years of hunting, which he began in 1925. His game ranch at Buffalo Range has now been taken over by his sons.

On numerous occasions George had to shoot marauding lions on the ranch, in order to protect his cattle herds. Many of his hunting stories have been printed in the BSA Police magazine, *Outpost*, under his pen name, *Nimrod*. But those times are past now, and when George's sons arranged to cope with the ranch, he retired comfortably in Salisbury.

Why did he decide to give up his new life of urban leisure for the job of riding shotgun in an area where his vehicle could be blown up by a landmine or he could walk into a terrorist ambush at any moment? 'I felt unhappy because I couldn't do anything for the country,' George told me. 'I applied to the rural ward police, signed a form and attended a lecture. Soon after this, I received a "Dear John" letter. It said: "Dear Mr Style, you are too old".'

Could he perhaps falsify his age on the application forms – as many enthusiastic elderly men did during the Second World War? George decided against this, it would be easy enough for officials to check his ostensible age by looking up his service record. Finally, it occurred to him that there might be an opening as regards guarding farms.

He advertised in the *Rhodesia Herald* accordingly: 'Retired farmer/rancher offers his service on a farm in any border area where genuinely required. No remuneration: own transport.'

Within a few days, the replies were flooding in. George selected as his first task what he considered to be the most urgent of these applications: a coffee farm belonging to Mr Clive Prince in the Chipinga area – where a family had been almost wiped out by a landmine explosion a few days before.

George took his sporting rifle and a revolver along with him, and spent a week on this farm while Mr Prince took a much-needed break.

An appeal from Mr Don Cocker at Chipa Farm, which overlooks the Burma Valley about four kilometres from the Mozambique border, was George's next assignment. Three battles had taken place against terrorists on this farm, and the house had been attacked by rockets and machine gun fire. More than 300 rounds of the latter had been fired.

Don Cocker was away with a PATU patrol on the night of the attack. His wife Fay had been forced to crawl down the passageway with their children, while bullets screamed overhead. Undaunted by this nightmare experience, she refused to leave the farm. 'Fay showed tremendous guts,' says George.

'She is one of many women in Rhodesia who insist upon remaining on their farms in the face of immense danger. They feel they have helped their husbands to build up the farm, and thus they intend to stand firm until the bitter end. I moved on to the farm as soon as I could, and took over from Fay. We were expecting trouble at any moment. And it came, too.'

George had tried to obtain an FN or an Uzi sub-machine gun for his guard duty stints, but an official at the Ministry of Internal Affairs turned down his application, saying that all automatic weapons available were urgently required for people permanently domiciled in the operational area. However, George managed to borrow a sporting .303 to supplement his 7 mm rifle and his revolver.

While he was at Chipa Farm, the Security Forces discovered a cache of arms on the lands there. They intercepted a band of terrorists, and a combined operation took place, resulting in 11 terrorists and six recruits being killed, and one terrorist captured.

Thereafter, the situation improved, and George was able to move on to his next job, guarding the coffee farm near Umtali of Mr Colin Campbell-Morrison. One evening, just after 6 p.m., Mr Campbell-Morrison heard shots, and called to George to listen. They heard the unmistakeable sounds of a contact between Security Forces and terrorists. Soon after, a Security Force patrol passed the farmhouse.

Later, George and Mr Campbell-Morrison heard that 11 terrorists had been killed on the farm's boundary. It was thought that they had been on their way to attack the farmhouse.

Another appeal from a plucky farmer's wife had George hastening to Bindura, and Frinton Farm, which is near Mtepatepa. This farm is owned by Mr Dave Turner, who had been taken to hospital with a head wound. He had been in a convoy travelling along the Mozambique/Rhodesia border, when they were ambushed by Frelimo troops. A bullet hit Dave behind the left ear, smashing his eardrum and jaw, and emerging via his mouth.

His wife had been trying to carry on alone on the farm. On one occasion when she was returning from town, she had missed a landmine by inches. A lorry just behind her detonated the mine, and was badly damaged. This, for Mrs Turner, was the last straw. So George took over from her, and she was able to spend a few well-earned weeks in town.

Here he sometimes heard Radio Maputo, which is easily obtainable on a transistor radio, and which blares out a never-ending monologue of hate and propaganda aimed at undermining the whites in Rhodesia. The broadcasts call for the Africans to rise up against their white employers: to take over their farms, goods, cars and wives. Fortunately, this is disregarded. George says that in his experience, the African population as a whole abhors terrorism. He has also noticed a growing spirit of goodwill between the races in Rhodesia, and can quote a recent instance of this.

At the end of August, George moved to Thackeray Farm, which overlooks Mount Darwin and Kipling, and which is owned by Mr Ralph Edwards and his wife Cynthia. Three years ago, before they had erected security fencing around their homestead, Ralph and Cynthia had been attacked by terrorists. One evening, the tractor driver had come to the house, calling out that his child was ill and needed medical attention. Cynthia had walked on to the veranda, switching on the light as she did so. Then she saw that the driver's hands were tied in front of him. She switched off the lights and dropped to the floor – just as a hail of bullets slammed into the wall behind her, at shoulder height. It later transpired that terrorists had forced the driver to go to the homestead with this trumped-up story, in order to induce the Edwards to appear.

While George was guarding the farm this August, so that Ralph and Cynthia could take a holiday, a group of terrorists walked into the compound of a neighbouring farm. An African labourer managed to creep away and telephone the police at Mount Darwin.

At 2 p.m. that afternoon, a party of Special Branch police went in civilian clothes to the compound, where they found the terrorists having a meal. They shot eight on the spot. The other two escaped.

The next evening, George was about to lock up the gate of the security fence when he saw an African walking away from the compound. When he challenged him, the man ran away. George thought nothing of it until he subsequently discovered that two terrorists had been in the vicinity. He says now that had he known this before, he would have shot the man without hesitation.

When I interviewed George, he was about to leave for another farm in the border area. 'This one is really a hot spot,' he told me with a twinkle in his eye. 'There have been reports that there are 30 terrorists in a nearby Tribal Trust Land. This assignment will probably be the toughest yet, but I couldn't be happier about it. I've never felt better. At least now I've got something to live for.'

The owner and his fiancée have gone to South Africa to attend to some business, get married and have a honeymoon. Their holiday will be all the more enjoyable for knowing that all will be well at home, now that a highly responsible old-timer is riding shotgun there.

George Style and shotgun – at 73

PART TWO

Stories by George Style
Bundu Jottings
Hunting Tales
Leopard Hunt
Personalities
Cape Hunting Dogs
A Lesson to All Concerned
... Camouflage

BUNDU JOTTINGS

Hunting Tales

One morning, back in 1954, 1 was trekking back from an elephant hunt in Chief Chironga's country, south of the Lundi, having been granted a permit by the Game Department to shoot one 'jumbo' in what was – and probably still is – a Tsetse Fly Area. I was accompanied by five Africans, one of them a former accomplice of the elephant poacher Barnard (known to the Shangaans as *Bvikenya* – the one who swaggers as he walks) and another, a onetime companion of Dr Jim Kennedy who had been for over thirty years GMO at Ndanga. Besides having shot many elephant, Dr Jim is reputed to have bagged over seven hundred buffalo in the Victoria lowveld. We were making for my truck which I had left about ten miles upstream.

The country we were crossing was, on the whole, covered with thick bush and in the course of our passage through it, we put up many Nyala, this being one of the few habitats in Rhodesia of this beautiful antelope which looks like a cross between a bushbuck and a kudu. Justifiably, it is protected under our Game Laws.

We eventually arrived at a large clearing, obviously an old Shangaan land. Our path was along the lower edge of the clearing. Suddenly, a large kudu bull broke cover from the edge of the forest behind us and galloped past at a distance of no more than 50 yards. Swinging round to the left, I raised my .470 double-barrel to take aim but the kudu was too quick for me and disappeared into the thick bush just ahead of us. While my rifle was still in the aiming position a second kudu bull appeared, galloping in the tracks of the first one. I fired for his shoulder and he dropped immediately and was quite dead when we reached him. The bullet, a hard-nose, had entered high behind the shoulder and just under the spine.

I was still gazing at the kill when the five Africans suddenly charged across the clearing and stood in a circle looking down at something and roaring with laughter. I could see nothing to cause such merriment until I walked over to them. To my surprise I found them gazing at another kudu, lying in the grass at his last gasp. We examined the bull, which was facing in the opposite direction to the first one shot, and found that my bullet had hit it in almost the identical place as the other, but on the opposite side. I realised what had happened and joined in the laughter. The Africans told me that the first bull we had sighted had turned as soon as it entered the bush ahead of us and they had seen it run back across the clearing. I had been concentrating on aiming at the second animal and had not seen this. In the instant that I fired at the second animal, the two bulls must have been completely opposite each other, crossing in opposite directions. My one fluke shot had killed both.

At the time we were camped at Chipinda Pools with a Schoolboys' Exploration Society party in charge of Mr 'Coney' Fleming, now Headmaster of Umtali Boys' High School. We severed the four hind legs of the kudu and presented them to the party. To this day, seventeen years later, ex-pupils who were on the expedition make a point of reminding me of one of my most successful kudu hunts.

My second fluke shot was a year later, in 1955. Not only was it a lucky shot from the marksmanship point of view, it was a very fortunate shot as far as my life was concerned.

Lions had been troublesome for some time and they had been difficult to get as they were not returning to their kills. Hoping to improve our chances of bagging the predators, I had offered the herd boys £1 each if they would come in at night, while the lions were actually killing, and report the fact. There were two boys in charge of each 200 head of cattle which at night were penned in large circular kraals made by simply chopping down Mopani trees and lying them one on top of the other to a height of about four feet. We crossed fingers that the cattle would not find their way through the branches. We still had to learn the necessity of building sound lion-proof and stampede-proof kraals with thick high thorn-bush.

In the early hours of a morning in the winter of 1955, one of the herd-boys, Samuel, and his assistant arrived to say that their cattle had been stampeded and that they had heard a lion killing a beast. I grabbed my old .375 Holland and Holland and my shooting lamp and we set off in the truck for the cattle kraal some five miles away. It was a pitch-dark night, ideal for our purpose. We walked around within a mile radius of the kraal but could find not a trace of lions, cattle or carcasses. The cattle had stampeded out of sight and we returned to bed.

At dawn we returned to the kraal and were able to spot where a beast had been killed by a lion about two hundred yards from the kraal. It was obvious that there was only one lion and that it had dragged the beast away. We followed the spoor for a full three miles before we came on the carcass of a large heifer hidden from vultures under a thick bush. The heifer would have weighed about 600 lbs. It had been neatly disembowelled and the innards and a portion of the hind legs eaten. The carcass had been dragged almost parallel with the road to just within two miles of the homestead confirming that the lion had lugged the 600 pound weight every inch of three miles.

I decided to try and trap the lion using the only two small traps we had at the time. (Later, four Canadian bear traps which were used with great success arrived from America.) I also planned to inspect the traps at 11 p.m. This would give the lion plenty of time to return to the kill as I had discovered that lions usually revisited the scene between 7 and 8 p.m. – if they returned at all. At 11 p.m. sharp, I set off with the boss-boy Phillimon, and my driver, Timot. We stopped the truck on the road some 80 yards from the kill and got out. I put on my shooting lamp, switched it on, and as I did so, picked up the glint of an eye near the kill. Without looking directly at us, the owner of the eye moved away to the left and I was convinced that it was either a leopard or a hyena.

We walked cautiously up to the carcass and found that both traps had been sprung. They had been set in gaps in the thick thorn-bush wall surrounding the carcass. We set off in the direction taken by the retreating animal and were suddenly faced by two eyes glaring out of the darkness. The moment the animal turned, I could tell by the spread of the eyes that it was a lion. Just then, Phillimon whispered to me: '*Shumba, Bwana!*' (Lion, Sir!) I politely informed him that I had already realised that and searched around looking for a tree from which to make a rest. There was none. We were surrounded by some very thin, pliable saplings and I had to be satisfied with holding the rifle against one of these to take aim.

My eyes were bad – I had not yet taken to a telescopic sight – and the sapling was bending as I tried to level the rifle. For the life of me, I could not see the foresight properly. It was just a blur. The lion was only about 50 yards from me as I desperately tried to keep the wavering muzzle still. I was very frightened, my heart was thumping in my chest as I had never known it thump, and I was only too well aware of what the noise of the shot would precipitate if I failed to hit the target. After what seemed about five minutes, I decided that it was hopeless trying to improve on my aim which was just below the glaring eyes – and I pulled the trigger. After the shot there was dead silence – a lion invariably roars when wounded (I say 'invariably', but I once wounded one in the stomach and he didn't roar) and the boys and I waited wondering what would happen in the next few seconds.

Nothing happened. I turned to the boys and said: '*Nda poshile!*' (I have missed!) My servants' confidence in their employer was voiced: '*Hono, Bwana, wa poshile! Ti ka zinzwa bumburu ku inda pa hlatini!*' (Yes, Sir, you missed! We heard the bullet go into the bush!) '*Kanjani tina amba tarira lapa pamberi?*' (How about going to have a look?) I asked in my best vernacular. '*Hikona, Bwana, moosh to na wuya kusasa!*' (No, Sir, it would be much better to come back in the early morning) replied Phillimon, much to my relief.

I thought this an excellent idea. I was not anxious to seek a wounded or unwounded lion in the dark and my heart was still pumping away in my chest. The next morning we located the sapling from which I had fired. Peering ahead, I spotted a light patch in the grass in a glade about 50 yards ahead. I ran forward, followed by the boys, and there, lying its back, was a young, full-grown male lion with a short, partly-white mane. We examined the head and found that my bullet had entered right between the eyes. It had been a clean brain shot – and hence, no roar. I could not resist turning to Timot and Phillimon and remarking: '*Hono. Bwana, to ka zinzwa bumburu ku ida pa hlatini.*' (Yes, so you heard the bullet go into the bush!)

The lion was duly loaded and we returned to the homestead with the two boys proudly chanting the Makaranga war song:

'*Raya wa baya! Mukono uno bay dzoze!*' (Stab! Stab! The large bull stabs all!)

Outpost, January 1968

BUNDU JOTTINGS

Leopard Hunt

One afternoon in 1954, I arrived back on the ranch after a visit to Salisbury. I was met by my younger son, who was assisting with the herds, and a young Cattle Inspector, a friend of my son's, who was spending a few days on the ranch. They greeted my homecoming with troubling news.

Two nights before, a leopardess and cub had tried, unsuccessfully, to break into the calf pen in the kraal just below the homestead where a small milk-herd was kept. Being thwarted in their attempt to get into the pen, the leopards had somehow managed to pull the two front legs of a calf through the poles forming the pen, and had eaten all the flesh off the legs. The calf was still alive when the attack was discovered at daybreak, but was quickly put out of its misery by having its throat cut.

My son and his friend followed the spoor of the leopards and traced it to the river-bed some 400 yards away. Here, lying in the reeds at the side of the drift, they found the half-eaten carcass of another calf. The predators had obviously come across the second animal which had unwittingly been left out of the pen by the herdboy. They decided to poison the meat with strychnine besides setting two traps in gaps in the thorn bush with which they surrounded the carcass.

On the morning of my return the traps had been inspected. Both had been sprung and some of the meat had been eaten. Following the spoor, it could be seen that the leopards had stopped further downstream to quench their thirst but the tracks were then lost in the thick undergrowth. There were no signs of vomiting so hopefully perhaps the leopards had gone away to die.

Having heard the news and knowing from experience what damage a pair of marauding leopards could do, I decided to make sure of their fate and sleep near the carcass in case they returned.

We dragged the remains of the carcass into the open drift so that visibility from the bank would be good, and pegged it down. Before dark I had my bed in position on the river-bank, behind a very large Baobab tree. Using large branches, I completed the camouflage of my hide. I intended to be comfortable during my vigil when not actually patrolling the bank with the shooting lamp, trying to pick up the eyes of the leopards.

That evening, after a couple of fortifying Scotches with the family, I made my way down to the river. I had enlisted the aid of my Boss-boy, Phillimon, and had armed him with a Browning automatic shotgun loaded with AAA cartridges – four in the magazine and one in the breech. I was equipped with a five-cell shooting lamp and my old .375 Holland and Holland rifle. Luckily, this weapon, which had long been a favourite of mine, had arrived only that day from London where it had been fitted with a new stock. I loaded with soft-nosed ammunition and applied the safety-catch.

As we neared the river-bank, I flashed the torch around in case the leopards were about. Phillimon was immediately behind me. We reached the bank and I shone the light in the direction of the kill and at once picked up a pair of eyes. I took aim just below the eyes and fired. There was not a sound. Either I had made a clean shot or had missed altogether. Suddenly a second pair of eyes came darting forward – a leopard obviously running. The eyes came to rest in the same position as I had seen the first pair, only fifteen yards from the river-bank where we stood.

As we were so close I decided to take no chances and use the shotgun. Keeping the torch on the eyes, I quickly exchanged weapons with Phillimon. I aimed for the eyes and squeezed the trigger. A grunt followed the report indicating that I had hit the leopard, but to be certain, I fired again. There was no further sound. I sent Phillimon back to the house for my Alsatian, Rin-tin-tin, a pedigree dog who was completely fearless when it came to lions, leopards, buffalo and anything else for that matter. One day he had tackled three hippo in a pool, diving after them to bite them when they were submerged and giving me a very anxious time in the process. Why he was not mauled by the hippo, I will never know, but perhaps the hippo enjoyed the game.

When Phillimon returned with Rin, we followed the dog into the drift until he stopped in front of some reeds with his tail going nineteen to the dozen. We approached cautiously with the shotgun at the ready and found Rin staring down at a pair of dead leopards lying side by side. We were overjoyed and on further examination discovered that there was no cub as had been thought, but that they were a male and small female, obviously hunting together while mating.

The farm hands were called from the compound and in no time the leopards were strapped to two poles. With a boy on either end of the pole, the victorious procession marched back to the homestead chanting their usual Shona war-song. My wife and son and the Cattle Inspector, hearing the song, were waiting in front of the homestead to view the leopards and offer their congratulations.

Why the leopards had not died from the poison, I just don't know. Perhaps they had vomited up the poisoned meat before the strychnine had done its work somewhere in the thick river-line undergrowth.

It had turned out to be a very satisfactory night hunt, bagging both the marauders. But, in fairness, those with hunting experience know that is often a simple matter – as it was in this case – shooting leopard or lion at night by taking advantage of them with a dazzling hunting lamp at close quarters.

In one of my Jottings, I mentioned Dr Jim Kennedy and forgot to give him his O.B.E. – which I used to say jokingly was the 'Order of Buffalo Exterminators.' I went to see Dr Jim in hospital in October to chat over old times but he was in great pain. I managed to ask him if his tally of over 700 buffalo was correct and he confirmed it although it seems an awful lot of buffalo to me. However, there's no doubt that, accompanied by his driver Benson, he shot a great number and had a few narrow escapes. On one particular occasion, he fell in front of a charging buffalo cow and narrowly missed being gored in the back. He got away with only a graze. Benson came to the rescue and finished off the animal.

It was with deep regret, shared by many old timers who knew Dr Jim, that I read of his death at the Salisbury Central Hospital on the 10th of November, 1967. His sister, Mrs Shelagh Johnson, lost her husband within a few days afterwards and on behalf of old friends of the family, I should like to offer our sincere condolences to Mrs Johnson at this tragic double loss, belated though such sentiments may be.

Outpost, February 1968

BUNDU JOTTINGS

Personalities

In 1927 Dame Clara Butt, the famous contralto, became very worried about the life her second son, Victor Kennerley-Rumford, was leading in London. He had fallen under the influence of a drug addict, and as a result was suffering both physically and mentally.

Dame Clara advertised for someone of strong character to take her son in hand and restore him to health, and the successful applicant was R.F. Dott of Angus Ranch in the Bikita district. Dott was a fine figure of a man, having been something of a champion boxer in Kimberley in his day, and he appeared to be just the man for the job.

Victor himself was no mean specimen of humanity, standing just over 6ft. 4in. in his socks, and built in proportion. There was a third very fine specimen of a man on the ranch in the person of Paddy Power, a partner of Dott's. Paddy was an ex-Trooper of the BSA Police who hailed from Waterford in Ireland, and it was the proud boast of the genial Paddy that he had never had a single case during his three years of service! Admittedly there was not much crime in the country in those days. Paddy and Victor shared a rondavel (round hut) on the ranch, and Victor, who was rapidly regaining his health as a result of the fine open-air life and Mrs Dott's good food, became something of a confidante of Paddy's.

One hot summer afternoon Victor was relaxing on the cool thatched veranda of the ranch homestead, when Dott came along. 'Hullo, Victor,' he exclaimed, 'what are you doing hanging around the house? Get a rifle and go out and get us some boys' meat!'

Victor wasn't at all pleased. It was a very hot afternoon and he was feeling particularly lazy after a good lunch. However, there was no gainsaying Dott, so picking up a rifle and ammunition and cursing to himself, he disappeared into the mopani bush in front of the homestead. Victor spent most of his time out shooting and was an excellent shot.

About half an hour later eight shots were heard in the distance. The ranch abounded in game in those days, and almost every species of animal in the area could be found within three miles of the homestead. Dott had high hopes of giving his boys a good dollop of meat that evening. He was not to be disappointed.

Another half hour passed and Victor was spotted approaching the homestead. Dott called out to him: 'Any luck?' 'Yes!' hailed Victor from a few hundred yards away, 'I got eight!' and he held aloft eight tails. As he came up to Dott he passed the tails over, and much to Dott's consternation he recognised them as coming from eight of his prime Aberdeen-Angus oxen. He was livid but felt that he could only put the mistake down to Victor's mental state.

That night, Victor, in the secrecy of their rondavel, admitted to Paddy that he knew exactly what he was doing, that he knew he would get away with it, but that he strongly objected to being bullied into going out shooting on a hot afternoon.

His health now improved by leaps and bounds. He became an excellent carpenter, making among other things endless tables, for which he was paid 10s. each. He also trained as a bricklayer, and was laying 300 bricks a day while assisting Paddy build tobacco barns on the ranch.

Victor did not take after his famous mother as regards singing, but he played the violin beautifully. He was good at cricket and an excellent tennis player, playing both games when opportunity offered. One day he and Dott had an argument in the lounge and this resulted in a wrestling match. In no time they were on the floor, and Victor had by now so recovered his strength that, powerful as Dott was, he succeeded in breaking three of his ribs.

After just over two years on Angus Ranch, and having, thanks to Dott, fully recovered his health, Victor had now to go out and fend for himself. After a short spell working on the King's Mine at Mashaba, he went down and worked for the Francis Brothers on their Bangala Ranch in the Zaka district.

By the winter of 1934 he had established himself on a farm in the Inyanga district and was doing well, and decided to have a short spell in Salisbury. After the visit he was to have returned with a friend by car, but was offered a seat in another friend's open plane and he accepted this. He was travelling in a shirt and shorts only, and he caught a severe cold in the plane, and this later turned to pneumonia.

Victor eventually became delirious where he was being looked after in the home of his friend, slipped away to his own farm house one night, got hold of his .303 rifle, and shot himself on the verandah of his kitchen. It was a sad ending for Victor after all he had been through and after he had apparently fully recovered his health.

Outpost, November 1968

Victor Kennerley-Rumford

BUNDU JOTTINGS

Cape Hunting Dogs

I was riding through Mpapa's country on Nuanetsi Ranch one morning just on forty years ago. The ranch had not been sub-divided then and the 10,000 square miles abounded in game particularly on Mpapa's section.

It was my first patrol of the area and i was being guided by Native Constable Tsamvisi, a Shangaan who knew the area like a book and who was, incidentally, a first-class shot and hunter who could be relied upon to procure meat for the pot when necessary. He was particularly useful in this respect when we had large numbers of prisoners to feed.

It was still early. Tsamvisi was about 25 yards behind me, travelling on foot as usual, and my personal servant, Sixpence, brought up the rear leading the pack mule. It was tiring enough sitting in the saddle at a walk for hours on end (and it's a wonder that our horses didn't suffer from sore backs more often as we lolled in the saddle) but how we walked the Africans off their feet in those days! Still, they never grumbled and I suppose they were used to it.

Suddenly, ahead of me I saw a large Alsatian dog with tail wagging run up an antheap. He was immediately followed by a second animal. As we were miles from the nearest habitation, I surmised that there must be hunters about and pulled up my horse, Prince, to consult Tsamvisi. He had seen the dogs and proceeded to enlighten me. They were not Alsatians but wild dogs, known to the Shangaans as '*hlolwa*' and to the Vakaranga as '*mapumi*'. It was the first time I had come across such animals but their resemblance to Alsatians was remarkable.

In the light of my experience since then, I realise now that we had come across a lair, Wild dogs usually produce their litters of up to 12 pups in abandoned antbear holes. The real significance of the find was lost on me at the time – I was not aware then that the Government offered a £5 bounty for the discovery of a lair; and they paid £2 for each wild dog killed and the Ranch Company chipped in with another £1. We were miles from water, it was getting hot and I wanted to move on as fast as possible. I knew that Tsamvisi, being a Shangaan, felt some sympathy towards the wild dogs as was customary among his people.

Some years later I was to encounter this same reluctance to kill the animals when I was hunting with two Shangaans in Crown Land north of the Sangwe Reserve. We were following the western bank of the Sabi at the time and the two old Shangaans were in the lead about five yards ahead of me. I suddenly noticed, immediately to their right and no more than 15 yards away, a pack of some twenty-five dogs squatting and lying about quite unconcerned about our intrusion. The Shangaans were equally unconcerned and walked on. I was quite nonplussed and called on them to stop. I had visions of augmenting my measly police pay. The two natives stopped and I explained the position to them. They were most unenthusiastic about my proposal. They looked upon the wild dogs as their benefactors and thus would not molest them. The dogs were a source of their tribal meat supplies, they would follow the packs when they heard their 'hoo! hoo!' hunting call and would recover part of the pack's kill for themselves. The dogs, for their part, seemed to accept this understanding with the Shangaans. Much to my chagrin we continued on our way. What else could I do?

The wild dog is a peculiar animal. Like the zebra, with its variation in the pattern of its stripes, no two dogs are marked alike. Their coats are irregular patches of black, white, brown and yellow, in every conceivable shade and pattern. In addition, the animal is peculiar in that it is not considered a true canine – as in the case of the wolf or jackal – because it has only four toes to each foot and lacks the fifth or 'dew claw' present in true canines. It stands about 2 ft. 6 in. at the shoulder, an overall length of about 5 ft. and weighs from 60 to 80 lb. The bushy tail, usually some 14 in. long, is generally tipped white. The large upstanding ears have rounded or oval tips.

Besides their characteristic 'hooo! hooo!' hunting call, two other sounds are associated with wild dogs. They utter a chattering 'kekkek-kek' cry when pulling down their prey and when surprised they utter a hoarse and abrupt bark, more like that of a bushbuck or baboon than an ordinary dog, and this bark is usually followed by a slurring growl.

As far as human beings are concerned, the wild dog is not aggressive like the wolf. They are very curious however, often standing on their hind legs to get a better view of what interests them. They have never been known to attack man in this country, but the late Mr Talbot-Bowe, who farmed many years ago on the Gwaai in the Nyamandhlovu district, related how a pack of dogs followed him for eight miles once when he was out riding. Every time he pulled up his horse, the dogs stopped, but try as he could, he was unable to throw them off. Eventually, to his relief he reached home. No doubt the horse was the attraction in this case.

On one occasion my hunting-boy, Johnny Bandura, and I trekked 12 miles to a water-hole in the Chipinga district in search of lion. I shall long remember this trip in view of the fact that I had left camp that morning wearing a new pair of soft, very comfortable 'brothelcreepers' or veldskoen. Unfortunately they were half a size too big for me and I had donned them without socks simply because they were so comfortable. By the time I got to the waterhole my feet were in a shocking state and in order to be able to hobble the 12 miles back to base next day, I was forced to tear up a pair of pyjamas with which to swathe my blistered feet.

That night after dark we sat under cover at the waterhole waiting for the lions. At about 8 p.m. a pack of about thirty wild dogs arrived and lined up several yards from the water. They sighted us and began growling. Suddenly the leader rushed towards me threateningly – and stopped only a few yards away from which point he stared and growled before retreating. He did this several times while I was in the act of donning my hunting lamp. I stood up to shoot and the leader disappeared behind the pack. I fired, shot one of the pack and the rest vanished into the night. I have heard since that had I been successful in shooting the leader, the rest would have remained and I might have been able to pick off a few more.

I don't think the dogs would actually have attacked us but they wanted us out of the way before they drank. A little later we had to move anyway, as a herd of elephant arrived to drink, squealed with rage when they got our wind, and forced us to abandon our hunt.

Wild dogs are the cruellest of killers without doubt. They literally eat their prey alive as they run it down. One after another they will dive in and snatch a morsel of flesh from the stricken animal until it drops from exhaustion or loss of blood.

My younger son and I were returning home one evening just after dark and were about a mile from the homestead when the lights of our car picked out a large pack of wild dogs on either side of the road. We knew the pack well, for they had been slaughtering impala for some weeks, impala being their favourite prey. There were as many as 30 to 40 in this particular pack.

We raced home, grabbed our shooting lamps and rifles, and returned to where we had met the dogs. We could hear them calling a few hundred yards south of the road and we followed quickly on foot. We soon had the dogs dashing all around us and next heard an impala bleating pitifully nearby. We ran the couple of hundred yards separating us from the kill in a few minutes. When we arrived we found the fresh skeleton of a full-grown impala doe, the pack having stripped it of all meat in the minutes it took us to cover the distance.

There was not even a morsel of flesh left on the head and I have never seen a skeleton left cleaner by carnivora. My son managed to shoot one dog before the pack moved off. They were still calling to each other on the hunt – the one impala had certainly not satisfied their appetites. This same pack seemed particularly fond of roaming up and down the road to the homestead, and one evening my son ran over a wild dog and killed it. The surrounding country was covered with very large antheaps and we suspected that there was a lair in the immediate vicinity. A few days later, the cattle boss-boy arrived to say that the lair had been found by one of the herd-boys so that same afternoon I set off with the two boys and a .375 rifle with telescopic sights. We approached the lair from behind a hill, from the top of which we could see at least a dozen dogs lying on and around the anthill. I managed to get four before the others ran away.

We walked down to the anthill and found several pieces of disgorged impala meat among the small pad-marks of several pups in the entrance to the lair. I bent my head towards the antbear hole and imitated the whining noise made by domestic dogs when calling to each other, A dozen small heads popped out of the hole! They didn't like what they saw and beat a hasty retreat into the depths. There was no time to dig the pups out that day so we decided to return with a gang of boys on the morrow.

As we had half-suspected, the pups had been moved when we arrived the next day. We located them a short distance away in another hole. None of the pack was around but it took most of the day to dig out the dozen pups. They were all equal in size, about as big as a half-grown cat, and had their eyes open. I tried to rear two of the pups but the nasty odour given off by wild dogs, coupled with the constant calling of the pair throughout the night, was too much for me. I gave them to a neighbour who brought them to maturity. In the end they became quite tame.

We knew that the pack would not be long in returning to the lair so we set four Canadian bear traps around the antheap and scattered chunks of impala meat poisoned with strychnine in the vicinity. We returned the next morning and found that we had trapped a dog and two bitches – one of the latter heavily in milk and probably the mother of the pups. We scouted around and picked up four more poisoned animals. The bounties were duly collected from the District Commissioner. The herd boy who had found the lair was given the £5 due to him plus another £5 from the proceeds of the 'tails', much to his delight. Altogether, we had accounted for a dozen adult animals and the same number of pups. It was essential to kill them whenever the opportunity was presented owing to the havoc they played with young calves on the ranch.

Wild dogs are not scavengers. In fact, they seldom return to previous kills once they have satisfied their immediate hunger. There are exceptions, however. One morning a small pack killed a heifer calf, ate their fill and ran off. My son poisoned the remains of the carcass and picked up five dead dogs the next day.

Once they start a hunt they are relentless in the pursuit of their quarry. On one occasion in 1927, the late Major E.W. Richens, MBE, then Corporal-in-Charge at Nuanetsi, was out hunting on the Sossonye River. Two miles from camp he heard wild dogs calling upstream. He investigated and discovered from the spoor that a pack of dogs were following a herd of sable. Some distance further on, with the noise of the hunt receding into the distance, he came across the carcass of a fully-grown sable bull which had dropped dead in its tracks, apparently from heart failure. There was not a mark on the animal.

In early South African days, the famous hunter

Gordon Cumming and others have recorded sight of bands of several hundred wild dogs. In view of the enormous number of herbivorous animals then in existence, there was probably nothing unusual in such huge packs. They had their part to play in preserving the balance of nature. Today, however, I would rather see man take on the role of these cruellest of predators when necessary. He can keep the numbers of game animals down by cropping cleanly and humanely and, at the same time, can make good use of the meat and skins.

Outpost, January 1969

BUNDU JOTTINGS

A Lesson to All Concerned

It was a very cold, overcast afternoon in 1928 when I set off from the police camp at Nuanetsi to look for something for the larder. We were very dependent on game meat in those days when almost every type of lowveld animal could be found within three miles of the camp and this added to the excitement of the hunt. We had heard lions roaring one morning down towards the Sossonye River two miles away, but owing to my inexperience Corporal Richens would not allow me to go after them – much to my disappointment. Not that my write-off would have been much of a loss as I had barely completed three years' service at the time and we troopers were not considered of much use until we had done at least five. However, I digress.

I was accompanied by a couple of Africans and after about an hour we managed to bag a large kudu bull, much to my delight. We returned to collect a gang of convicts to bring in the meat and as I approached camp I was shivering with cold, being dressed in open-necked shirt and shorts. As I entered the gauze-doored veranda of our very new barracks, our cook, a Nyasa named Mataka, stepped forward in his spotless *kanza* (a long white gown worn by Africans from what is now Malawi northwards to Abyssinia). He held a tray on which was piping-hot tea and a plate containing .a few straight-from-the-oven jam tarts made with real puff pastry. Nothing could have been more welcome and it was obvious that Mataka must have been watching the clearing round the camp for my return. He was a cook in a thousand and Richie and I were largely reaping the benefit of a very good training received at the hands of Mrs Henry Nash Watters, wife of the Native Commissioner (and himself a former member of the Force). Mataka had worked for them at Bikita for many years.

We certainly appreciated Mataka. Until his arrival, a week or so before, we had depended on two very raw Africans from Portuguese territory for our welfare. When tea had been called for then, no tray was used and they would approach with refreshment firmly clasping the top of the cup to the saucer with the palms of their largely unwashed hands.

Mataka, apart from his excellent cooking, kept a spotless table. The cloth and serviettes were always without blemish, while fresh wild flowers were always in evidence on the table, an old pickle jar being used as a vase. After breakfast in the mornings he would attend to our two bedrooms, dusting and polishing everywhere and thus revealing his training at the hands of a woman. To this day I have never seen anywhere in Africa a better cook or cleaner, or more conscientious domestic servant.

The circumstances in which we came by Mataka's services were somewhat out of the ordinary. After leaving the Watters family he had been cook for several months at Nuanetsi Ranch Headquarters. One evening, after he and the waiter, Tatata, had finished their chores, they set off for the compound together, the waiter leading. Mataka had armed himself with a carving knife before leaving the kitchen and he suddenly overtook the unsuspecting Tatata, pulled back his head and slit the waiter's throat, leaving him on the ground for dead. In the early hours of the morning Tatata crawled into one of the huts in the compound but was unable to talk. Not only had his windpipe been severed, but he had lost great quantities of blood. After some local first aid, he was sent to Fort Victoria hospital where he eventually made a good recovery although he was left with a rather weak voice.

Corporal Richens had carried out the investigation and Mataka had been charged with attempted murder. No stronger motive for the crime was revealed other than that Mataka appeared jealous of Tatata and was afraid he might lose his job to the waiter. He was committed for trial at the next session of the High Court in Fort Victoria and until then was an 'awaiting trial prisoner' in camp.

Our living conditions with the two raw Portuguese Africans had been far from pleasant and Richie decided to take a chance. He knew Mataka's worth as a cook, felt that he was not the type to do a bunk, and reckoned that there were always enough of the Black Watch near our quarters to act as guards.

Under Mataka's ministrations we lived like lords for three weeks. Then Richie suddenly decided get away from the dull routine of office work and escape on the annual patrol of the district. He planned to be away for a fortnight.

Now we kept about a hundred laying hens in camp and consequently were never short of eggs. At daybreak on the morning that Richie was to leave on patrol, my personal servant, Sixpence, brought my morning tea and told me that a large eagle was hovering over the hens with malice aforethought. At once I took the keys of the office and exhibit box from Richie and removed the shotgun and a couple of rounds from the latter. The two shots I fired at the eagle were ineffective as it was much too high but at least it scared the bird off. When I returned to the barracks Richie was in the bathroom, but knowing that it was customary to take a shotgun on patrol (to keep ourselves in birds for the pot), I placed the gun in Richie's room – quite sure in my own mind that he would want to take the weapon with him.

After breakfast Richie set off in good humour. He was intent on enjoying his spell in the bundu. He left the camp alone after instructing the two African constables and his personal servant to meet him at ranch headquarters, his first port of call some eight miles away. By the time Richie had disappeared it was nine o'clock and as I strolled over to the office with African Sergeant Taruwona following, I noticed Mataka sitting in the doorway of Richie's room, meticulously polishing a silver picture frame. I had just sat down to discuss with Taruwona our duties for the day when we heard a thud. We both came to the same conclusion – that the noise was caused by the collapse of a kit shelf in either Richie's or my room.

We walked across to the barrack rooms and pushing open the door of my room, the first reached, we found all in order. We then went to Richie's room next door and found the door closed. I opened it and a shocking sight met our eyes. Taruwona grasped his head in both hands and turned in circles, moaning continually.

In the middle of the floor lay Mataka. An ever-widening pool of blood was centred where his skull should have been. The shotgun lay on one side of him and a carved imitation army cane on the other.

Richie's tunics hanging in an open corner wardrobe were spattered with blood and brains, as was a large portion of the ceiling and one wall. I noticed a few rounds of shotgun cartridges on Richie's bookshelf and it was apparent that Mataka had seen these and the weapon I had discarded, had loaded the shotgun, placed the muzzle in his mouth and, using the army cane, had pressed the trigger. To say that I was shocked is to put it mildly, especially as Mataka had always undertaken his duties so cheerfully. I hurried to the Native Commissioner's office a couple of hundred yards away and reported the suicide to Mr King-Hall, a nephew of the Admiral of that name. While gasping for breath I related to him and his new clerk (Stanley Morris, who retired as Secretary for Native Affairs a few years ago) what had happened. Mr King-Hall took the matter very calmly, told me to have Mataka buried, and said that he would hold an enquiry on Richie's return. I went back to camp, saw to the burial, had the room cleaned up and moved Richie's things into the adjoining spare room.

The incident caused quite a stir in the district and the gloom-mongers considered that Richie, as well as myself, would be discharged as a result.

Two weeks later Richie returned from patrol having heard of the tragedy much earlier by bush telegraph. He was very nice about it although he claimed to have told me that he would not be taking the shotgun on patrol with him and that he had instructed me to lock it up again. Unfortunately I had no recollection of this.

The enquiry was duly held and Richie in evidence pointed out that the gaol at Nuanetsi was a wood and iron building; that the heat inside was intense; and that the awaiting-trial prisoners much preferred to work around the camp than remain in the unbearably hot building. When the suicide occurred Mataka was unfortunately out of sight of the native constables around the building.

The proceedings were forwarded to Salisbury while our fate hung in the balance. Feeling that I was to blame, I was more concerned for Richie's future. I had never lived with a finer gentleman or policeman. It was an anxious time for both of us.

What a relief it was when a week or two later the record of the enquiry was returned with a simple foot-note made by the Commissioner, Colonel Georgie Stops: 'Let this be a lesson to all concerned.'

The tragedy was doubled when, a few months later, the mind of Tatata the waiter became deranged and he threw himself into the Nuanetsi River, then in flood, and was drowned.

BUNDU JOTTINGS

... Camouflage

One experiences some remarkable cases of camouflage when hunting in the 'bundu' and I should like to relate one such case experienced by me when at Nuanetsi in 1927.

It was a hot summer's day and I had off-saddled at about 10 a.m. intending to continue the patrol in the cool of the afternoon. Although we had left the previous night's camp soon after daybreak, we had covered only about 12 miles. Going was essentially slow, as not knowing the area, I was compelled to ride at the walking pace of Native Constable Tsamvisi, one of the few Shangaans in the Force and a first class hunter, and my personal servant Sixpence, who was leading the pack mule.

After a hearty brunch of boiled bully-beef mixed with onions, served with mashed potato, and washed down with a mug of hot coffee, I decided to walk out and look for something for the pot. I was accompanied by the two Africans, and as was invariably my custom, I took the lead. I had found from bitter experience that I was quicker at spotting animals than they were, and always walked at a very slow pace so as to spot the animal before being seen, something often possible. An African in the lead was apt to walk too fast, be noisy and scare the animals off.

The weather had become overcast since making camp and walking was not unpleasant. Game in the area was plentiful and varied and the exciting feeling of not knowing what you were going to meet around the corner always kept one alert. It could be anything from a duiker to an elephant or lion.

We had been walking for about half an hour when I saw, about 200 yards ahead of us, in the middle of an old native land, a very old, large and dead tree from which extended several gnarled branches. Something caused me to glance at the tree a second time and I noticed that on the left side a portion of it looked remarkably like a large waterbuck bull, with its hindquarters towards us. Two thin dead branches leading off a bigger one strongly resembled the back of a pair of horns, and the large gnarled end of the left-hand branch looked very like the white ring encircling the hindquarters of a waterbuck. If it were indeed a waterbuck, the left side and shoulder were just visible, for it would be facing almost directly away from us.

The two Africans were about twenty paces behind me and I stood staring at the tree until they joined me. I then pointed at the tree and in a whisper asked them if we were looking at both a waterbuck and a tree. They both shook their heads and said they did not know. We stood for a full five minutes trying to make up our minds and hoping for the flick of a tail or the twitch of an ear. There was no movement whatsoever.

We had all decided that there was no animal there and that what we were looking at was purely an old gnarled tree, when I thought I would take a shot to make sure. Using my Service .303 with which I hunted regularly, as we were allowed to buy ammunition at only ten shillings per hundred rounds, and hunting was encouraged, I took aim behind what would be the shoulder if indeed it were a buck. I pulled the trigger and immediately the left hand portion of the old tree sprang to life. The large waterbuck bull, as it turned out to be after all, must have been fast asleep until struck by the bullet. It galloped ahead for about 100 yards before dropping dead from a heart shot.

I have seen many animals well camouflaged in the bush, such as the red impala standing on, and harmonising with, a red antheap; the striped zebra standing in a thicket, when the stripes became part and parcel of the thicket; the black sable antelope standing among black tree trunks in a forest and not spotted until some movement was made, and buffalo lying down among large black rocks, so that it was difficult to tell which were the buffalo and which the rocks, but never have I seen such perfect camouflage as was represented by the waterbuck and the old gnarled tree. The grey hide of the waterbuck harmonised perfectly with the colour of the dead tree, its horns were similar to many other dead branches projecting from the tree, while from where we stood, the white ringed hindquarters looked exactly the same as two or three other broken off and gnarled branches.

To have foxed two meat-hungry Africans, and the one an experienced

Shangaan hunter, it will be appreciated that the camouflage must have been exceptionally good.

In no time Africans appeared from nowhere, as is so often the case when an animal is shot and you think that you are miles from the nearest habitation. There was much feasting that night and the two Africans with me gorged themselves in the company of several others who had joined us at our camp. Unfortunately for me I had to stick to bully-beef, as the meat of a waterbuck bull has such a strong, musty flavour, that it cannot be stomached by Europeans. It would be interesting to hear if others have had similar experiences in the 'bundu'?

Outpost, November 1975

PART THREE

General Interest Stories by George Style

The Crawl
Good or Bad? The Story of Scotty Smith
Lundi River Rescues
Those Pointed Shoes
The Charge of the Light Brigade
When Rhodesia Abandoned the Gold Standard
Barnard, the Elephant Poacher
A Stolen Person
Night Hunt
Nda Rashika Torch!
When the Lion Walks
Tagati?
The Marauding Leopards of Bikita
Vermin Eradicator Extraordinary

THE CRAWL

I wish I could forget it but the trauma was such that only blessed sleep brings relief. I was under the impression that the word applied only to emotional shock until my Concise Oxford informed that, in addition, it is a 'morbid condition of body produced by wound or external violence'. The words 'external violence' put my 'trauma' into a nutshell.

It was fifty years ago that I found myself stationed at Bikita with one of the oldest troopers in the Corps – 'Busky' Knight, who was in charge of the two-man station. Busky was perfectly happy and had, he hoped, dug himself in for life. Like so many other 'outside' officials of that period, he had amassed his own herd of cattle which supplied plenty of milk and, in addition, owned a large flock of pedigreed White Leghorns taken over from Trooper Richards who, whilst on leave in England, had decided to take his discharge. I remember that eggs were so plentiful that Busky took a walk behind his brick hut every night in order to dispose of the surplus. I also recall that he suspected the Native Commissioner's wife of wanting to rival his flock. All eggs sold to her were carefully pricked with a needle. How frustrated her broody hens must have become!

Apart from the nightly sundowner of Commando brandy – and when in camp it was Busky's Regimental Order (not unwillingly obeyed) that l drink with him – Busky had provided himself with various other amenities and diversions. But after six months in the bundu I was getting browned off and longed to see a girl of my own race again. It was a known, if rarely admitted, fact that fellows who spent too long in the bush found that the complexion of the locals seemed to pale into insignificance. Anyway, the question was how to get back to Salisbury and civilisation for a spell? I was one of the lucky ones for there I had my own sweet and pure girl-friend – doubly lucky, for in those days we outnumbered the opposite sex by ten to one.

Now when collecting recommendations from men of note in my home village of King William's Town the previous year in order to support my application for the BSA Police, one of the leading lawyers of the town, R.W. Rose-Innes Esq., JP, had mentioned that 'this young man is one of the best, if not the best, rugger forward in this town.' No doubt this exaggeration, modestly disclaimed by me of course, had helped my acceptance into the Force. In 1925 I managed to get into the BSA Police and into the BSA Police XV. Thus, in debating ways and means of getting back to Salisbury, I came upon the answer. I would apply to return for the 1926 rugby season, a sporting request that was not thought unreasonable in those days. Again, my application was successful – it showed a great keenness on the game as well as a desire to enhance the reputation of the Corps – and, packing my kit and bidding Busky a fond farewell I arrived in Depot early in May to get down to some solid training – for rugby, that is.

The rugger enthusiasts who returned from outstations annually to winter in Depot presented something of a problem for RSM Jock Douglas. From long experience he had been given cause to regret the threat posed by sportsmen with more time on their hands than was good for them. Faced with the 1926 invasion, he planned accordingly. He put up his proposal to the Depot Commandant, Captain Rochester. 'I've got it, sirr,' he announced in his husky brogue. 'I'll put these ruggerr players on to breaking in remounts!' The Commandant agreed and breaking in the wild batches of horses brought up each year from the de Beers studfarm near Kimberley became the order of the day for the rugger players. One of the consequences was that Corporal Jack Betts, whose lion skin hangs in the bar of the Police Club today, became a regular Depot visitor in winter but saw precious little rugby as he was almost continually hospitalised. But there was more, it seemed, in the RSM's devilish plans than full employment for the sportsmen. Perhaps it was an element of revenge for past wrongs committed by his charges.

Jock's happiest moments were spent watching us perform in the riding school. He was generous with his help in assisting one or two of the luckier victims to hold a vicious brute. He was kindness itself as he patted the untamed horse and whispered in its ear before turning to the recipient of his vengeance. 'There you are, Betts, a nice quiet animal ... quiet as a mouse. Just jump up into the saddle, there's nothing to be afraid of.' Having given such kind advice, Jock would retreat a few yards to a position of safety. But when Jack Betts, or some other unfortunate, hit the dust, the Old Man would be facing the other way with his shoulders shaking, giggling to himself and trying unsuccessfully to restrain his laughter.

Then came the fatal day for me. As I breathed a sigh of relief at having survived another morning of Jock's entertainment, the RSM turned to me, 'Look, me lad. At two o'clock I want you to take out Remount No. 342. He's a very quiet animal – just give him some exercise!' 'Very good, sir,' I replied unhappily, knowing full well that it was anything but good.

We had given Remount No. 342 the name of Socks and not only because of the animal's colouring on both hind legs and near fore. Socks was a treacherous and angular brute. He had thrown and injured several men and was fast earning a reputation akin to that of Long Tom. The latter was so intractable that our acknowledged 'RoughRider', Sergeant Hampton, had attempted to break him by inspanning Long Tom with the mules to draw the buckboard. Taking the mules with him, Long Tom had tried to argue with a barbed-wire fence and was so badly injured that he had to be destroyed.

At the appointed time of 2 p.m. I was sitting nervously in the saddle. So far, so good. Keeping the animal at a walk, something I intended to do for the whole of the exercise, I set out for the golf course, riding past the barrack rooms cautiously in case any one of my more fortunate companions had planned an upset. By 2.25 p.m. I had reached the far side of the golf course and was at least a mile from camp. At 2.26 p.m. I was writhing in agony on the ground.

Without any warning Socks had taken a great leap forward and thrown up his hind legs. I had flown over his head to land with a resounding bump on the right side of the spine, where the backbone meets the pelvis. For the first hour I sprawled on my back in tremendous pain, groaning and unable to move, while constantly calling for help. Predictably there was not a soul in sight or earshot. Socks had long disappeared over the top of Gun Kopje. The shortest day of the year, 21 June, was not far off. By 5.30 p.m. it would be almost dark and freezingly cold. I knew that if I did not get back to camp that night I could well die of exposure.

I don't know how long it took but it must have been at least an hour before I was able to roll over on to my stomach. It was quite impossible for me to get to my feet and I was convinced my spine was broken. There was only one thing for it – and that was to crawl home. I set off, using my knees and forearms, and with very necessary and frequent rests made a little headway. I met no one on my painful travels and by the time I had reached the road in front of the barrack rooms it was dusk. All was quiet. The troops as usual were no doubt in the canteen swigging beer and eating Over's bread and cheese.

My accommodation was a room in the sick lines, behind the stables, which I was sharing with old 'Murph', Farrier-Corporal Murphin. I continued my crawl on what was now hard gravel, past the water-troughs and the stables, and eventually reached my room. After creeping in and another long rest, I eventually managed to pull myself up on to the hard iron issue-bed and its three almost equally hard coir-stuffed biscuits. Very soon afterwards, at a most opportune moment, Murph walked in and passed me an empty rifle-oil can. He left almost immediately to report my condition to the RSM.

A few minutes later and Jock's bulky figure filled the doorway. After many huffs and puffs, he opened the conversation. 'Well, me lad, who told you to take out that horse?' 'Excuse me, sir, but you did! You told me to exercise Horse No. 342 at two o'clock.' 'No! No! No!' Jock argued. "There must have been some misunderstanding. Get up now and I'll give you a nice soft job. Go up to the Mess and act as mess orderly – just see that the tables are set correctly. Off you go now.'

'But sir, I can't move!' 'Nonsense, you're quite all right, my lad! Just get on your feet and go up to the mess, it's a nice soft job!' 'Very good, sir.' There was no point in arguing. It was obvious that Jock wouldn't take no for an answer and it was also obvious that he was very worried and wanted to see me walking. As recruits we had often wondered about the 'legality' of being used as rough-riders and Jock's concern now increased my suspicions.

A few minutes after Jock's departure, the grinning 'Tommy', Sergeant Blake-Thompson of the Camp Hospital, showed up. After only a cursory examination he packed me off to the General Hospital by ambulance. The next day I was told that the X-ray showed my spine to be intact although there was serious bruising. Later in the morning the Medical Director, Dr A.P. Martin, an enormous man, called in to see me and put me at ease. 'All you need, my boy, is a few days of rest in bed,' he announced in his sonorous voice. 'Then you'll be quite fit to go back on full duty.'

I must say that the period which followed was one of the happiest and most relaxing of my many spells in hospital. I was thoroughly spoilt by the two girls who nursed me, a couple who will always be remembered by the Old Hands for their beauty and charm – Sisters Lilian Frith and Lorna Du Preez. With an appetite that had suffered in no way from the fall, they fed me like a lord. But all good things come to an end and after just a week I was back on full duty – including remount riding – and again playing rugby.

Now, after fifty years, my chiropractor tells me that the fall from Socks pushed some of my lower vertebrae to one side to press on the sciatic nerve. For all that, I have no regrets over the damage revealed by a subsequent X-ray. Getting away from Bikita to see my girlfriend and escape from the bush for a time was worth all the discomforts.

And so, no doubt, many other rough-riding remount breakers of that day, suffer similarly. Without even the comfort of a disability pension. Memories linger – some of the more painful ones as long as the most pleasurable.

Outpost, November 1976

GOOD or BAD?

The Story of Scotty Smith

Scotty Smith has been described as one of the world's most picturesque bad men, along with Dick Turpin, Robin Hood and Rob Roy of Britain, and others. Few have achieved the lasting fame or notoriety of Scotty, the cattle-rustler and horse-thief, highwayman and outlaw, secret service agent and patriot, IDB trafficker, confidence trickster and soldier of fortune among other things.

Smith claimed to have been born in Perth, Scotland, in 1845, and always maintained that his real name was George St. Leger Gordon Lennox; that he was the eldest son of a fairly wealthy Perthshire landowner; and that his father, the Laird of the estate, had given him a good education including courses in land surveying and veterinary science.

Mr F.C. Metrowich (in his book, *SCOTTY SMITH, South Africa's Robin Hood*) writes that; 'while Scotty was undoubtedly well-connected, his pretensions to legitimate relationship with the Gordon Lennox family and to the fact that his birthplace was Perth are difficult to substantiate. Obviously, if these claims have any validity, some record of a man bearing so illustrious a name would have been preserved in the neighbourhood where he was born and educated. But although at my request the Town Clerk of Perth consulted various reference books and made certain other investigations, he drew a complete blank.'

At the age of 18, Scotty joined a cavalry regiment which was posted to India, where he saw action on the North-West Frontier. During a skirmish in the hills he ignored the order to retreat after his officer had been killed, assumed command, and ordered the men to charge. Although the objective was reached, heavy casualties were suffered, and Gordon Lennox was court-martialled and cashiered. Although as a result of intervention by the Duke of Cambridge the verdict was set aside and he was reinstated, he decided the army was no place for him, took his discharge and returned home. Scotty's father now wished him to marry the eldest daughter of a landowning neighbour who had no sons, and thus unite the two estates. This young Gordon Lennox refused to do, as a result of which he was disinherited by his father, boarded a ship and sailed for Australia. On board were two thoroughbred horses and Gordon Lennox noticed that the one was in considerable pain from a badly fitting shoe. With the Captain's permission, he removed the shoe, pared the hoof and expertly replaced the shoe. The passengers had already called him Scotty because of his nationality, but after this he was known as 'Scotty the Blacksmith' which was soon abbreviated to Scotty Smith.

For a time Scotty practised as a veterinary surgeon in Australia but later went gold mining. Here he ran into trouble when he found a miner bullying a youngster and intervened. The miner drew his revolver, but Scotty was quicker on the draw, shot first, and killed him. As a result he sailed for America and after a short spell there he returned to Europe and fought for the French in the Franco-Prussian war, in which he was wounded and taken prisoner by the Germans.

He was released on the cessation of hostilities and a couple of years later he fought for the Carlists in the Spanish war of 1872-76, but when the attempt to restore Don Carlos of Bourbon to the Spanish throne failed, he moved to South Africa where he joined the Frontier Armed and Mounted Police.

Scotty was just in time to take part in the last of the nine official Kaffir wars, the Galeka-Gaika revolt of 1877, and when the campaign ended the following year he was stationed at Kokstad as a farrier. About this time he deserted to return to Scotland to put his financial affairs in order. It seems that his desertion was only temporary for he returned to the mounted police and was later stationed in King William's Town as a farrier. From this appointment he later again absconded, taking with him two of the best police horses, and thus began his career of horse and cattle thieving and brigandage.

At this time, Scotty, who stood six feet two inches in height, was described as being powerfully built, beautifully proportioned, as hard as nails, and a very striking personality with a thick red beard, heavy eyebrows, bright blue eyes and a ruddy face. He operated around Kimberley for a time, raiding the farms of the more prosperous farmers in the Transvaal and Free State. Being unable to resist the temptations offered by illicit diamond buying and gunrunning, Scotty was soon forced by the police to move north to the small isolated village of Zeerust in the Transvaal. Here law and order were non-existent and he and other toughs haunted the notorious 'Zeerust Club' which had its headquarters at the 'Bucket of Blood' hotel.

Scotty did not remain long in Zeerust but moved southwards to the new republics of Goshen and StellaIand, where there was little, if any, law and order. For some years he made the wild country bordering on Taungs, Vryburg and Mafeking and extending westwards through the Kalahari Desert to the frontier of German South West Africa, his hunting grounds. He had an amazing and profitable career, and at one time the old South African Republic of the Transvaal put a price of £500 on his head, but to no avail. His cool brain and proverbial luck extricated him from the most perilous situations and on the few occasions when he was actually caught and jailed, the police quickly discovered that their lock-ups were no match for the ingenuity of the bandit.

It was Scotty's many deeds of chivalry that endeared him to so many people, and the following incident was typical. In the Vryburg district he called at a farm to find a mother and daughter in great distress. The daughter confided that her father had died recently and there was a large debt owing to the Vryburg store. If this was not paid within the next few weeks the farm would be sold. Scotty drove the mother and daughter to town, drew the required amount from the bank, walked into the shop, threw the money on the counter and shouted: 'There's the sum owed you. Give me the receipt, and if I ever hear of you oppressing people like this again, I'll come back and put a couple of bullets into you.'

It was his better nature too, that saved the BSA Police the loss of 102 remounts and the two incidents in connection with this are quoted in full in the book.

'Major Jesser Coope, who afterwards became a well-known citizen of Southern Rhodesia, also had an encounter about this time with the famous freebooter, which redounds much to the latter's credit. It was the year 1890, and Jesser Coope, then a young subaltern in the British South African (sic) Police, was in charge of a number of remounts which had been purchased in the Vryburg district. It was his custom to have the horses counted each morning before leaving the place where they had stayed for the night. At the very first camp after leaving Vryburg he found that two of the mounts were missing.

'Now Jesser Coope had a tremendous battle rounding up his tough, hard-drinking men and getting them out of the Vryburg canteens on the previous day. He had no illusions about what would happen if they were sent out to search for the missing steeds. They would make a bee-line back to the town, and he would have all his trouble over again.

'He therefore gave strict instructions that they were to remain in the camp. Then with an old hand who knew a good deal about the art of tracking, he followed the trail of the missing animals until he came to a cart outspanned not very far from Vryburg. A tall man with a beard came out to see what he wanted. The tracker immediately whispered to his officer, 'That's Scotty Smith. He's sure to have pinched the horses.'

'But when Jesser Coope taxed Scotty with the theft, the latter blandly denied that he knew anything about it. Jesser Coope, however, refused to believe this and after a while Scotty admitted that he had taken the horses. Then with an impudent grin on his face he offered to fight the officer for them.

'Now Jesser Coope was an old English public school boy, and like so many of his kind he had shown more prowess on the sports field and in the gymnasium than in the classroom. He was a first-class boxer, so he immediately accepted the challenge. But Scotty was only testing him out, or perhaps his unfortunate encounter with the young farmer was still fresh in his memory and had made him more cautious than he would otherwise have been.[1] At any rate he roared with laughter, and treated the whole matter as a joke.

'All right, you win,' he cried. 'You can have your horses back.'

'They shook hands on it and Scotty sent his man to fetch the missing animals. Then he rode back with the officer to his camp and they made a night of it.'

The second confrontation between Scotty Smith and the BSA Police was in very similar circumstances.

'One day a young officer of that famous corps arrived in Mafeking. He was in charge of a hundred remounts, which he and two troopers were taking back to the force. They attended to the horses and then picketed

---

[1] Some time before Scotty had held up a prominent Free State farmer who was riding back with the proceeds of the sale of his wool clip. The Boer suggested that, as he had always heard Scotty was a good sport, they should fight it out, he wagering his cash against Scotty's pistol. Scotty thought that it would be a walkover for him and agreed, but the Boer must have been a potential champion and Scotty, much to his surprise, got the thrashing of his life.

them in a large open space in the middle of the town, after which, hot, dusty and exhausted, they retired to the hotel for the night. Before dawn the officer awoke with an uneasy feeling. Suddenly realising that he had not taken the elementary precaution of appointing a night guard over the horses he hurried out to see whether they were all right. And then he stopped dead. There was not a single horse in sight.

'With growing panic he hastily summoned his men. For three days they searched frantically but without success for the missing stock. The horses appeared to have vanished into thin air. There was one clue, however, to their fate. At widely scattered points on the veld the troopers picked up a few halter ropes, halters and picket pegs, which seemed to indicate that something must have stampeded the animals. At last, in a state of profound dejection and with visions of being court-martialled and cashiered floating before his eyes, the young officer decided to consult the barman about the possibility of obtaining a number of Baralong tribesmen to help him in his search. The barman, however, was not very encouraging. He had a pretty shrewd idea who the culprit was, and suggested that the best thing the subaltern could do would be to reconcile himself to his loss.

'At this stage a tall, silent man, who had been standing on one side listening to the conversation, suddenly intervened. Impressed by the young officer's obvious distress, he walked up to him and in a friendly manner asked, 'What year were you at Sandhurst?'

'Taken aback by this unexpected question, the youngster told him, and then poured out his trouble into the stranger's sympathetic ear. The latter listened in silence until he had finished and then patted him on the shoulder. 'Don't worry, my boy,' he remarked kindly. 'I know this part of the country extremely well and I'll see what I can do for you. Send your men off to have a good rest.' Then dropping his voice he added in a much sharper tone:

'Now pull yourself together, young man, and don't give way like this. Just imagine what impression your present state would have on your colonel, were he to get wind of it. It's fortunate for you that I'm not your adjutant!'

'The officer retired in a very crestfallen mood. But at dawn the next morning he was awakened by the unexpected sound of the neighing and whinnying of a large number of horses. Hardly able to believe his ears, he jumped out of bed and rushed in the direction of the noise. An amazing sight met his eyes. About a hundred horses were standing tethered to the picket posts.

'When he recovered from his first shock the subaltern counted them and found that not a mount was missing. He also noticed that, although most of their halters bore the BSAP stamp, in some cases improvised ropes and reims had been used. It was only later that he realised that the animals could not possibly have stampeded, because they bore none of the cuts and abrasions which they would undoubtedly have done had they been frightened into breaking loose.

'At the moment, however, his only desire was to find the man who had performed this miracle and had restored his self-respect. But the mild-mannered, soft-spoken stranger was nowhere to be found. All enquiries were met with a blank wall of reserve. For some reason no one seemed willing to acknowledge that they knew anything about the man. The barman would say, for example:

'Oh 'im. 'E comes 'ere now and then. Don't know 'is name, but a bloke 'ere once called 'im Scotty. Best leave 'im, son, to 'is own secrets. It'll pay you better that way.'

Scotty was one of the first to offer his services to the Union authorities at the outbreak of the 1914-18 war, when, in spite of his 69 years, he was remarkably fit. He was attached to the Military Intelligence and served with distinction in the German South West African campaign.

After contracting 'flu in 1919, Scotty died at the age of 74, and was buried in the Upington cemetery. A simple metal plaque was erected over his grave, and this read:

> George St. Leger Gordon Lennox. Gone but not forgotten.
> Never will his memory fade. Wife and children.

In 1913, Major C.A. Anderson who died at Marandellas last year, and was an authority on the underground water resources of South Africa, spent two and a half months travelling for the Union Government in the Kalahari Desert with Scotty as guide and got to know him well. 'I would like to stress,' he wrote, 'that Scotty was a well-educated man, with a clear brain, a magnificent stamina (he was nearly seventy years old when we went on our trip together), and a keen sense of sarcastic humour. He certainly was not a criminal in the usual sense of the word, although he broke the law on numerous occasions. If he had remained in the Army, and his regiment had been engaged on continual active service, George St. Leger Gordon Lennox would undoubtedly have made an honoured name for himself. That Scotty fully appreciated his position was made clear to me one night when we were sitting at the camp fire sipping our cocoa before turning into our blankets which were already spread out on the soft, desert sands.

'My only trouble,' he told me, 'has been that I was born two hundred years too late.'

'How do you make that out?' I asked. He then said, 'My great weakness is, if I see a bunch of good cattle I want to annex them. In modern times this is looked upon as stealing and calls for police intervention, which may lead to imprisonment without the option of a fine.'

To this I replied: 'Quite so.'

He then continued: 'Two hundred years ago annexing other people's cattle was known as rieving. A successful riever was a highly honoured member of his family group, and if the cattle had been rieved from south of the Scottish border the riever was acclaimed as a Scottish hero. You see my point.'

'I assured him that I fully appreciated his argument.'

Outpost, October 1968

LUNDI RIVER RESCUES

After three years of drought, this last season could not have started better — much to the relief of all in the Lowveld. A steady soaking drizzle set in on the night of November 10 1968, and continued intermittently for three days, followed by a few isolated falls on November 14. Later, for just over seven weeks until February 9, fairly regular and soaking rains were experienced and by this time the Lowveld was looking really beautiful. Then abruptly the rains stopped. By the end of February we were in the throes of another drought with the grazing badly parched and the sprouting crops threatened. The spectre of a long term threat loomed — that Kyle and Bangala Dams and Lake MacDougall would be unable to supply water for the irrigation of the dependent area through to the next rainy season. The prospects were far from cheering: we prayed for the paradox of a much gloomier horizon.

And then, in March as some had predicted, the rains came ...

By March 14, the Lundi River was in spate. It had risen 18 feet, had overflowed its banks and now presented the picture of a foaming, debris-strewn torrent some five hundred yards across. The low-level bridge on the Triangle-Mbizi road was buried four feet below the swirling waters.  On March 17, Section Officer Graham of BSA Police, Triangle, received a message from Field Reservist Ken Tilbury (a former member of the Force) of Mpapa Section, on the southern side of the Lundi, to the effect that several Africans were stranded on an island in the middle of the torrent some distance below the railway bridge. The island was about 250 feet from either bank and the lives of those marooned were in peril. Because of the tree trunks and other debris being carried downstream, rescue by boat would be no simple matter. Such a venture was threatened to a greater extent by two sets of rapids above and below the island. The rock-strewn shallows about a hundred yards downstream from the island promised to batter into match-wood any craft embroiled in their clutches.

Section Officer Graham left for the river on receipt of the SOS, taking with him African Constables Muchada and Magola and a lifeline discharger rifle with some 150 feet of rope. The truck was halted by the swollen river but Ken Tilbury was on the lookout for the policemen and managed to cross from the southern bank in his 14-foot run-about powered by a 45 h.p. motor. With Ken was the mechanical engineer of the Mpapa Section, Mr Karl Howells, and between them they managed to ferry Section Officer Graham and Constable Muchada across to the south bank. The dangers ahead were underlined by the sight of a ten-foot crocodile which slid into the water as the small boat reached the bank.

The boat was then loaded with the available rescue equipment and several blankets (in case the marooned Africans were suffering from exposure). The resultant load was such that the boat wallowed through the water instead of planing although the ten knot current ensured a swift if hair-raising passage downstream. The railway bridge was passed about three miles down the river, and then the rapids above the island forced the rescuers to land to take a closer look at the helpless Africans from the bank.

The reconnaissance revealed that there was no alternative to a rescue by means of the boat although there was a smaller island near the bank between the two groups of people. The river was still rising and it was already 5.20 p.m. so there was no time to be lost. Tilbury returned upstream to fetch the boat, having decided that he stood the best chance of navigating the rapids alone in a lightened boat. Twenty minutes later he was back, had beached the craft opposite the island and the heavier equipment had been unloaded. Karl Howells volunteered to go with Tilbury on the first attempt to reach the island but it was decided that he should remain on the bank with the rescue equipment and a rope in case the boat was swept downstream. It was essential that two people should crew the small craft since its engine had to be hand-started and it was most likely that the propeller would become fouled in the flotsam of grass and reeds evident in the river. Speedily Section Officer Graham and Ken Tilbury waded waist-deep into the torrent to manhandle the boat into a relatively grass-free area. They clambered aboard and started the engine. The venture seemed doomed. Only minimal headway was possible against the tearing current and in a very short time the earlier fears were realised and the propeller jammed in a tangle of grass. In the anxious moments while the propeller was freed, the boat drifted to within a hundred yards of the lower rapids. A long battle against the current followed by which time it was apparent that the only possible method of making a landfall on the island was by virtually ramming it from an upstream direction.

The three men and the woman had been marooned on the island for three days, since March 14. In that time they had eaten nothing. Having baled out the water that been shipped in the outward passage, the rescuers prepared to ferry the woman to safety. There was a mere four inches of freeboard and to have taken more than one of the marooned Africans at a time would have been impossible. The remaining trio pushed the boat into deep water but no sooner had the engine been started than the propeller jammed again in the weeds. While Section Officer Graham struggled to free the choked drive the boat rocked violently and more water was shipped. Eventually the safety of the bank was reached where Mr Howells and Constable Muchada helped the woman ashore.

The second journey to the island was equally hazardous. Having pushed the boat clear of the reeds and clambered aboard once more, the two men reached midstream before the propeller again became tangled in the reeds and the small engine stalled. This time the boat drifted to within thirty yards of the lower rapids before the engine could be restarted. Reaching the island and beaching in the same manner as before, the water which had slopped into the boat again had to be bailed out.

The next candidate for rescue was a very frail old African called Peter. He clambered aboard, shivering with fright, and after a few yards the three men were drifting downstream towards the rocks with a stalled engine once more. Ken Tilbury managed to grasp a bush which protruded through the water to halt the rush towards the rapids while Section Officer Graham cleared the propeller yet again. The bank was finally reached as the engine spluttered and resigned itself again to the stranglehold of the debris.

It was 6.15 p.m. and getting dark. Further attempts to reach the island would have been suicidal so the rescuers shouted to the remaining two Africans that they would have to remain on the island until morning. The river continued to rise but the patch of dry land about 20 by 40 feet in area was still some four feet above the rushing waters.

The rescue party and the two Africans who had been brought off the island walked the four miles to Mpapa Section where they were greeted by the news that six more Africans were similarly stranded on an island further downstream.

On returning to the river next morning, it was discovered that the water level had dropped. The small boat which had been anchored to a tree was high and dry and it was impossible to launch the craft into the river in which further islands had appeared. The waving tips of grass above the water indicated that even if the boat was launched, progress through the shallows would be hampered by the repetition of a tangled propeller. Graham and Tilbury were able to wade to the nearer island from which they attempted to fire a rope across to the stranded Africans. The wooden block carrying the line shattered in mid-air and the attempt ended in failure. Finally it was decided that if the river continued to fall as indicated the two Africans should be able to wade ashore in a matter of hours.

The rescuers then tramped downstream through the mud to investigate the plight of the other six Africans which had been reported the previous evening. There was little that could be done for them immediately. Their island was situated in a narrower part of the river but the speed of the torrent at this point would have swept the small boat or the strongest swimmer away in a matter of seconds.

The river continued to fall during the morning until Section Officer Graham was able to drive a Land Rover across the low-level bridge and return to the station to report. Inspector Ray, the Member-in-Charge at Triangle, agreed that there was little more that could be done as long as the river continued to fall.

On the following day it was found that the level of the water was not dropping as swiftly as anticipated. Something would have to be done about those who had now been marooned without food for five days. To add to the problem, Chibi reported that more Africans were stranded about thirty miles from the station opposite Nyahombe Range.

Inspector Ray contacted Police Reservist Rodney Style of Buffalo Range and asked him if he could mount an air reconnaissance in his Cessna. Mr Style readily agreed and Section Officer Graham was again pressed into the search, this time more comfortably from the air, and accompanied by Police Reservist Peter Knivett, also of Buffalo Range. Having taken off from the airport, the two Africans who had been left behind on the island near the railway bridge were soon located. With the supplies left to them by Ken Tilbury and Section Officer Graham, they appeared to be as comfortable as could be expected and in no immediate danger. The search party were unsuccessful in locating the other stranded Africans and it later turned out that they were hiding under some trees, probably in fear of the low-flying aircraft. Having returned to Triangle, the situation was reported to Inspector Ray.

On the morning of March 20, it was decided to air-drop rations to the stranded groups. Rodney Style removed the passenger door of his aircraft, rations were stacked on the passenger seat and Peter Knivett and Section Officer Graham squeezed into the back of the plane. Again, the first two Africans were located without difficulty and a one hundred pound sack of food was dropped to them. Attempts to locate the other groups were again unsuccessful on the first flight, but a later sortie revealed their presence and Style and Knivett were able to supply food from the air in the afternoon.

The excitement would have been over and the remainder of the rescue operation would have become merely a matter of patience until it was reported that the river was rising again in the catchment area. It was decided to evacuate all the remaining Africans by helicopter and RRAF headquarters at New Sarum were contacted to this end.

Flying Officer Peter Bristow landed in his Alouette at Triangle on the morning of March 21. Guided by Section Officer Graham, each of the islands was visited and with great skill the pilot managed to land in the very restricted areas to evacuate the marooned people to safety. Two men and two boys were first rescued from the Nyahombe Range area, then the two from the island below the railway bridge, and finally the six Africans were picked off the island further down the river.

Thus ended a drama which could well have had the most tragic results had it not been for the courage, persistence and skill of all involved in the rescue operations. The Acting Commissioner of Police has directed that a memorandum of good work performed be awarded to Section Officer Graham and personal letters of congratulation directed to Field Reservists Style and Tilbury for their part in the rescue.

Outpost, July 1969

I Shall Never Forget ...

... THOSE POINTED SHOES

They were the first I'd ever owned and will certainly be the last. I have just remembered how I came to buy them.

It was while on Recruits' Course in 1925 that Molly A., the belle of Salisbury, asked me to take her to the dance at the Grand Hotel that coming Saturday evening. As I was a very poor dancer I was highly flattered and agreed immediately. The snag was that I had no dress suit, so the following afternoon, after the last parade of the day, a Law and Police lecture by 'H.H.', I walked down to Over's store where Trixie, for ten guineas, sold me one off the peg and insisted on me buying a pair of black pointed shoes to match.

Unfortunately, a little later, it was the suit I lost, but not the shoes. They pinched badly, and in any case I had never liked pointed shoes, always associating them with the effeminate type. By then I had passed out of Depot and was stationed in Fort Victoria. About the end of the year the new hospital was completed and a dance was given in celebration. The band struck up and, hastily stubbing a cigarette, I walked across the floor of what is now the men's ward to claim my partner. We were gaily waltzing around when she exclaimed that she smelt something burning, and all of a sudden the right-hand pocket of my dinner jacket burst into flame. After all, £12.10s. a month did not go far even in those days, and half-smoked fags were never discarded.

It must have been a week or two later that Corporal 'J.J.' invited me one Saturday morning to make a fourth in a party to Zimbabwe that night with two attractive young sisters. I accepted with alacrity. You could count the girls in Fort Victoria on one hand. I couldn't wear my dress suit, but did, unfortunately, don my pointed shoes. One of the three European-owned taxis was engaged and off we set, the European driver, like all good drivers, looking straight ahead. After showing the girls the Ruins by moonlight while our taxi waited, we eventually returned to the hotel. While the others waited in the car, I went into the bar to order a round of drinks from my host the late Mr Stappard, an old-timer of the BSA Police. You can imagine my surprise, disappointment and anger when, stepping out with the tray, I found that my party had disappeared, taxi and all.

About an hour later a car pulled up and the taxi-driver walked in for a round of drinks. He had quite a reputation as a boxer, but I was too angry to let this worry me and although expecting to come off the worse, honour was satisfied with a few good clouts and punches. He had, of course, been spending the evening with my partner. Thinking things over today, it was Corporal 'J.J.' who should have collected the punches — or the point of my shoe — but he had remained cuddling in the car.

After closing time they very kindly called for me: but being too angry and proud to travel with them I invited them to push off, which they promptly did. After all, there were at least a dozen cars outside, so there would be no difficulty in getting home. So I thought, anyway.

After finishing my last drink at leisure I looked round for a lift to camp, eighteen miles away, to find that all the cars except one belonged to tourists spending the night. This one happened to be another of the three European-owned taxis, and on my asking the driver to give me a lift he informed me that he dare not do so, as he was a friend of the man I had assaulted and had no wish to fall out with him.

Once again pride came to the fore and I assured the driver that he need not worry — I would walk home. What was 18 miles after all? I had been compelled to tramp a similar distance at night once before, when, as a young bank clerk, I had accompanied a girl friend by train to a junction 16 miles from home. While we were sitting in the carriage holding hands, the return train had silently pulled out. I was posting my ledger at 9 o'clock the next morning.

I set off from the Zimbabwe Hotel on my trek back to camp soon after 11 p.m., and it was then I cursed those pointed shoes. The further I walked the more they pinched, and the soles were so thin that my feet ached with every step along the gravelled road of those days. It must have been about 3 a.m. when I reached the hills of farm Brucehaeme, bought later by my Sergeant-Major, the late Bill Hewlett. I could go no further. My feet ached unbearably and the drinks consumed that evening had made me extremely drowsy. Despite the bitter cold I lay down by the side of the road and slept.

I could not have slept for too long, it was far too cold. I had to continue walking to keep warm, and the fact that I had already covered 10 of the 18 miles urged me on, despite my aching and, by now, blistered feet. Eventually there was one small rise ahead of me and I knew I would see Fort Victoria.

I topped the rise just as the sun rose and there, on the veranda of Zimbabwe Hotel, standing in his pyjamas suspiciously close to the pub, was old 'Stap'. It was too late to hide and he spotted me at once, calling out cheerfully to know whether I had spent the night sleeping in the bush. I was too shy to tell him about my 20-mile walk and how, after my sleep, I must have walked back the way I had come. I was grateful for the room 'Stap' gave me and the hot tea he sent me and it did not take me long to remove my shoes and fall asleep.

About 1 p.m. I awoke to the sound of a motorcycle arriving. It was Trooper Storr Garlake (now Major-General), who had come to look for me. My presence in camp had eventually been missed. I was soon on the pillion, clutching my shoes in one hand.

There are two things that I shall never forget. The wonderful comradeship of those days and *those pointed shoes*.

Outpost, July 1962

THE CHARGE of the LIGHT BRIGADE

It all came back to me while soaping myself in the bath this morning. Two large brown scars were clearly visible on the inside of my left leg just above the knee, that portion of the leg with which one grips the saddle if properly trained, as we certainly were by Rough-Rider Sergeant 'Hampie' Hampton and Corporal George Sewell.

The early part of our recruits' course during the month of May and part of June, 1925, had been taken up very largely with escort training for the visit in June of H.R.H. the Prince of Wales. How proud we were when the day after meeting His Royal Highness and escorting him from the Railway Station in Bulawayo to Government House, Force Orders for the day carried in very large type the headlines:

'THE FINEST BODY OF CAVALRY I HAVE SEEN SINCE LANDING ON THE SHORES OF AFRICA.'

Inspection by the Prince of Wales

Much to our disappointment, the presentation of a medal which it was rumoured we were to get from the Prince never eventuated!

Re-trucking our horses we returned to Salisbury where a few days later we rode to the Station to again escort His Royal Highness to Government House. Here we sat holding our rifles at attention for a full three-quarters of an hour before he emerged from the Royal Train rubbing his eyes and looking somewhat the worse for wear. I heard him remark as he passed with the O.C. Escort, Captain Bugler: 'I seem to have seen several of these faces before!'

Tired as we were, we soon forgave our popular Prince for having kept us waiting so long, apparently, as we learnt later, as a result of a party held on the train the night before. When at the Police Sports that afternoon he successfully took Cromwell, Sergeant Simpson's horse, over the jumps he was much applauded by us all.

Eventually September came, our squad had completed training and we were due to be drafted to the outside districts. Now in those days Umtali district was the most popular in the country and how thrilled I was when one afternoon our gruff but much esteemed RSM, Jock Douglas, burst into the lecture room where 'H.H.' was holding forth on the subject of Law and Police, and exclaimed, while holding a sheaf of papers in his hand: – 'Style, you will leave for Umtali in the morning!'

It so happened that I was on Sick Report as with two very large but unripe boils on the inside of my left leg just above the knee, I was unable to ride. Without thinking and in great excitement I jumped to my feet calling out: 'Very good, Sir. I am at present on Sick Report but immediately after this lecture I will go up to the hospital and get taken off.'

Jock muttered about having to send someone else in that case and left the room. Nothing daunted, as soon as the lecture was over at 5 p.m. I went with all possible speed to the Camp Hospital where I explained the position to our Medical Sergeant, 'Tommy' Blake-Thompson. 'That's all right,' said Tommy, 'we'll soon get you off Sick Report. Show me these boils!'

He then proceeded to take each unripe boil in turn between his two thumbs and squeezed with all his might but to no avail. Meanwhile the pain was so excruciating that the tears were streaming down my face. The boils, now much bruised and still retaining their cores, were if anything larger than ever. However, Tommy very kindly wrote 'Discharged for full duty' across the Sick Report, and thanking him sincerely for making it now possible for me to go to Umtali, I returned to my barrack-room.

Now we recruits had found that if we wanted a Late Pass through having neglected to obtain one from the Orderly Corporal during the day, we could always obtain one from Jock at his house provided he had consumed his second sundowner. He was then in very good spirits in more ways than one and always affable and obliging. Thus it was with high hopes that at the estimated time I proceeded to Jock's house carrying my Sick Report.

He was in a very good mood when he opened the door in response to my knock. I informed him that I had been taken off Sick Report and asked if I might now proceed to Umtali. Jock seemed genuinely sorry when he told me that I was too late as he had already detailed someone else. This was a great blow to me, and the fact that I was now on 'Full Duty' meant that I would have to ride in the morning.

The first parade for next day was for all recruits to ride down to the Inoculation Camp near Salisbury Kopje and each lead back one of the last batch of remounts which had recently arrived from the de Beers' breeding farms near Kimberley. Donning a pair of slacks – as the size of the boils would not allow of the wearing of riding breeches – I duly fell in with the rest of the recruits and was detailed to ride Captain Bugler's horse Punch, a very beautiful chestnut with a long light tawny mane flowing over a permanently arched neck. Corporal Peetz who hailed from Natal was in charge of the troop.

Eventually we were given the orders: 'Prepare to mount! Mount!"

Off we rode in troop formation, four abreast. We passed through the Depot gates into Montagu Avenue and had ridden only a few yards when Punch broke ranks from near the middle of the troop. At once Corporal Peetz called out to me: 'Hold him, Style, or he'll get away!' 'Don't worry,' I replied, 'I'm alright!'

All of a sudden Punch began to quicken his pace. I tried to check him but with one leg out of action I found I could get no leverage on the reins. Next minute he broke into a canter followed by an all-out gallop and away we sped down Montagu Avenue with the wind sweeping by at what seemed to be gale force. Ahead I could see a gang of about 40 natives picking up a section of the tarmac and laying stone. I well remember the gang parting like the waves of the Red Sea as we clattered over the stones between them. It took me all my time to keep my balance and to say that I was terrified is to put it mildly. I had always heard that one should try to turn a run-away horse and with great difficulty managed to turn him up one of the streets into North Avenue, down which we continued the race.

To cut a long story and a long race short, we finished up in the veld near Salisbury Kopje without the horse having once slackened his pace. Here I managed to turn him in a circle until after about five minutes he had had enough. I then headed Punch for the Inoculation Camp where we arrived a few minutes later. As can be imagined he was in an absolute lather of sweat, so tying him to a tree I offsaddled and gave him a thorough rub down with hay. I then entered the Mess where I found the troops drinking tea kindly dispensed by Sergeant Bill Ansell of the Camp and looking at copies of his *La Vie Parisienne* magazines. From the pictures of the beautiful nude and semi-nude girls no eyes were lifted to greet me as I found myself a seat. Eventually Corporal Peetz deigned to glance up and remark: 'So you've arrived, have you?'

After tea and a suitable rest we rode back to Depot leading a remount each and I had no further trouble with Punch who had had all the exercise he wanted for that day. On our return 1 learnt something about Punch which no one had bothered to tell me. He was never ridden without a martingale owing to the hardness of his mouth and on one occasion had run away with Captain Bugler and headed for the stables. Either to unseat Bugler or because it was the shortest route home, he ran underneath some loquat trees. Bugler's scalp was apparently lifted and as a result it was said he suffered from severe headaches for many years.

Even with a martingale I doubt whether, with one leg out of action, I could have held Punch in. Racing down the avenues certainly gave me the biggest fright I have had from run-away horses and it was thanks to the early hour of the day and the fact that there was not much traffic in Salisbury 45 years ago that I did not come to grief. I am sure that in the famous charge of the Light Brigade at Balaclava, the 17th Lancers (the famous *Death or Glory* boys and my father's old regiment) galloped no faster into the Valley of Death than did Punch down those two avenues.

A few days later Tommy was able to remove the cores from the boils and I was transferred to the Victoria District where, with Umtali forgotten, I spent five very happy years in the Corps.

Outpost, March 1971

When Rhodesia Abandoned the Gold Standard

Gravel Mining during the Great Depression

The Great Depression of nearly forty years ago took many Rhodesian farmers off the land and saw them labouring to mine gravel (photo above) and build the strip roads which are an unforgettable part of our history. The Depression and the abandonment of the gold standard by Rhodesia – but not South Africa – also brought a minor crime wave.

The Wall Street Crash of 1929, with its echoes throughout Europe, began an era of crisis for gold, and ushered in the great world depression, the days of which I often recall. Very many of our farmers had to abandon their farms and seek jobs. The price of maize had dropped to five shillings a bag, and the price of tobacco to a few pence a pound. It was in these days that so many farmers worked on our roads, laying the tarmac strips for a few bob a day.

The United States stayed uneasily on gold until March 1933. On 21 September 1931 Britain abandoned the gold standard after a suspension since 20 June. A week before, foreign countries had been withdrawing gold from the Bank of England at an alarming rate. The South African government decided not to follow the British example in the mistaken belief that the South African economy was strong enough to stand on its own feet. The results of this policy were disastrous and South Africa's overseas market for its agricultural products collapsed. Despite the most stringent regulations, gold flowed out of the country. The banks accumulated a huge balance of depreciated sterling in London. It was not until 29 December 1932, that Mr Havenga, the Minister of Finance, yielded to mounting political and economic pressure and announced that banks had been told that the South African pound had to find its own level, which was another way of saying that he was abandoning the gold standard. Within days the South African pound was at parity with sterling.

Pressure on Mr Havenga to finally make the decision was largely caused by two men. One of them was Mr Justice Tielman Roos, a former Cabinet Minister who had been made a Judge of Appeal but had resigned from the Bench in a protest of disapproval of the South African Government and afterwards stumped up and down the country, telling everyone that unless the South African pound was devalued the nation would be ruined. The other man was Sir Ernest Oppenheimer, the mining magnate, who pointed out that the world situation had changed, the gold standard had ceased to be international and that it was in fact 'managed' by the United States and France. Sir Ernest pointed out that to follow sterling would increase the price South Africa received for its products in the markets of the world.

Meanwhile Northern and Southern Rhodesia had followed close on the heels of Britain and abandoned the Gold Standard on 12 October 1931. And from this time onwards, until South Africa abandoned the gold standard in December 1932, much gold and silver was smuggled out of Southern Rhodesia into South Africa at a premium, despite the fact that severe penalties had been promulgated by our government for this offence. I know that for smuggling gold out of Southern Rhodesia the profit was five shillings in the pound, but what the premium was on our silver – presumably less – I have forgotten and been unable to find out, even from the Research Department of the Standard Bank in Johannesburg. Travellers leaving this country were allowed to take out with them only £5 in gold and £5 in silver. The prevailing great depression was, of course, an additional incentive to smuggling.

I had resigned from the BSA Police after just over five years undistinguished service the year before and, as I have so often said, a policeman learns much after he has left the Force. In the days of which I write there was virtually no serious crime among the Europeans in the Colony owing to our very strict immigration laws. But as a civilian I was to hear of many offences, mostly minor, that had been committed.

My first offer of a job was that of junior clerk in the office of the Native Commissioner, Bikita, but having been a bank clerk for four-and-a-half unhappy years, miserable years, I had a horror of working between four walls. And thus I came to take over the humble job of Dip Supervisor from ex-Trooper Paddy Hodgins, an Irishman from Waterford, and became responsible for the cleanliness of over 30,000 head of cattle.

At about 11 o'clock one morning in 1932, I drove over from Chesuko Dip Tank to the nearby 'Mission-in-the Sunshine' to pay my respects to the Afrikaans missionary-in-charge and his wife. I received a warm welcome from the lady whom we will call *Mevrouw* (Mrs) van de Grote Borste, who immediately invited me into the *zitkamer* and called for coffee, at the same time apologising for the absence of the dominee who was instructing a class.

After berating me for not being able to speak the *taal*, seeing I had been born in South Africa, and at the same time vowing that she did not believe my ignorance, she told me of the wonderful holiday from which they had just returned, a few weeks spent at the coast down south. 'You know, *Menheer*, we had a lovely time, and the extra money I made came in so useful. Before leaving, I stitched golden sovereigns all around my corsets!'

How many coins she smuggled out in this way she never told me, but it could have been a great number as the corsets needed to engulf her enormous figure would certainly be extra-outsize. On discussing this incident with a friend recently, he informed me that he knew of a missionary's wife at Gutu who had smuggled out gold in the same way. No doubt I was very guilty of not living up to the adage of 'Once a policeman, always a policeman', in not reporting the misdemeanour of *Mevrouw* van de Grote Borste, as I am sure all you other ex-policemen would have done in similar circumstances. My 'blind eye' became more serious when the smuggling out of Southern Rhodesian coinage began to assume really alarming proportions.

Railwaymen were largely involved, secreting large quantities of specie behind the panelling of carriages after some deft carpentry. More specie was found hidden under coal in the tenders of locomotives. Many members of the public were caught at the border with coin secreted in their cars, hidden in the tyres, in batteries and behind panelling. Two well-known ranchers were prosecuted, one receiving a seven-year gaol sentence, for trying to smuggle out coin in this way. The temptation was so great that otherwise respectable citizens were becoming involved, as the following incident will prove.

There are not so many people in Rhodesia today who remember these days of 1931-32 when so much of our coin was smuggled into South Africa. Even retired bank managers I have consulted have been unable to tell me of the premium paid on silver. And so, the other day, I telephoned a friend I have known a lifetime to see if she could help me. I knew that she was teaching at one of Bulawayo's leading schools at the time. We will call her Betty Byrom.

'Hullo Betty!' I said, 'I've phoned to ask you what you can remember about the days when we went off the Gold Standard. I want to know what premium was paid on silver coins exported into South Africa.' 'Well!' Betty replied, 'I can't really remember, but did I never tell you my story?' 'No!' I said, 'let's have it!'

'Well!' she said, 'It was the school holidays, and I was going home to Naboomspruit where I was looking forward to buying some new clothes. John saw me off at the station – we were engaged at the time – and after waving good-bye from the train as it was pulling out, I went to my compartment. I sat down and began to feel really miserable. I was in an awful state of mind and did not know what to do about it. You see, I had drawn the whole of my salary in half-crowns. I had then removed the linings from the bottom and the lid of my suitcase, and after sticking all the half-crowns into the suitcase with glue, replaced the lining. I felt on the verge of tears when a charming young man appeared in the doorway. I recognised him as being a resident of the same boarding-house as my own, but did not know his name.' 'Good evening, Miss Byrom, I am Jack Smith, and I have seen you at the boarding-house. Won't you come along to the dining-car and have a drink and dinner with me?' 'Thank you very much, I would love to!' said I.

We sat down, and Jack ordered the drinks. As the steward left I blurted out: 'You know, Jack, I feel terrible!' 'Why, Betty, what's the trouble?' 'Well, you see, I'm smuggling out some silver coins I have in my suitcase!'

Jack pushed back his chair, stood up, and roared with laughter. 'What are you laughing at?' I asked. 'I'm terribly unhappy!' 'Don't worry, Betty,' said Jack, while trying to stop laughing. 'You're telling the right person; I am on the train to keep an eye open for smuggling. You see, I am in the CID!'

'You can imagine how I felt, but, thank God, Jack let me off.' Well, there you are, Betty's charms won the day. One thing, at least, I can say for myself and the corsets – and there certainly was not the charm behind *them* – I was not a serving member! I often wonder if Jack is still with us and remembers the incident.

Outpost, November 1977

The African population of the time was also confused by the departure from the Gold Standard. The following skit is from the December, 1933, issue of The Outpost.

'Baas!'

'Yes, Sixpence?'

'Enedaba lo golstandar?' 'Lo what?' 'Lo golstander, baas.'

'Oh, the gold standard! What do you know about the gold standard?'

'Lo golstandar plenty skellum, baas. Him stealing me four shillings.'

'What do you mean, stealing your money?'

'Long time ago baas gave me one pound paper money. Me keep him. Last week me go buy shirt one shilling. Chinaman say him golstandar money. Ikona twenty shillings, sixteen shillings. Enedaba lo golstandar?"

'Well, Sixpence, the Government made the gold standard.'

'Ow! Lo Baas Hertzog take all money!'

'Ikona, Sixpence; lo South Africa pound twenty shillings, lo English pound sixteen shillings. English money ikona gold standard.'

'Baas, King George, him got plenty money, no good him take my four shillings.'

'Hang it all, let me explain.' 'Ya, baas, lo ...'

'Shut up! Wena iaz lo sovereign?'

'Ya, baas, him yellow shilling.'

'Yes, well, lo South Africa plenty sovereigns. Lo bank lapa side England piccanniny sovereigns, nearly finish. England ikona gold standard. Nobody steal your money!'

'Ya, baas. Somebody steal me four shillings!'

'You're a fathead, Sixpence.'

'Ow! Dat dam' Chinaman steal me four shillings.'

'Ikona, Sixpence. The Chinaman will only get sixteen shillings for the note. Besides, you mustn't swear.'

'You no swear, baas, when somebody steal your four shillings, baas? Golstandar plenty skellum.'

'Look here, Sixpence! Suppose you buy an ox for five pounds. Bye and bye you sell it for four pounds. Nobody steals your money, but you lose one pound.'

'Me no buy ox, baas, me buy cow. Byembye cow get plenty piccaninny. Me buy two, three more wife. Lo ox ikona mooshi, no get piccaninny.'

'Well, suppose I buy an ox and lose one pound when I sell it. Nobody steals my money.'

'You no buy ox, baas. You got motor car.'

'Oh, hellup ...! I'm fed up with your four shillings, Sixpence. You had better keep your note. Perhaps bye and bye English Government get plenty sovereigns and then you get twenty shillings for Bulawayo note.'

'Me want buy one shirt, baas. Why Government not steal sovereign from bank? Plenty sovereigns lapa side for bank. No good steal four shillings from me. Me poorman.'

'Oh, dash it all! Bring your note along, l will give you twenty shillings for it.'

'No want twenty shillings for note, baas. Paper money finish.'

'What do you want, then?'

'Me fix him, golstandar alright, baas. Me go buy one shilling skokiaan by 'nother boy. Me get change nineteen shillings for Bulawayo money.'

'You batty scoundrel! Then why do you come worrying me if you have got your money?'

'Want you help me, baas.' 'Help you? How?'

'Ya, baas. You got 'nother Bulawayo note, baas?'

'What?'

'Please, baas, me give you sixteen shillings for 'nother Bulawayo note, then me go buy 'nother shilling skokiaan. Me fix golstandar!'

BARNARD, the ELEPHANT POACHER

You will do your best to apprehend Barnard, the elephant poacher, known locally as 'Bvikenya'.

It was in the late 1920s that I was sent on patrol by the late Major 'Paddy' Richens, then Corporal-in-Charge at Nuanetsi, with the above instructions, among others, on my patrol sheet. It was an impossible task, really, for Barnard was worshipped by the local Shangaans, whom he kept well supplied with meat. They would do their best to see that he was not arrested, and could usually advise him a week beforehand of the approach of a patrol. Horse patrols were comparatively slow and distances great, and thus there was ample time for warning by so-called 'bush telegraph,' when word of the troopers' movements was sent ahead rapidly from kraal to kraal.

In his *The Ivory Trail*, Bulpin tells how, on one occasion, Barnard had shot an elephant alongside the road leading to Crooks' Corner. A police patrol was due along this road the following day, so the local chief instructed his followers to cut a deviation well away from the by-now vulture-infested remains of the carcass, and had the women tramping up and down the new section of road all night in order to deceive the patrol. The ruse worked, apparently, and I could well have been the trooper involved, for I later discovered that Barnard was travelling ahead of me.

I left camp mounted on my small but stocky black pony, Prince, to carry out a patrol lasting approximately a month. I was accompanied by a 'Black Watch,' Native Constable Tsamwisi, a Shangaan and a first-class game shot, as well as my personal servant Sixpence, leading the pack mule. Prince added considerably to the enjoyment of this patrol, which was through country abounding in almost every species of game. He was a horse in a thousand, for I could shoot from the saddle or take a standing shot resting the rifle on the saddle. He never so much as flicked an ear. If wanting to stalk game, I simply dropped the reins to the ground and would find him an hour later grazing contentedly not more than twenty-five yards from where I had left him.

We arrived at Crooks' Corner about ten days later, having visited several kraals en route, and made camp on the north bank of the Limpopo. Crooks' Corner is the extreme south-eastern corner of Rhodesia, and was then the junction of four territories, Southern Rhodesia, the Transvaal, Mozambique, and Portuguese East Africa. If my memory serves me correctly, there were two Portuguese governments at the time.

It was here that poachers and others wanted by the police of any of the territories so often took up their abode, slipping across on to foreign soil if a patrol from their own country arrived on the scene. According to Bulpin, Barnard did not always bother to do this, but simply moved the frontier beacon between his camp and the approaching patrol, of which he had had ample warning.

He had only once been arrested by a British South Africa Police patrol, and then somewhat unfairly. Two troopers had been sent down from Fort Victoria, and on getting wind of their approach he crossed to the Transvaal side of the Limpopo. The troopers crossed the river at night, took him by surprise in a hut, and without an extradition warrant took him back to Fort Victoria, where he stood trial for poaching a hippo, the only charge that could be proved against him. He was fined £5, the fine being paid by the late Tom MacDougall, the intrepid lowveld pioneer, who opened up the Triangle Sugar Estates. Old Mac has told me that he enjoyed many a hunt with Barnard in the early days.

While making camp, Tsamwisi informed me that there was a European living just across the river, who was in charge of a Witwatersrand Native Labour Association recruiting station, so I decided to go over and pay my respects. It was the tail end of the dry season and the river was running only about a yard wide, so I stepped across and found myself just east of the Pafuri River, in a large pool in which could be seen dozens of crocodiles.

The station was situated on a high kopje on the Portuguese side of the border, and consisted of a collection of very attractive and spacious thatched huts surrounded by gauzed-in verandas. Here I met the European, whose name was Chapman. He was a most charming personality, and very pleased he was to see one of his own kind again as his only neighbour was a Portuguese Chef-de-Poste living a few miles away.

In the course of conversation over a drink, Chapman told me that he was leaving in the morning for Louis Trichardt to collect a new car and an Alsatian dog which had been promised him by an Afrikaans lawyer.

'Come along with me,' he said. 'You say your Corporal's told you to take three or four days off while down here, so what difference does it make?'

'How can I leave Rhodesia?' I replied. 'I'm in the BSAP, I'd get the sack. Besides, I'm looking for Barnard.'

'Nonsense,' said Chapman. 'Who's going to know anyway? And as for Barnard, he passed through here heading for Louis Trichardt two days ago.'

After making certain enquiries I assured myself that he was not bluffing, and that Barnard had in fact gone south, so I decided to take a chance and make the trip, and we had a final drink on the strength of it. At the crack of dawn I was up, and donning a civvy shirt, my khaki shorts and some stockings and shoes, I joined Chapman, and we set off in his old jalopy. For several miles we travelled through what is now the northern portion of the Kruger National Park, the land being annexed later, and game was seen in large numbers. At about 3 p.m. we arrived at Louis Trichardt, booked in at the hotel, and then took delivery of the new car.

Back at the hotel, Chapman met friends from a farm fourteen miles from town, and they invited us to a braaivleis and dance to be held at the farm that evening. It appeared that we had come to town on the right day! At 5 p.m. we followed the lawyer, a man called Kruger, to his home eight miles from town in order to collect the dog. I was introduced as a friend of Chapman's and we were invited in for drinks. The two old friends were soon chatting merrily away, while I sat back and listened. In the course of conversation Kruger confirmed that Barnard had just returned from Rhodesia.

'You know, Chapman, I've just seen old Barnard, and he's most anxious that I should return to Rhodesia with him on a hunting trip this coming winter. I'd very much like to go, but I'm scared of those Rhodesian police. They're a cantankerous crowd and, as you know, they're after him.'

'Well,' replied Chapman, 'as a matter of fact, you have one of those cantankerous Rhodesian police sitting right here!'

He simply could not resist disclosing my identity, and the look on Kruger's face had to be seen to be believed. However, after the initial shock to Kruger and myself, we had a good laugh. We thoroughly enjoyed the braaivleis and dance that evening, and it was good to be among so many pretty girls again. They were certainly few and far between at Nuanetsi. I was escorting my partner to a seat after dancing an arm-pumping 'vastrap' to the tune of an accordion, when I was called over to the bar table by Chapman. Next to him was standing a burly-looking man about 5ft. 10in. in height. He had a close-cropped head of fair hair and a small clipped moustache. On his right cheek was a very prominent wart. I had seen him arrive while we were dancing.

'I'd like you to meet Mr Barnard,' said Chapman, while grinning from ear to ear. Turning to Barnard he said, 'Meet a cantankerous Rhodesian policeman.' I now had evidence beyond doubt that it would have been a waste of time looking for Barnard on the Rhodesian side of the border. Again we had a good laugh.

Next day we returned to Pafuri, and I crossed over to my camp at Crooks' Corner having had an interesting and enjoyable trip, which, after nearly forty years, can – I hope – safely be revealed. As a result of threatened blackwater fever I was transferred soon after my return to Nuanetsi, so I was unable to attempt Barnard's capture during his forthcoming poaching trip. He was never again arrested by the Rhodesian police.

Barnard had shot his three-hundredth elephant in the Sabi-Lundi area of Rhodesia, when he one day met the famous Zhulamiti (*Taller-than-Trees*), a magnificent specimen, whose tusks were reported to reach the ground. He was about to fire when he lowered his rifle. He could not bring himself to kill this outstanding animal, and he then and there gave up elephant hunting for all time. With the proceeds of the sale of his ivory, he is reported to have bought two farms in the Louis Trichardt district.

Barnard passed away to happier hunting grounds, free from 'cantankerous Rhodesian policemen,' about eighteen months ago. According to the local Shangaans – and recently confirmed by Geoff Gillett, who is in charge of tsetse fly operations there – Zhulamiti still inhabits the Gona-re-Zhou forest, a living memorial to a once-famous elephant poacher.

Because of a change of heart by an elephant hunter forty years ago the mighty Zhulamiti (*Taller-than-Trees*) roams the forests of Gona-re-Zhou. This recent photograph by Geoff Gillett shows the immense left tusk, reaching almost to the ground. Elephants do not attain maturity until over 30 years of age. Zhulamiti was a full-grown specimen and already a legend among the local Shangaans when Barnard encountered him in the Gona-re-Zhou forty years ago. He must today therefore be some 80 years old. He may have as much as another 70 years of life before him. The largest known elephant was that shot in Angola in 1955 by Count Fenykovi of Madrid. It weighed nearly 12 tons and stood 13 feet 2 inches at the shoulder: its tusks were poor. This elephant is now mounted and on display at the Smithsonian Institute in Washington.

Outpost, May 1965

A STOLEN PERSON

The Story of L/Cpl. Nkosana Pompey, BSA Police

These reminiscences were not written by ex-Lance-Corporal Pompey but were related by him to Mr George Style of Buffalo Range. Mr Style first met Pompey at Bikita in 1925 and says that in those days he spoke with a cultured English accent and would have been mistaken for someone just down from Oxford. Assuming that Pompey was about 14 at the time of Queen Victoria's Diamond Jubilee in 1897, he would be about 82 today, which is about the age he appears to be.

I have always considered myself a stolen person. It happened many years ago, when I was a very small boy living with my Matabele parents in Puhle's Kraal, Inyati. I never saw my parents again, have never returned to the kraal, and do not know if I have any relatives in the district.

I was playing alone in the clearing in front of the huts one morning, when I saw two horsemen arriving. They were the first Europeans I had seen, and were carrying rifles on their backs. All the others in the kraal ran into the bush leaving me alone. I was too small and terrified to run away, and can remember crying bitterly. I suppose my parents thought I would come to no harm as I was so small. I was wearing just a small front and back apron of skins.

The two horsemen pulled up near me and sat talking for some time while gazing at me. Then one dismounted, handed his horse to the other and walked over to me. He walked round me, looking at me, and eventually took me by the hand leading me over to his horse. He placed on the front of his saddle, mounted, and we all rode off. We came to Bulawayo, and I remember entering a big laager there. There were many soldiers about, and I can well remember the sandbag emplacements, with large guns protruding from between the bags. I was immediately made to wash, and was given a shirt to wear. I stayed some time in the laager, possibly a year or more, and was kindly treated. While there I learned that the man who stole me was Dr Jameson, and that his fellow rider was Mr Cecil Rhodes.

One day a Captain Vearey told me that he was returning to England, and he made arrangements to take me with him. We travelled in a coach drawn by about 12 mules, and drove all the way to Cape Town. Here we boarded a ship called the *Tantallon*. I do not remember how many days we were at sea, but we eventually arrived at Southampton. I learned the names of the places later.

From Southampton we went to London where we stayed about a week. Here I can remember holding on to my master's coat for fear of losing him in the crowd. I can remember at one time skating on the ice outside London. 'What-ho! She bumps! If she cracks, she bears!' we used to cry while skating. I will never forget my impression of all the traffic in London, and the large Clydesdale horses.

From London we went to Yorkshire, and also Kent, where I saw hops growing for the first time. We also visited Manchester, and a place where the Princess of Wales lived. We went to Norfolk, and I can remember attending a garden party there, and being the centre of attraction, having to wrestle in turn with all the little boys. Many years later, when stationed at Bikita, the late Gordon Hughes who was first mining and then trading there, recognised me. He was one of those who had wrestled with me at the garden party. People appeared to be frightened of me because they had not seen a black boy before. I can well remember boys wetting their handkerchiefs and rubbing away at my arms trying to remove what they said was black paint. They could not understand why the palms of my hands should be white and the rest of my body black.

I was well looked after in England. I was taken regularly to theatres. I will never forget the cold, and men removing the snow from the doorways in the mornings. I attended Queen Victoria's Jubilee in London, but could not see her through the crowds. Some sports were held during the jubilee, and I won a silver cup for running.

After about five years in England, Captain Vearey told me one day that we would be returning to Africa. We embarked and travelled as far as Durban. We continued on to Beira, where we disembarked and came up by wagon and on foot to Umtali. I remember seeing a lot of soldiers there. There were no roads at the time, and no road to Salisbury. Trees were cut down ahead of us as we travelled. I well remember a compass being used.

On arrival in Salisbury I went with Captain Vearey to the Police Depot. He was leaving with a mounted column – I presume for the Boer War – and left me in the charge of the CID, who then engaged me. He told them to look after me till his return, but I never saw him again. He had left me a lot of clothes, including his own – quite a box full.

Lance-Corporal Pompey, ex-BSA Police who was in charge of the African Police at Bikita in 1926. Photograph taken in 1965.

From the CID, I went to work at the Commercial Hotel, Bulawayo, as a waiter, the proprietor being Mr Mountford. While there the BSA Company formed their police, and I decided to enlist. After a recruit's course, I was transferred to Fort Victoria. Later I was transferred to Ndanga, where I was promoted to Lance-Corporal. In 1915 I was transferred to Old Bikita, at Denga. Some years later we moved to the present Bikita station, where the late Mr Paddy Power, then a trooper, built the new camp. Here I took my discharge in 1929. I served for many years at Bikita under Trooper 'Busky' Knight, it being then a Trooper's station.

I have had a happy life on the whole, but am hard-up today. I draw a pioneer's pension of 30s. a month from the District Commissioner, Fort Victoria. It costs me 9s. to go in by bus from Bikita Minerals where I live, to collect this! When I left the Police I drew a gratuity of, I think, about £36. I have five sons and six daughters, all living, and born during my Police service. They never give me so much as a box of matches!

The name Pompey was given me by Mr Cecil Rhodes when in the laager in Bulawayo.

Outpost, March 1965

NIGHT HUNT

'Look here, my lad, behind a night lamp you've nothing to fear. A lion will never charge a light. And what's more, if you wound one at night, rush up close and finish it off before it can get away.'

It was the late Ali Hamman speaking, himself a fearless and most successful lion hunter and official vermin destroyer for the Devuli Ranching Company at Bikita in the 1920s. In the course of conversation with him, I had been expressing a wish to shoot a lion. Hamman, using a 7.9 Mauser rifle, had accounted for 64 lions in all, most of them along the Sabi River. He was able to call them up at night by grunting into a calabash and had in fact bagged several by this means. Advice from such a source was something to be remembered, and I remembered it in September 1933. I was out hunting for lion in the Zaka District near Rupongwana Dip on the Sabi. It was a very dark night and ideal for my purpose. Three Shangaans accompanied me – Cement, who had a stiff leg as a result of a mining accident, Hathlani and Herani. The last two had been reluctant to join us, Hathlani remarking: 'Bwana, hunting lions at night can be very dangerous!' 'As long as you stay behind, you will be quite safe,' I replied, thinking of Hamman's advice. 'What's more,' I added jokingly, 'surely it's better to be killed by a lion than to die in bed.' They did not think so, but eventually agreed to go with me.

About 1 a.m. my five-cell electric shooting lamp picked up a row of nine pairs of eyes. Earlier we had met a herd of impala from which I had shot one as bait. Naturally I thought we had come upon more impala. We closed up on the eyes to a range of about fifty yards and it was then that I observed nine pairs of massive lion forelegs, with the lower half of the chests showing above them. The pride was standing behind a low outcrop of rock beside a well-used game track leading to the river.

My first inclination was to beat a retreat. But remembering my brave words to the Shangaans and since this was what we had been up half the night looking for, I felt obliged to put on some sort of a show, frightened as I was. In the back of my mind I still had Hamman's comforting assurance – but I had not expected to meet quite such a large pride.

As confidence came flooding back, I decided to start on the left and drop the whole pride like ninepins in a skittle alley. Aiming two inches below the eyes of the first on the left, I fired. A lion dropped dead. But all thoughts of a skittle alley were soon forgotten when the rest of the pride began moving about restlessly, all grunting at the same time. It became impossible to fire again so, keeping my light on them, I told Cement to lead me by my left hand to the nearest tree. When I had the tree safely to hand, I told my companions to climb some of the numerous mopani trees immediately behind mine and they promptly disappeared.

Suddenly the remaining eight lions began advancing towards me in close formation. I was now terrified and moved to the left, ready to shin up my tree – only to find that Cement and Herani had returned and chosen the same tree. Cement was frantically trying to scramble up but with his stiff knee could make no progress and kept slipping back. I was tempted to push him away in a bid to save my own skin. All sorts of considerations began to flash through my mind. What weighed most in the end was the thought of the shameful story that would be told of me. I decided to die fighting. But at the same time I was busy cursing myself for having come on the hunt.

A second or two later, one of the lions charged with a roar. I could see the pair of eyes leaping towards me and followed them with my sights. For an instant they were steady and I fired, instinctively stepping behind the tree, which had hurriedly been vacated by my companions as the charge began. The sound of the shot was still in the air as I felt a heavy thud on my right. Looking down I saw an enormous lioness lying where I had stood a second before. She lay, gasping for breath and facing away from me, with her tail across my shoes and touching the tree. The rest of the pride had vanished. Before the lioness could recover, I finished her off with a shot in the neck immediately behind the head.

We now examined the kill and found that the earlier bullet, a .303 had entered just above the left eye, where there was less than an inch of skull. Without fracturing the skull it had come out a few inches further on. My shot had done no more than knock her unconscious. She was so old that her fangs were worn to the level of the rest of her teeth and she could only have been able to keep her wonderful condition by hunting with a large pride. My first shot had killed an almost fully-grown lioness and perhaps it was this that had enraged the old girl. From the pug marks, we found that she had sprung from a spot just over eight paces – some twenty-five feet – from where I had fired.

Once I had recovered from the shock of the charge, I suggested that for a lion to charge a night lamp was so unusual that it could not occur twice in a night, and that we now follow up on the rest of the pride. '*Aikona,*' piped up Hathlani, 'we'd rather die in bed!'

Loading the animals in the dicky-seat of my old two-seater Ford, we proudly returned to camp, my companions chanting the Shona war song: *Baya wa baya! Mukono uno baya dzose*! (Stab! Stab! The bull stabs everything!) They were very pleased to receive the tasty lion meat and the valuable fat which, rubbed over the heart, is reputed to make a man extraordinarily brave. I thanked them sincerely for accompanying me, unarmed as they were, on my first lion hunt.

I will not go so far as to say that Hamman's advice was wrong. I think rather that I chanced upon an exception to the rule. I have heard dozens of stories of lions shot at night (apart from all those bagged by Hamman) and have never heard of a similar charge – in this case straight at the light. At the same time it must be remembered that when we came on the pride of nine, they were strung out in a line over about fifteen yards. When I fired at the one on the extreme left, several of those on the right would have been able to see me clearly. They probably also saw my companions when they moved back to climb trees and this probably caused their advance, which in turn stimulated the old lioness to charge.

A leopard once charged my light at night, but that is another story.

Outpost, July 1965

NDA RASHIKA TORCH!

'*Bwana, nda rashika torch!*'

These are words I'll always remember.

I have the greatest respect for the courage of Africans on occasions and I'll never forget the night in the early 1930s in the Zaka district when I went after a lion at Ndari dip tank on the Sabi.

This lion had been feeding on the carcass of his mate for just a week, as we discovered later. At full moon a Shangaan had shot the lioness with a muzzle-loader from a platform. Two of his cows had been killed. My companion was Johnny Bandura, my hunting boy who'd been with me on many previous expeditions after leopard and lion. I was hard up in those days and the only firearm I possessed was an old long-barrelled .303 Lee-Enfield. Johnnie's weapons consisted of an axe and a hunting knife.

It was a very dark night, the moon having not yet risen. As we approached the Ndari River just below the dip, the lion got wind of our approach from where he was feeding and bounded on to the bank. I fired, aiming just below the eyes. He roared as the bullet hit him and the eyes promptly disappeared. I immediately flashed my lamp to one side to look for him, when Johnnie shouted:

'*Ishe, basopo! Isa torch uko, shumba ya wuya*'

(Boss, look out! Shine the torch there. The lion is coming!)

He immediately jumped in front of me, his axe raised, to take the brunt of the charge. Fortunately the lion turned and ran downstream.

He was found dead next morning, my bullet having severed his jugular vein.

For years I'd been conscious of the unfairness of taking African escorts unarmed after dangerous game. But I had no money so there was not much I could do about it – other than go it alone. By 1957, my financial position had improved and I was having a lot of lion trouble on the ranch. A pride of three had killed 36 head of cattle over a period of three weeks. They just would not behave 'normally' and return to finish gnawing at their prey but killed afresh almost nightly. I decided that the only thing to do was to hunt them at night on the ground. But, having had a few narrow shaves in the past, I was determined to take along an armed escort this time.

Many hours were spent in training the driver Timot, and the bossboy, Kebi, in the use of an automatic and a double-barrelled shotgun. Long pieces of string were attached to cardboard cartons that were then dragged past them at the double by a suitably bribed youngster. Eventually they became fairly proficient and rarely missed but it took a lot of patience and a great deal of ammunition to reach this stage. However, I was confident that we were now ready for the hunt.

'Truly, *Bwana*,' they both assured me, 'now that we have these shotguns, we shall never run from a lion. You have nothing to fear!' At sunset a few days later a driver came in to get water for borehole operations and told me that he had just met three lions on the road, six miles back. The hunt was on. I summoned my bodyguard. Kebi was given the Browning automatic and Timot the double-barrelled Winchester, as well as a spare hunting torch. I decided to use a very accurate .303 Lee-Enfield, but one of the gang, Herani, was instructed to keep close behind me with my .375 Holland & Holland rifle. The two houseboys, Peter and Johan, were keen to come so I put them in charge of the two dogs: an Alsatian, Rin, and a crossbred wire-haired terrier, Socks. I told them to keep well to the rear with the two dogs on leads.

We set off soon after dark and very shortly afterwards the Africans reckoned they could hear the lions grunting in the distance. We followed the grunts. At about 8 p.m. I saw three pairs of eyes directly ahead. From the spread of the eyes, we knew they were lion. Two were standing cheek by jowl but the third was about twenty-five yards to the left and he moved still further to the left as we stopped some fifty yards from him. I got the distinct impression that this one wanted to get behind us and decided to shoot him first. I was sure he was the male of the pride. Trouble was that he just would not face the light and continued to show only one eye. There was nothing for it but to aim at this eye. I fired and the lion roared. The two dogs ran past me barking and I let off two shots well to the left of where the other two lions had stood, hoping to scare them off. The lion continued to roar and it was then that I realised that I was all alone. It was a pitch-dark night, overcast, and with no moon, and to say that I was frightened is to put it mildly. I decided to back behind a tree while keeping my light in the direction of the roaring. I tripped over a log and fell backwards. My headlamp fell off and was extinguished. Not only had the batteries fallen out, but also the wires had become disconnected. From the sound of the roars, I was quite sure the lion was creeping up on me. Terrified, I called out to Timot: 'Timot, *faka lo torch*! (Timot, put on your torch!)

I must have called out a dozen times. Eventually, I got a very weak response from the top of a mopani tree: '*Bwana! Nda rashika torch!*' (Bwana, I have lost the torch!)

At this stage Kebi very pluckily clambered down from his tree and joined me. He caught me by the hand and suggested we run for it. I thought this might be a fatal mistake and, assuming his night vision to be better than mine, got him to lead me to Timot's tree, at the base of which I stumbled on his shotgun. The lion continued to roar in the immediate vicinity and it was some time before we could persuade Timot to descend. As his feet touched the ground, he tried to run and we had to restrain him. I handed him his shotgun. He had no idea where he'd dropped the lamp. My gun bearer now joined us.

'Where have you been, Herani?' I asked none too gently.

'*Bwana*,' he replied, 'I have never left your side.' There was no time to argue so we shuffled over to the tree, where the two houseboys were giggling hysterically from on high. 'If you two b...s don't come down at once,' I shouted, 'I'll leave you up there all night.'

They came down and we all moved rapidly through the bush towards the road. As we reached the road, the lion's roars appeared to be even closer behind us and we sprinted the last few hundred yards to the truck. We were all badly shaken. As there was no canopy on the truck to shield those in the back from the wounded lion, we decided not to chance our luck and to abandon the hunt and return home. Kim the Alsatian suddenly joined us but of Socks there was no sign. We set off with the still roaring lion speeding us on our way. On reaching the homestead, I swallowed a couple of stiff whiskies while recounting the hunt to my wife. We decided there was unfinished business and, re-equipped with torches, to return to the scene. We discovered the poor brute lying down and he weakly raised his head on our approach. I put him out of his misery.

My first shot had entered the left eye (at which I'd aimed) and exited immediately behind it, missing the brain. The wound had affected his balance and while he thought he was getting away, he had walked round and round in a circle of about ten yards diameter. As he had turned towards us in the circle, so it had sounded as though he was creeping up on us. He was a full-grown male, in wonderful condition but with a smallish mane.

Socks I found lying dead next morning, well to the left of where the two lionesses had stood. I thought one of them must have killed him with a blow from her paw, but on examining him I saw that one of the two bullets fired at random had gone through his heart. It was a great loss, made worse by the manner of his death. It had been Socks who gave tongue when following wounded animals while Rin remained silent.

I shall forever be grateful to Kebi for helping me out of a tight corner, but I could not help comparing my two armed escorts with Johnny Bandura and his axe – now being used in happier hunting grounds.

Outpost, August 1965

WHEN THE LION WALKS

THE man had obviously never listened as an eland approached a water-hole at night. An authority on game – no less a person in fact than a former Chief Game Officer for Burma, and author of the lavishly illustrated *Game Book for Burma* – he could perhaps be excused for the few gaps in his knowledge of African game.

'Nonsense,' he said. 'You're talking tripe. For one thing, nature would not allow eland to make such a noise – the sound would betray them to predators.' 'Well,' I replied, 'I can only assure you that what I have told you about the eland – and the lion too – is correct.' And we left it at that. One does not argue with authorities.

The conversation took place over lunch one day during the second half of 1941 at an OCTU at Njoro in Kenya. The speaker was the late Colonel Edgar Peacock, DSO, MC and Bar, who later was to have such a distinguished career in the Burmese theatre. With his second-in-command, Major W.E. Poles, MC (ex-Corporal Poles of the BSA Police, and after the war to become Chief Game Warden of Northern Rhodesia, now Zambia) and a small force of trained guerillas, he was parachuted behind the Japanese lines, where he trained a force of Karen tribesmen and, east of the Sittang River, wiped out 13,000 Japs for the loss of only a few of his own men.

Poles was also at the OCTU (where he won the Belt). By then he was already an authority on African game, and had he been at our table he would soon have settled the argument.

I was to meet Peacock again. He dropped in on his way through to Nuanetsi, a few years before passing on to happier hunting grounds, 'to hunt pink wildebeest there, and blue lions and tigers' as he put it when he wrote shortly before the end. The heavy strain of the Burmese campaign had told on him, and on doctor's orders he was returning to the wild in the hope of recovering his health. It was a little while before I recognised him, as he had aged considerably. When I did, I invited him back for a cup of tea and a chat. He came back with me and stayed nine days, trying hard to shoot an impala with a bow and arrow. However, the impala were too wily, and eventually he had to resort to his old .303 rifle. What happy days they were, *as they continued the remedy Nimrod of old began: the healing hand of the jungle on the fevered brow of man.*

But to get back to my story. One hot summer's night in the early 1930s, I was sharing with Johnny Bandura a platform built in a large mopani tree. I had shot a zebra during the morning as bait for a lion which (we had learned from spoor) had been drinking nightly at a pan near the Sabi River, just north of the Sangwe Reserve. With my car we dragged the carcass of the zebra to the vicinity of the pan. We had built the platform overlooking it, hoping the lion would, after quenching its thirst, come over for a feed. It was a disappointing night. About 9 o'clock we distinctly heard the lion lapping water at the pan. Unfortunately the animal was hidden from us by bushes and reeds, and having had its fill of water wandered off obviously having already eaten its evening meal. We never got so much as a glimpse of it. As the night wore on, we were alerted by the sound of a herd of eland arriving. We knew they were eland by the regular click-click-click (the sound which Peacock was later to scoff at) which we could hear from a couple of hundred yards away. Suddenly all would be quiet as they stopped periodically, listening and looking to see if danger lurked near the pan.

The eland is the largest and heaviest of the antelopes, a large bull weighing from 1,500 to 2,000 lb. As he treads, so the cleft in the hoof expands, and as he lifts his foot, so a click results as the two sides of the cloven hoof come together again. The eland reached the pan, drank their fill and departed. The clicking receded into the distance.

Johnny turned to me and I passed him a cigarette. Presently he said, 'I can remember my father telling me that when a lion has fed, and is really satisfied, he makes the same clicking sound as the eland when he walks.' I had occasion to remember this a year or two later when, while hunting on the Chipinga side of the Sabi, Johnny and I again found where a lion had been drinking regularly at a pool in the river. We built a platform in one of the large trees beside the track, just where it entered a clearing. That evening, before sunset, we settled down on the platform, the sides of which we had built up with poles covered with grass and branches to make us completely invisible from below. Soon after dark we heard the steady click-click-click of eland coming down to drink. Then there would be a pause, and then the clicking would continue until it stopped in the clearing just upstream of the platform.

I switched on my five-cell head lamp and saw two eland, which immediately ran off. I was very comfortably seated in a camp chair, and settled down to wait for the lion. It was just on eight o'clock when we heard a lion roar, followed by the bellowing of a kudu. I had always thought adult lions were quick killers, but that kudu took a long time to die, and it was pitiful to hear the continuous bellowing until at last all was quiet.

An hour later I heard clicking again. This time it sounded as if a single eland was approaching. There were again pauses as the animal stopped to listen for danger, and eventually the clicking ceased in the clearing where earlier the herd of eland had stood.

I switched on my light, and the beam completely encircled a large lion with a half black and half tawny mane. He was standing looking upstream towards the lights of our camp across the river. I had the back of his head in my sights and was about to pull the trigger, when I realised that Johnny was asleep with his head under his blanket. Taking my right hand off the rifle, I shook him, as I wanted him to see the lion. There was a flash as the lion's head came round and I caught the glint of his eyes. Then he bounded out of the clearing. While he was running across the vlei at a distance of about 200 yards from us I had two shots at him but missed, and I realised for the second time that one should shoot first and rouse any sleepers later. I had lost a magnificent black-maned lion in exactly similar circumstances only a short while before.

I now had evidence beyond doubt of the truth of the story told by Johnny's father. The lion had just fed well on the kudu and had come down to drink. The clicking made by the lion as it approached was indistinguishable from that made by the eland – in fact, when I switched on my light, I had been expecting to see a large eland bull. Whether the sound is made by a contraction of muscles or by the swing of a full stomach I do not know, but there must be others who have heard it. Since that incident I have paid a visit to Mr and Mrs Denis Townley, the well known former crocodile hunters, who are now living on the Devuli River near its junction with the Sabi.

The Townleys, hunting together, have accounted for more than 600 crocodiles in the Sabi River and its tributaries, and their name is legendary. When I used to go on police patrols in the late twenties and early thirties I would hear stories from the Shangaans of the remarkable white woman who would dive into the Sabi and help her husband haul out the crocodiles. It was said that it was Denis Townley's practice to use a .22 rifle merely to stun the crocodiles. He and his wife would then remove them from the river while they were still alive and kill them on the bank, presumably to prevent them sinking. When I met them eventually, on the Sabi, they had just accounted for their up-till-then record, a 14-foot monster.

While I was spending the morning with them the other day, Mrs Townley called up for me her pet adult crocodile, Waidoko. The pool is about 40 feet below their lodge, and after Mrs Townley had called Waidoko two or three times in quite a moderate voice the crocodile came swimming down the pool from higher up-river where it had been lying out of sight, left-turned smartly and all but came to heel. When we left it was still gazing up at us, disappointed no doubt at not getting its usual piece of meat.

Crocodiles, according to Townley, have very good hearing. From what I witnessed this must be so.

My purpose, incidentally, in mentioning the Townleys is to say that they too have heard the click of the well-fed lion at night, and believe that it is made by the muscles in the shoulders.

Outpost, April 1966

TAGATI?

On Nuanetsi Ranch many years ago, a young section manager told me of a remarkable bag he had collected on one occasion. He was hunting on the banks of the Nuanetsi River towards sundown, and came on a lone buffalo bull drinking at a pool in the river. He fired, killing the bull instantly with a shot through both shoulders. The bullet continued on its course and killed a crocodile floating in the water beyond. After passing through the crocodile it ricocheted off a rock, killed a bushbuck standing on the bank, and continuing its upward flight went through the head of a guinea-fowl roosting in a tree. I raised an eyebrow.

Nevertheless, one does have some remarkable experiences when out hunting in the bush, and what I am about to relate is true. I record the three experiences, partly because I would like someone to explain them. In each case frontal head shots were taken and I aimed just below the eyes.

The first occasion was in the early hours of 30 September 1933, when I met a pride of nine lions near Ruponkwana Kraal, on the Sabi River in the Zaka district. I was using a five-cell electric head lamp, and of the two lionesses shot that night, the first dropped dead with a roar. I was just fifty yards away when I fired, and was using a long barrelled .303 Lee-Enfield. As I had only solid bullets I had cut off the ends with a pair of pliers, exposing the lead, and thus converting them into soft nose. These bullets inflicted a terrible wound on any animal hit, and a wound easily visible.

Next morning, when we came to skin this lioness, no wound could be found. Anyone who has hunted with Africans will know that one of the first things they do before skinning a carcass is to find out where the animal was hit, particularly with dangerous game. We examined the head closely, looking into the mouth, up the nostrils and into the eyes and ears, but without avail. There was no wound on the head or in the neck, chest or body, and no speck of blood. We skinned the animal and closely examined the skull. Once again there was no sign of any fracture, blood or discoloration. We examined the body carefully, but there was no sign of any wound and nowhere a drop of blood. We then examined the skin, and nowhere was it punctured or discoloured. On dissecting the carcass, there was no sign whatsoever of any internal wound. This was no cursory examination, but an extremely thorough one, and eventually we had to give it up, completely baffled.

A year or two later, there was a leopard grunting nightly on the slopes of Biri Hill at Bikita, and I decided to go after it. I went out one afternoon and shot a baboon as bait, and tied it to a tree on the slopes of the hill after having it dragged for some distance. That night, accompanied by my bodyguard, Johnny Bandura, with his axe, I walked out with my head lamp, and found a leopard on the kill. It sprang on to a low rock as we approached and looked at the light. Again, aiming just below the eyes I fired and it rolled over dead. It turned out to be a leopardess, no doubt in season, and calling for a mate each night. I had used a 7.9 mm. rifle and a soft nose bullet.

Next morning we went through the same procedure of looking for the fatal shot, but again, without avail. When I went on leave some time later and presented the tanned skin to my late father's greatest friend, I felt rather foolish. He wanted to know where I had hit the animal.

The third occasion was during the latter part of the last war, when I was with the King's African Rifles in Zomba, Nyasaland, now Malawi. A pride of six man-eating lions, after killing an African cripple near Liwonde one night, had gradually worked their way into the outskirts of Zomba, living on warthogs and native dogs. The cripple had left his hut to relieve himself, when the lions pounced on him. I had gone after them, and though they had killed an ox after eating the man, they did not return. All that was left of the cripple was his skull.

The CO had a report one morning that the pride had been seen at about 8 o'clock near Mr Thorneycroft's farm, Chimpeni, and he asked me if I would like to go after them. I at once set off with the African who had come in to report, taking with me an army .303 Lee-Enfield, which was very accurate, and with which I had done a lot of shooting. It had rained the night before, and the pride was easily tracked. We soon had quite a concourse of Africans following us. At about 10 a.m. we came up with the lions, heard them grunting as they disappeared behind a ridge, and found where they had been lying in the long grass. Presently a lioness appeared on top of the ridge looking in my direction, and I fired for the head. It dropped with a grunt, dead as I thought. A second lioness now appeared, and I fired hurriedly for the chest, hoping for a heart shot. She roared and charged, while at the same time the first lioness also got up and charged, but dropped dead after running about 30 yards. The second lioness did not travel far, her right shoulder being broken, and I finished her off. I had once again used the hard nose army bullets with the ends snipped off, exposing the lead.

With the first lioness killed – I won't say shot – we went through the same procedure and could not find any sign of a hit. It was examined by dozens of Nyasas living in the vicinity of Somanje's village, situated a few miles behind the police camp, but they could only put it down to tagati (witchcraft). After skinning the two lionesses, and knowing that lions are cannibals, I tied the two carcasses together around a tree. The rest of the pride came back that night, and from a platform I shot a large male, the others running off.

One explanation put to me is that possibly the bullet in each case went so close to the top of the skull as to paralyse the brain. I certainly cannot think of any other explanation other than that shock or fright had caused heart failure, but would have been more ready to believe this had the rifle used been of heavy calibre, such as a .500 express. It must be remembered, as I have said, that all three shots were frontal head shots, and that there is barely an inch of skull above the eyes of a leopard or lion.

It would be interesting to know if others have had similar experiences.

Outpost, March 1966

The MARAUDING LEOPARDS of BIKITA

Bikita is probably the most beautiful outstation in Rhodesia, surrounded as it is by picturesque hills, the slopes of which are thickly wooded with wild loquat trees. The rounded Chigure to the east, the precipitous and rocky Rukunguwo (Hill of Crows) to the south, the long Biri running to the east from behind the station, and the longer Gurundema, across the Rozwa River, running to the west, abounded in leopards thirty to forty years ago and probably still do to this day. They could be heard grunting on one or other of these hills almost nightly, and it was in this vicinity that I bagged 23 of my total of 30 leopards shot with a rifle.

Leopards are now protected in most agricultural areas of Africa, as they are the most efficient natural controlling factor where bushpig, baboons and monkeys are concerned, and there was a grave danger of their extermination in some areas owing to the value of their pelts, and the fact that they are so easily trapped or shot at night. However, in ranching and tribal trust areas they cannot be protected owing to the heavy toll they take of stock. On many occasions they kill for the sheer lust of killing, as was instanced in the adjoining district of Zaka one night, when a trader friend, Jock Ferrie, had 72 sheep killed by a single leopard.

Although considered by many hunters to be the most dangerous of Africa's animals when wounded, they seldom attack man if unprovoked, and then it is very often the result of a wound that turns them man-eater. This was probably the case with the man-eating leopard of the Hunyani River in the lower Sipolilo district, which was shot by Mr Orla O. Blair, an American with the Evangelical Alliance Mission, whom I met soon after the incident in April 1949, while hunting elephant on the Angwa. It appeared from the scars on its left foot that it had been hurt in a trap at some time or other. It was known to have killed at least 16 Africans of all sizes and ages. Soon after the arrival of the Blairs it decapitated a woman.

'It took a child from the back of a mother walking along the path; again, two grown boys were walking through the field and one was killed by the animal,' writes Blair. The leopard's last human kill was made one evening in April 1949, when it leaped into a village and took a child right before the mother's eyes. It was said the mother took the leopard by the tail as it took the child away, but, of course, she did not hold it. Men came and recovered the body of the child, 3 years old, out in the woods. The following night Blair tied a live kid goat to a post at the spot from which the child had been taken. He and three Africans waited in a hut 17 paces from the goat, which bleated incessantly. After about two hours the leopard was heard to pounce on the goat, and switching on his torch, Blair shot it with his shotgun through the doorway of the hut. For months the inhabitants of the villages in the area had been indoors by sundown, and their joy at the kill can be imagined.

Among leopards, the most notorious was perhaps the man-eater of Rudraprayag, in the Garhwal district of India, shot by Jim Corbett in 1926. Corbett's theory was that the leopard had turned man-eater after feeding on the corpses of Hindus who had died during the Spanish 'flu epidemic of 1918. Owing to the large number of deaths at this time, the customary cremation ceremonies had been dispensed with for a simplified rite, which consisted of placing a live coal in the mouth of the deceased and then throwing the body from a hilltop into the valley below. The man-eater made his first killing after the epidemic had subsided, and is known to have killed at least 125 persons during the following seven years.

My first leopard hunt was not quite so successful. I was sitting by the fire in my hut in the old police camp in Bikita one cold winter's night in 1926, when there was a knock at the door. 'Come in!' I shouted, and Lance-Corporal Pompey opened the door. 'Sir,' he said in his cultured English accent (he had spent five years in England as a boy), 'there is a leopard in the Black Watch (Native police) lines and they've been throwing firebrands at it. Won't you come and shoot it?'

I responded with alacrity, for it had been my ambition to bag a leopard for some time. We set off, and passing through the police lines, circled a kopje near the Rozwa River. I picked up in the light of my Bulala lamp – the old carbide type – a pair of eyes and fired. The eyes disappeared, and walking cautiously up to where we had seen them, we found I had shot Jock, the half-bred Collie dog of Trooper Richards, who was on leave in England.

My second hunt was more successful, and thereby perhaps I atoned in some small way to Richards. He was a great poultry fancier, and in the camp had bred up a large flock of pedigreed White Leghorns, the pride of the flock being a beautiful cock imported from England for the sum of six guineas – a lot of money in those days, when a trooper's starting pay had been reduced to £12 10s. a month. After a game of bridge at the Native Commissioner's one night, I returned wearily to camp at about 11 o'clock and entered my hut. As I lit my candle I heard loud squawking coming from several of the fowls which slept in one of two rondavels immediately behind my hut, the other being used as a box room. Half asleep, I picked up my candle, went out, peered into the box room, saw nothing and went to bed. Next morning when Sixpence brought my tea, he told me that there was a lot of leopard spoor at the back of my hut. We found that a pair of leopards – they must have been mating, the only time that leopards hunt as a pair – had gone round and round the fowl hut killing the inmates. We followed their spoor, and over a distance of about a mile, parallel with Biri hill, found 22 White Leghorns and one turkey strewn about. Among the Leghorns was the six guinea imported cock, complete with leg ring.

I decided to have my revenge, and that evening, having no night-hunting lamp, I tied a long five-cell hand torch to my issue helmet, and carrying my service .303, set off with Lance-Corporal Pompey. Down in the garden, soon after dark, we picked up two pairs of eyes. The leopards, as we knew they must be, walked away, each showing the glint of the left eye. I fired at the front eye which immediately disappeared, and there was a grunt as we heard the second leopard spring away. We found I had shot the male, a magnificent specimen, the bullet entering just behind the ear.

For the next ten years, accompanied by my hunting boy, Johnny Bandura, armed with an axe only, I hunted many leopards, missing many too, as the head does not present a very large target at night, and my old long-barrelled .303 Lee-Enfield, with its service sights, was not the best of weapons. Africans frequently called me out to avenge the death of their calves, sheep and goats. Although unfair to Johnny, in that he was not better armed, it was a great comfort to me to know that he was always just behind me with his axe.

One evening soon after dark, I arrived at the late Chief Ziki's kraal to make arrangements for a cattle sale. We were sitting outside his house in Morris chairs, draped with leopard skins, and sipping tea made by his son, Punch, when we heard a calf bellow. Presently Ziki's police boy arrived in some excitement.

'*Mamba,*' he said, '*muru ya rumwe ne ingwe!*' (Chief, a calf has been killed by a leopard.) 'Turning to me, Ziki asked me if I would go and shoot the leopard. I had with me a modern five-cell shooting lamp, but unfortunately the batteries were very weak, and I told Ziki. "That's all right,' he said, 'you can take my lamp.'

I found that the batteries in his lamp were as weak as mine, so, difficult as it was, I decided to wear both head lamps. Accompanied by the police boy I set off for the cattle kraal which was at the foot of a rocky kopje at the back of the house. As we approached the kraal, my lamps picked up a pair of eyes on the kopje, about 100 yards from the kraal. I decided to enter the kraal and shoot from behind the cattle in case of a charge. I had just bought a new rifle from Trooper Henry Freese, ex-Mercantile Marine. It was a beautiful weapon, a 7.9 mm. Mauser, fitted with a telescopic sight. I rested the rifle on one of the many tree stumps in the kraal. I was among a large herd of the chief's cattle, many of which were between me and the leopard. Resting the rifle guaranteed a steady shot, but I now found that the torch batteries were so weak that I could not clearly see the aiming mark in the telescope, though I could clearly see the leopard's eyes.

I was several minutes taking aim, and eventually deciding that this could not be improved on, I fired. Immediately I saw the eyes leaping towards me, and at the same time realised that the cattle had, in a flash, moved behind me. The police boy had disappeared. Terrified I kept my light on the eyes as I moved backwards to get out of the kraal. Suddenly the eyes disappeared and just then the police boy appeared and led me backwards to the kraal fence. We scrambled through and hastily made our way to Ziki's house to collect my car.

We drove to the kraal and found the leopard sitting up immediately outside it, and I finished it off with a shot in the head. It was a huge male, the biggest leopard I have seen, and would certainly have qualified for entry in *Rowland Ward*'s, something we did not worry about in those days. It had the whitest coat I have seen on a leopard and was altogether a magnificent specimen. My first shot had broken its lower jaw.

What had saved me from possibly a fatal mauling was the fact that the leopard had been temporarily blinded owing to the length of time I had kept the light on it, and had charged head on into the poles of the cattle kraal. This was the moment when the eyes disappeared. In its rage after hitting the kraal it had torn up shrubs and stones over several square yards, so I hate to think what it would have done to me had I been in the open and not been able to stop the charge.

We loaded the leopard in the dicky-seat of my old two-seater Ford, and after showing it off to Chief Ziki, and receiving his profuse thanks, I returned to Bikita where the animal was photographed next morning before being skinned.

Those who have experienced it will agree that a night charge by a dangerous animal is not a pleasant experience, and something long remembered.

Outpost, December 1965

VERMIN ERADICATOR EXTRAORDINARY

The Texan, tall and lean in his wide-brimmed hat and with a pair of six-guns holstered at his hips in the best traditions of the screen cowboy, lounged in the shade of the orange tree. A stranger walked up and remarked upon the arsenal, whereupon the guns were drawn in a flash and fired. Two oranges dropped from the tree. The scene was not the American mid-West and the oranges were not grown in California. This was Rhodesia in 1923 and the tall Texan was George 'Yank' Allen, the country's most famous lion hunter.

Yank Allen was a legend on the cattle ranches of Rhodesia and is reputed to have shot and trapped over three hundred lions, or 'dawgs, bitches or pups' as he described them, on Liebig's and Nuanetsi ranches. His total bag of lions, including those he shot in Northern Rhodesia (now Zambia) and the Congo must have exceeded five hundred. He seems to have led a charmed life and had many hairbreadth escapes. Graham Bowker, who worked for Liebig's for 33 years from 1918 to 1951 and who is now enjoying a hard-earned retirement at Glen Kermus Farm, Bindura, knew Yank Allen well:

'He stood about 6ft. 3½ in. in his socks, was slightly built and angular looking. He was fair and always cleanly shaved. His mouth contained only two teeth – one in upper and one in the lower jaw. These two teeth, which were directly opposite each other, always gripped his pipe when he smoked. He would use the pipe to gesticulate while he talked and having said his piece, the pipe would be thrust back into the mouth to be grasped in the vice. Yank's set of false teeth was kept in his 'skoff-box', to be used at meal times only.

'He did not dress the part of a Mexican cowboy as did three others on Liebig's later – Oscar Dahl, Collins and Gush – but he simply wore an open khaki shirt and khaki slacks. As a rule, he packed only one of his two guns and this on the left hip to be shot with left-handed. The right hand was kept for his rifle. On the right side of his belt was a hunting knife and his tobacco pouch. His head was covered by a floppy, wide-brimmed bush hat.'

Many are the stories told about Yank and about his marksmanship with his two .44 six-shooters and rifle. Some of these stories were absolutely true, some of them perhaps a trifle exaggerated. Another acquaintance of mine was telling me of his first meeting with Yank on Nuanetsi Ranch in 1923. He walked up to Yank, who was sitting under a kaffir-orange tree and introduced himself. 'I understand,' he said, 'that you are quite useful with those two guns of yours.'

Yank drew his two guns in a flash and shot two oranges out of the tree. He told the other to throw them into the air and blew the fruit to smithereens as they fell to the ground. 'Now,' said Yank, 'would you like to see me make one roll?' Placing an orange a few yards from him, he again drew his guns and sent it rolling along the ground with the bullets just skimming the surface of the fruit.

There is no doubt that Yank was a deadly shot. It was reported that it was common practice for barmen to ask him to open whisky bottles while they held them at arm's length and he neatly blew off the tops. Many were the men who had to dance to Yank's tune – so the saying goes – when he shot under their feet in the bar.

One Section Manager on Nuanetsi Ranch came back from town to find his wife in great distress. In the manager's absence, Yank had been sent over from Headquarters to check the cattle. He was ensconced on the cattle-race counting the cattle and, at the same time, shooting the heads off all the fowls as they wandered past. Keeping his eye in on chickens seems to have been a favourite of Yank's. Graham Bowker tells of the time when he and a few other ranch hands were shopping at Mazunga store one Sunday morning. The Jew who ran the store was letting the purchasers in through the back door, one by one, as he had already been warned by the police for trading on Sundays. Who should turn up but Yank Allen, very much under the weather. 'Hullo,' said Yank. 'What are you chaps talking about?' 'Shooting,' replied Bowker. 'Shooting!' said Yank. 'What do you know about shooting?' With that he drew the only six-shooter he was wearing and promptly shot six of the trader's fowls. He reloaded as the owner walked out of the back door to see what the commotion was all about and Yank promptly emptied his gun to dispatch another six of the trader's chickens. The consternation of the trader was amusing, but thinking discretion the better part of valour, he re-entered the store and said nothing.

Bowker had been itching to accompany Yank on a lion hunt, but it was

Yank's policy always to hunt alone, a policy he found wisest from bitter experience. According to him, all natives were the same in this lion-hunting business. They were even frightened and trembled all over when they saw a dead lion. If they saw a live one, they ran to the nearest tree and were up it 'like a bunch of baboons'. The commotion was distracting to him. In his own story of his adventures Yank wrote that he would not have native or white man with him when hunting. He preferred to rely on his three dogs, Nigger, Bully and Chocolate, who would always follow wounded or trapped lions into the thickets.

Yank complained of the occasion when he condescended to take someone with him on a hunt. This is his story: 'He wanted to shoot a lion. When we came on the lions, I was about to ask him if he was ready, but when I looked at his gun I saw that he still had the safety catch on. I wanted to make sure that he had an easy shot and when we were lined up, I said, "Shoot! Shoot!" But no fear. I looked at him and saw he had the buck ague so badly that he couldn't have looked paler had he been dead. I missed my shot through giving him a chance.'

After a great deal of persuasion, Bowker relates that he was finally successful in getting Yank to take him on a hunt. 'It was amazing how the man seemed to know just where to find lions,' says Bowker. They came upon two, a lion and a lioness. Yank fired and killed the male stone dead. He then deliberately wounded the lioness by shooting her in the stomach to provoke her into a charge. As the lioness sprang a few paces away, Yank fired from the hip with his .303 and broke her neck. She fell dead with her tail lying across his shoes. Bowker says that Yank with a .303 was a deadly shot firing from the hip. Apparently his only rifle was the long-barrelled Lee Metford which he carried in a long army gun-bucket when riding his horse, Toby.

Baiting the cats as he had provoked the lioness seemed to be an idiosyncrasy of Yank Allen. If there is any truth in the following story told about him, he certainly did take chances on occasions. Accompanied by a visitor to the Nuanetsi Ranch, he went out one morning to inspect the carcass of one of the cows which had reportedly been killed by lions. As they approached, they saw a large male lion feeding on the carcass but the beast was so engrossed in his meal that he failed to notice the approach of the men. When they were only a few yards from the kill, Yank threw his hat at the lion which jumped away with a grunt. Yank calmly focused the camera brought with them and took a 'snap'. He then discarded the camera and shot the lion – to the untold relief of his companion.

The professional hunter had patently little respect for the enthusiastic amateur. Otherwise he was a very friendly character who loved children and animals. He took a very special pride in his horse, Toby. Two lions escaped Yank's gun one night when he was too occupied in keeping them away from Toby. The cats made continual attempts to stampede the horse and Yank was equally determined to save the animal. Shortly before daybreak, the two lions moved away to the Nuanetsi-Liebig's boundary where a bunch of Liebig's weaners were paddocked. They ravaged the cattle and killed what to my mind must be a record number for a pair of lions. They killed thirty-six of the weaners and fed on only one! Dan Swart, Head Stockman of the Nuanetsi Ranch happened to be in the vicinity at daybreak and he followed the lions to the banks of the Sossonye River where he killed both of them.

Toby was often to be found grazing out of sight of Yank's camp and Yank would whistle him up for a feed of maize, using two fingers in his mouth. On Toby's arrival, Yank would put down a double handful of maize but if Toby was very hungry, he would look away and continue to ignore the food while Yank cursed him. This would go on until Toby considered that the appropriate amount of maize had been offered – and on some occasions, he would not be content with less than six handfuls. Only then would he commence feeding. If Toby failed to respond to Yank's whistle immediately, he would be called all the names Yank could think of and he had a vocabulary that could scarcely be equalled.

Although Yank's language in front of men was at times not all that was desired, when in the company of women – or 'marms' as he called them – his manners were perfect. He never fraternised with the Africans as did so many in those days. As a matter of fact, he found it extremely difficult to keep a personal servant. They always seemed afraid of him as the following story will show:

> Young Zeederberg, a nephew of the man who originated the famous coach service, was manager of Section Six on Liebig's. At Yank's request, he found him a servant and some time later called at Yank's camp and enquired how the new servant was making out.
>
> 'Well,' said Yank, 'when I set up camp here a couple of days ago, I

sent him off with a bucket to get water. I was sharpening my knife at the time. He picked up the bucket and went off and that's the last I saw of him.'

Despite this rather fearsome reputation, Yank was an extremely hospitable type and an excellent cook. He would offer a meal to any callers at his camp and would cook and serve the victuals himself. One story tells of the time when Yank was returning from Messina with his trap and mules, bringing with him a case of whisky. Reaching the Limpopo, which was running low at the time, he made camp in the shade of a large tree near the river-bed. Unfortunately for Yank, Corporal 'Blanco' White was on patrol at the time and duly arrived at the camp. On seeing the case of whisky White insisted that duty must be paid on it before it could be brought into Rhodesia.

Yank was most annoyed. 'To hell with that!' he exclaimed. 'I will not pay customs duty on the whisky, but will stay right here and drink the lot.' Soon afterwards, a transport rider named Roos arrived with his wagon. Yank invited Roos to stay with him and drink until the whisky was finished. Roos declined at first with the excuse that he was too busy, whereupon Yank drew his six-gun, took a bead on Roos's stomach and repeated the invitation. The result was that the oxen were outspanned and Yank and Roos spent six happy days together on the banks of the Limpopo finishing off the whisky.

Yank's generosity was not always so forcefully offered. Eben Mocke, Trooper 1437 of the BSA Police (who will be known to readers for his own adventures) and who is now living on Good Hope Farm, Box 8470, Causeway, just outside of Salisbury, knew Yank and gives the following character sketch of him: 'I met Yank on three occasions at the farm of "Surveyor" Campbell-Nettlethorn, near Hunter's Road. Yank and Campbell had become acquainted when the latter surveyed Nuanetsi Ranch and again later when he measured up the Mazunga Ranch. At that time, Yank had the contract to destroy carnivorous animals on the respective ranches and according to Campbell (Yank was not the type to brag) he made a first-class job of ridding the ranches of the predators. Returning from Que Que to my farm Riverdale one day, my wife told me that she had received a visitor. 'Such a nice lanky tall but ugly American had lunch with me. He gave me a revolver for my protection!'

'My wife was reluctant to accept the gift, pointing out that there was a shot-gun and a rifle in the house and that in any case, the natives would not molest her or give her trouble. Yank was insistent and told her: 'By the time you have your armoury loaded, your throat will have been slit, whereas with this six-shooter, you push the safety catch forward and in the wink of an eye you can fill him with lead. You stick to this shooter, Marm, and my conscience will be at rest.' A few days later, Mrs Mocke and I went over to Nettlethorn, taking the six-shooter with us. When we arrived, I greeted Campbell and asked him: 'Where's this American who goes around distributing revolvers to lonely women.' 'The damned old fool – he'll give his soul away,' replied Campbell with a loud laugh. 'He told me all about it. He's one of those characters who never possess a thing. He's too kind-hearted – I've known him to give his only spare shirt to a new-born native baby.'

'Later, in the afternoon, Yank Allen arrived for his tea and I was introduced to him. He was exceptionally tall – Campbell was 6ft. 1in. and the American topped him easily. He was obviously surprised at finding us there and as soon as he saw us, he seemed to switch off the amazing and vital energy with which he had swept on to the veranda – an impression which was in no way impeded by his considerable height and obvious strength–and lapsed into that casual lethargy which is seen so often displayed by professional dancers, boxers or acrobats. 'How d'you do,' he said and, despite his harsh twang, his voice had that clear honest bluff quality about it. His eyes were small, piercing and unblinking but kindly. My wife had said that Yank was ugly but I was of the opinion that dressed properly, shaved and groomed and with a decent set of dentures, he would have been handsome. As it was, his two 'fangs' continually gnawed at the stem of a short 'nose-warmer' pipe.

'Well, Mr Allen…' 'Yank is my name. I get embarrassed when people "Mr" me.' 'Well, Yank,' I continued, 'I've brought back your revolver. It was very kind of you but we really do not require it and it's of much more use to you than it will be to us.'

'That six-gun I gave to the Marm here and I'll be most offended if you insist on returning it to me.' 'Well, in that case, thank you very much for your handsome gift.'

Campbell, trying to get a rise out of Yank, asked: 'Why are you so keen to get rid of the gun? Can the damned thing shoot?'

'Shoot!' exploded Yank, 'I'll show you how the damned thing can shoot!'

The American grabbed a small paint tin from the window sill and threw it some five yards from the veranda. Raising the gun, he fired four shots in as many seconds to send the tin spinning over the ground. Each shot was a strike and never before had I seen such shooting. 'Y'know, Marm,' he said to my wife, 'Scotchmen are unbelievers. They believe no one, especially the likes of this lanky fellow here. If I was to give him a gold sovereign, he'd bite it to see if it was genuine.' (Yank pronounced it 'gen-you-ine'.)

... he fired four shots in as many seconds ... and that was the last I saw of him

'Yank Allan was no braggart and no one would ever know many of the narrow escapes he had had with wild animals and especially lions. To him, it was all quite natural, part of his work and his business and his alone.

'The second time that I met him he did tell us of an adventure that he had experienced with a lioness but only because we were discussing the necessity of quick action in the bush.

'This old she-cat became a general nuisance round my camp. She coughed, growled and grunted for no other purpose than to keep me from my lawful, hard-earned sleep. I decided to kill her and followed her fresh tracks down to the river. She had ignored the hole from which I took my water and had marched up the dry river-bed. I followed the tracks in the sand and some fifty yards up the river, came to a spot where the flood waters had carved through the earth to leave high walls on either side. Suddenly I heard a slight rustle and, wheeling round, I saw the lion in mid-air diving straight for me with extended claws. I fired and jumped to one side as fast as I could. The lioness dropped with a thud on the sand on which I had stood a moment before. The gawd-damned cat was dead – the bullet had entered her chest, travelled through her body and made an exit next to her tail. It shows you how quick you have to be in the bush at all times.'

I fired and jumped to one side... ... stopped the charge

'When he came to the end of his story, his hand moved in one quick jerk towards a biscuit on a small plate resting on his knee. He squeezed something between thumb and forefinger and threw it away, remarking as he did so: 'Flies are a pest and carry disease!' My astonishment can best be imagined and I asked him: 'Did you just catch a fly with your fingers? 'Yes,' he replied. 'It's quite easy when you know how. As soon as the fly settles, he invariably lifts his hind legs over his wings to make sure that there is nothing to impede his take-off. When thus occupied with his legs over his wings, you make a quick grab and you've got him.' 'Oh, please, Yank,' said my wife, 'do it again.' 'Sure, Marm,' he replied, and spilled some sugar on the table and settled back to await the arrival of the flies.

'The movement of an aggressive snake's head was slow in comparison to the movement of Yank's arm and fingers. To our great amusement, he caught several of the pests. He was steady-handed and had nerves of steel. His eyes never seemed to waste time with blinking. Had he become a matador and moved to Spain, I am convinced that he would have become a champion bull fighter and landed a fortune.'

In the National Archives in Harare is Yank's autobiography written in longhand, half of it being in a foolscap book and the remainder in an old writing pad. It makes extremely difficult reading in view of the fact that Yank wrote without a single paragraph and with no punctuation whatsoever. His story was paraphrased by the late N.H.D. Spicer, one time Editor of *NADA (Native Affairs Department Annual)* and is serialised in Issues 26, 27, 29 and 30, from 1949 onwards.

Spicer mentions in NADA that Yank had the names of *Mbulawa* and *Mararakuteni* but that the meanings of these could not be traced. It is presumed that he was known as *Mbulawa* (the killer) by the Matabele and that the Makaranga called him not *Mararakuteni* but *Mararakuseni* (the one who sleeps late). Yank was known to the Bavenda on Liebig's as *Ndau* (the lion).

This is the opening of Yank's story in his own words:

> The Title of This Book is Lion hunting in South Africa in Southern Rhodesia and Northern Rhodesia and Congo for peard of 14 years Lions and Big game hunting the most of people like to no wher you corn from I will tell you I was Borned in North America in the State of Texas on the Colorado River in 1867 that is South West Texas I ust to fancy myself as a Cow Boy I have ben on the Cattle Ranches in the Westerns Teritores for 15 years I sailed from New York in 1896 for Bonazers (Buenos Aires) South America and went up the River Plat on Stalk (stock) ranches till the Boar Ware then I ran Stalk to South Africa as Stalk forman on Ships Reeked in Cape Town'.

Mr Spicer thinks that the word 'reeked' means 'reached', as from enquiries made there were no wrecks at that time. However, whether wrecked or not, Yank remained in South Africa.

Many years later, when employed on Liebig's Ranch in the Gwanda district, Yank told Graham Bowker, the manager of Section 6 at the time, of his reason for emigrating to South America.

> It was like this, Booker (as he called Bowker), in Wyoming I was in love with a beautiful gal.
>
> 'I'm telling you' he said, thrusting his pipe at a doubtful looking 'Booker', 'she was beautiful.' Another guy was also in love with her and when I walked into a saloon one evening he was there and immediately drew his gun. I was quicker on the draw and shot first.

After peace was declared in 1902, Yank went up to Johannesburg on 15 July 1902. There he operated two cabs for a time and was doing very well *until the Jew Boys got purmites to git up. They put the tin cap on me.*

So he sold out and worked in the mines on rock drilling. This, he writes, also nearly *put the tin cap on him*. (Phthisis was thought to be a contributory cause of his death many years later.) At the time of the strike in 1907 he came up to Southern Rhodesia with pack donkeys and crossed the Limpopo. He fell in with a trader who told him he needed a permit to enter the country, and advised him to report to the Police at Fort Tuli. which he did. As a result, he had to appear in Court at Gwanda.

> The magistrate asked me which away I entered Rhodesia I told him by a Kaffir Corral by the name of Cockbula that was all rite then he started to tell me what a sirous crime it was to enter a new Countery with out a purmit he went on to say I had played the game then he finded me 1/- shilon and said if I would write to the Aturnal Genal Salisbury he would write also to git my gunes back I got then back in a forth night.

This may have been Yank's first brush with the law in Rhodesia. But it was not to be his last. Much later on, the police at Nuanetsi made themselves very unpopular with Yank. He had made camp very close to the Police Station and one day, sent one of his boys out with a rifle to get a buck. It was a case of arms to natives, a heinous offence in those days, and the late Major E.W. Richens, MBE, then Corporal-in-Charge, summoned Yank to Court. Yank was fined £25 and afterwards refused the usual warm hospitality offered at the police camp and went off in a great huff. He had not been gone long before he returned in a worse temper than ever. He was met by Trooper S.D. 'Sandy' Sandes (later Sergeant Sandes of the CID) who is now farming at Sallow Glen Farm, Fort Victoria.

> Gol darn it all, you git me fink £25 and when I gits back to my camp I finds all me guns stolen! exclaimed Yank.

Richie was very perturbed and left with Yank to make enquiries himself. He had a wonderful command of the Chikaranga language and shone when it came to investigations. He returned to camp saying that he was sure that Yank's cook-boy had stolen the guns and had brought him in for questioning. He was locked up for the night. Now a few days before a pair of telephones had arrived, complete with batteries, and intended for linking a line with Ranch Headquarters, eight miles away. This was about 1923. Trooper Sandes had a brain-wave. He took the one telephone out on the veranda, connected it to a battery and then led a wire from the telephone through the window and attached it to two pairs of handcuffs lying on the Charge Office floor.

Next morning the cook was brought into the office for questioning but he stuck to his story and denied all knowledge of the case. There were no witnesses, it was a serious case and Ritchie was baffled. Finally, Ritchie addressed himself to the suspect. 'If you can pick up those handcuffs from the floor, one in each hand, and then let go of them, you are not guilty.' Sandy, who was squatting on the veranda took this as his cue and started to turn the handle of the telephone. Suddenly the cook cried out. 'I have hidden the rifles. I will show you where they are.' Ritchie promptly set off with the cook and returned in no time with the missing guns which had been hidden at the top of a baobab. Yank's relations with the Police were consequently restored. Possibly the mild method of third degree used to solve the case would have been frowned upon by the Bench had it come to light. On the other hand, had it not been used then the rifles would never have been recovered.

Yank had only one known enemy, a fellow Texan by the name of Bill Lusk who was a prospector and who was buried at Gatooma by Sandy sometime between 1926 and 1930. Nobody ever knew what started the feud but Bill had told Sandy that if he and Yank ever met they would shoot it out. Another story current in those days was that Yank had been deported from Northern Rhodesia after he had had a set-to with a Native and had subsequently disembowelled him with his Bowie knife. This happened long after his first entry into Rhodesia and much was to happen in the interim.

Having recovered his guns from the Attorney General, Yank's diary continues: *Now I am off like a bird I dont no where.*

Yank then met a man who was down on his luck and they joined forces. At no time did he himself appear to be short of cash. A few days later he shot a waterbuck – he had at first mistaken them for donkeys – and on going out to inspect the meat that night was attacked by a leopard. He had to fight for his life having only his knife with him. He caught it by the lower jaw and tongue and stabbed it three or four times till it dropped. He was in a bad way with scratches, and as he puts it, *Ioanaly had a belt left on me.* He was much annoyed with his half-section and their natives who, despite his cries for help, had remained in the laager thinking Yank had been caught by a lion.

He then trekked on to *Belingway* and Victoria. Here he got rid of his pal, giving him £5. *He haden seen so much money in a life time.* Yank then moved on to *Slukeway* (Selukwe), where he took a job on the *Umtebekway* Mine. Here he was eventually involved in some sort of trouble, and he was injured by a billiard ball apparently. He writes:

> I got along nicely for two month I was outside they seem to be a click rutting the mine they had a frend come up from Johannesburg wanted a job, so they put ther frend up to play a game of cricket on my Head with a 8 ounce Billiard Ball he played a good game he got me just betwene the eyes cracking my coknut 3 ways. The sun noks me out after 14 years I waited for jug (judge) and jury for 5 month and then I went to Northern Rhodesia among the Lions Safter than with men.

He subsequently found, on many occasions, that he was not to be safer among the lions than among men. Yank reached Livingstone on 23 July 1908. He went on to Broken Hill where he fell in with a Dr Pollard who was out hunting and was a *chane drinker*. They got stuck into a bottle of absinthe and then sent for more. *If there would of ben a larg Bull Elephant came along neather one of us could have seen it It a lon Shoot it.*

After a certain amount of hunting Yank got fed up and joined a man called Ben Johnson, who had recently come down from the Congo, and they went shooting marabou storks on the Kafue, being paid 7/6d to 25/- for the plumes. This did not turn out to be very profitable for Yank, as a Jewish trader would take the plumes for groceries only – so his partner said – and Yank had to pay their boys from his 'Box'.

> 'I begone to cratch my head' writes Yank, 'Thinking the Treasure wasin much of a cop if Box had to keep things on the go I mit as well be siting under the shad of a tree as hunting he was pulling me on like a old par of socks.'

Yank did a lot of hunting on the Kafue at one time and on one occasion bagged a whole pride of seven lions, but the last one nearly got him.

> The lion jumped up mad Wrore and came for me I don't know why I turned tail to run when I turned tail I went as cold as a peace of ice and Har went up like porkpine quiles my hat went off I never sean since My advice to any man going out Lion hunting should tak a Extry Hat and a Extery par of pants.

Yank jumped into a boat after running from the lion but the lion followed and jumped on to the boat as Yank slipped out the far side.

He was pulled into a dug-out from where he was bobbing about in the water, got ashore and finished off the lion:

> ... then I went over and sit on the lion that had put me in the River I am going to have a talk to George Allen if you are going to mak a practic of Lion Hunting you have got to make a practic of being as furm as a tree and dont turn tale if you do you wont mak a success you will be in a Lion Beley if you haden a turn tail you woulden of ben so near killed you could of beat him on the spot you had a good gun and can use it I must make up my mind what I am going to do if I going to turn tail I wont shoot any more lions.

According to Yank he often gave himself a talking to after a narrow shave or when in danger. On one occasion a lion had dragged a trap into thick bush. Yank writes as follows about the incident:

> Seen no lion nothen but hollars and thick Bush I thought George wher ar you going you haven seen your mother lataly you stay out of ther I did.

After shooting in the Luangwa Valley in 1909 and doing quite well in ivory and skins, he reached Elizabethville on 16 November 1909. There he got as much as £11 for some marabou plumes, and a fair price for leopard skins.

In March 1910 he trekked north to Lake Tanganyika. In continuing the journey he had a narrow shave when attacked by a party of Africans, possibly cannibals as he suggests:

> I tracked from the lakes North I seen rather more than the natives of the countery and they rather like the flesh of a white man I tracking 3 months seaking my forchen finaly I found it I had been tracking hard 4 ower sruck camp 10 oclock Eaten lunch I lay down to rest and went to sleep I was wakn up by Runing and holing from my natives when I looked I Seen 50 or 60 armd natives charging torge Wher I was Thunder Struck I got holt of my Gun When they got in 30 yards threw Badl axes and assigies at me and stcks 2 of Them old blunder buss They diden shoot I was watching the gunes I soped ther charg at 20 yaz they ran a way I had lots of axes and assigies my natives all gone they all showed up 4 oclock afternoon we wasen long giting a all natives had a axes and assigies I left lit footed I went South I think next morning we was 30 miles from wher I decovered the forchen

and I kept the pass up Till reached Kambala Copper Mine and back to Elizbeth Vill by this time it was 3 day of June 1910.

Yank then spent some time hunting elephant on the border of the Congo and Northern Rhodesia. He reached Elisabethville on 7 September 1910 and sold his ivory for 13/- per lb.

> I had no permit to shoot elephants so I taken the ofer. My ivery wayed 337 lbs My lions skins I bumped the lot off at £7 each Leopards £2 each.

This was certainly not a bad price for lion skins in those days as the average price for a lion skin in Rhodesia up to the last war was only about £5. Today a good lion skin could fetch £40 and a really good leopard skin over double that amount.

After nearly three years absence in the Congo and Northern Rhodesia, during which time he did a lot of hunting and a little mining, Yank returned to Bulawayo on December 10 1910. He writes:

> After a good long peard (period) of Rest picturs and theatars and motor cars funes (funds) running be off to try my han on prospecting.

Yank discovered a fortune, as he thought, in the Gwanda district but the gold turned out to be fool's gold – iron pyrites. In January 1912, he saw in the papers that lions were troublesome at Mazunga, on Liebig's ranch. He writes that at that time the ranch had been operating for two years under Mr Delasso, who was running 20,000 head of cattle.

> I writen to the manager ofing my surfaces to exturmate the liones on the ranch I Resived Reply at once £10 per head and furnac me Boys and Transport writin the manager OK. The people looked at a darn fool probaly they ar write they told me they had heard of men taking on som jobes but never heard of anyone Taking lion hunting up to the present time on the Ranch one mangy Lion poisoned the men telles me a bout seeing lions but never shot them.

There is no doubt about it that Yank came within an inch of losing his life on many occasions, and I quote two such instances as paraphrased by Mr Spicer:

> 'On 20 December 1912, 1 was on the road thirty miles out of Mazunga. I had trekked about seven and a half miles when I came to

a small spruit. I went to look for water. About 150 yards down the spruit I came upon nine lions eating a kudu which they had killed. They cleared off up a steep bank.

It took me some time to get up the bank. When I got to the top I saw one female lion running up the bed of the spruit towards the road where I had left the oxen and the boys. I stood still looking about to see if there were any others. I saw a small lion quite near me partly hidden in the bush. Suddenly it galloped off. I had a shot. It went on. I had another. It let out a roar, jumped into the air, and then went down. Then I saw a large female lion walk out of the bush. She stopped about a hundred yards away and stood looking at me. I had a pot at her. She ran a short distance and then went down. I went up to the little one; it was dead. I went over to the second one and saw her lying behind a bunch of bushes watching me.

I put gun to shoulder, but just as I pulled off the lion made a charge at me. I missed its head and body. It came at me snorting. I saw that I must put a brake on that charge somehow. I stopped it when she was within six feet of me. She somersaulted and her hindquarters struck me on the hips and knocked me for two somersaults. The lion was dead. I smiled to myself and called to the boys to come and get some meat which I had shot. I said I had killed a buck.'

On 2 January 1913, Yank wounded a lion near TowIa Mountain on Liebig's, while hunting a pride. Here is his story, again in Mr Spicer's words:

'Just then there was a tremendous roar and a lion hidden behind a small ant hill sprang and landed within six feet of me before I could have said 'Goodbye, Mother.' The lion came on me in one clear spring five feet in the air. I put the gun to my shoulder and shot her in the head. I think it was her intention to break my neck when in the air for one paw struck me on the shoulder making it black and blue and the other hit me on the knee sending me flying through the air backwards. I struck the ground eight feet away from where I was when the lion charged me. I had kept hold of my gun and I tried to get up but could not. When I could move and raised myself I saw that my head had been lying on the lion's head. My hair was drenched with blood from the wound where I had shot her. This large lioness had the strap of my rifle twisted around her front paw and my eyes were full of dirt. I jerked the screw out of the stock of the gun and fired another bullet into her head but she was dead.

A sable antelope nearly got Yank on one occasion. He writes (as paraphrased):

'One morning I was on the Bubye River and went out hunting. I had two dogs with me, Nigger and Bully. They baled up a sable antelope near a stony kopje. I went up to where they had the sable cornered. When I got near the buck he gave one snort and came for me. He nearly caught me but I jumped behind a tree. The sable struck the tree four feet up and knocked the bark off. The shock stunned the sable and I shot it in the neck killing it. Its horns were forty-seven inches long – he was an old bull.' (Rowland Ward gives the record sable horns as $60^{3}/_{4}$ in. and the record for the Giant Sable as $64^{3}/_{4}$.)'

Having shot many lions on Liebig's, Yank moved to Nuanetsi in July, 1914. He writes that he saw Mr Gilpin, who was Tokwe Ranch manager, and was sent to Nuanetsi Ranch, managed by the Pollitt Brothers. He crossed the Lundi and went to Mr Whitfield James' store eight miles further on at Chitanga to get groceries. It was a very wet season and when Yank got to the river (Nuanetsi?) opposite the main camp on 28 December 1914, he fired off his gun.

Mr Parsloe came done to the river and we hollered to each other across the water.

Yank moved about quite a lot, alternately working for Nuanetsi and Liebig's ranches and also for a spell on Rhodesdale. In January 1916, he took over the management of the farm at Hunters' Road for the surveyor, Mr E.A. Campbell, mentioned by Mr Mocke.

'Now for a forchen' writes Yank, 'it won't be so dangous as lion hunting'.

However, the weather was unkind and the 100 acres of maize that Yank planted suffered from the drought. He reaped 300 bags.

I had got a telegram wanting me to com and exteurmat varmants just as soon as Mr Campbell got to farm I was redy to git off I got 13/- per bag for meales I inspanned my mules and off lik a bird for more lions more money in lion hunting with the danger then Runing (ruining) your eye site looking for rain. I got more than 100 miles to go to libigs Extract Meat Company Ltd Mazunga 9 days I arrived They told me lions had com in since I killed them out in 1913 and 1914 I off to try my luck I felt like I had got out of gaol.

Yank again got down to business and wiped out many lions, wild dogs and leopard. On 28 September 1917, Yank had a letter from Mr Campbell asking him if he would accompany him on a survey of Nuanetsi Ranch.

£25 per month and all found written him I would except the job I setled up with the Company and off to Bulawayo for a blow out which I had I kept up the ase (pace) till 16 december then I went to Gwelo.

Yank joined Campbell and says he learned a new job, climbing up kopjes and putting up a pole with a yard of calico on the top and making a beacon of stones sometimes twelve feet across and twelve feet high. Some of the beacons were as much as 20 miles apart. He writes that he was at that job of beaconing mountains and shooting buck for natives for eight months, travelling all over the ranch with Campbell, and three times round it.

Thi the British South Africa Company noen as the Nuanetsi Ranch Grat Zimbabwe the eary (area) of this is 2100000 acres caring 110000 head of cattle at present time.

Yank used to feel the loneliness at time and writes (paraphrased) as follows: The weather had cleared up and promised better hunting. Birds were calling in all directions. Even that broke the monotony and somehow I did not feel quite so lonely as you do when the weather is cloudy, the days long and you have nothing to do and no one to talk to. Dogs and mules and Natives are not really much company for one. Natives can only talk about eating, and they do not lie when they say they can eat. I had fourteen boys on a survey job once, and they used to eat the whole of a large buck in two days, together with mealie-meal in proportion. They used to eat day and night.

However, he took frequent holidays in Gwelo, Bulawayo, Messina and Johannesburg, and thoroughly enjoyed these excursions and his drinking bouts. Normally he never took drink into the bush with him but there were exceptions, such as at Christmas time 1917, when after getting four lions on the Bubye, he set off for Mazunga on 18 December. He writes:

> Went Mazunga for Christmas they was a number of us went to Section 5 on the Umsagwanda River for a picnic on Christmas Day 2 or 3 fttes we had som Cap brandy 3 fits (fights) in each bottle sun down we got on ox wagon and off to Mazunga Most with a thick head no brandy left or beer.

By 10 December 1918, Campbell had finished his survey.

> E.A. Campbell going to farm I going to Johannesburg Transvall for a livy time I got to Johannesburg 23 december I spent 6 weeks I got to the limet and come back to Rhodesia mor in my line hunting lions.

Yank returned to Mazunga to hunt lions and wild dogs. He was paid £30 a month. He writes that he also made a bit out of biltong which he sent down to the Transvaal, making £35 a month on the average, and he kept this up for two years.

One day Yank's three dogs bayed up a waterbuck in a large pool of water near the Messina road and he was heartbroken when he lost his favourite dog Nigger, the name being always spelt by Yank with one 'g'. Here is the story:

> My dogs went in for Water Buck I never seen dogs sinc my lion dog Niger went with 2 other ones a crockdale got the lot I heard a yelp my old dog Buley I run I jumped in and got old Buley out mit ben caught my self dog cut one foot on back I put 14 stitches in it losing my dogs brake me up I did hate it the best friend I ever had was dog Niger I had no mor hart to hunt lions while on the ranch.

Yank writes that he killed only 13 lions in the second year and found wild dogs getting scarce. He knew of only 11 left and says he could not get them. He got disgusted, settled up with the Company and went off to Bulawayo until after Christmas and then paid a flying visit to Northern Rhodesia where he hunted for a time, 'but', he writes, '*the law woulden let shoot maribut stalk for ther plumes the law got strict sinc I ben a way.*'

He took a train to Elisabethville, collected carriers and went on a two months' hunt shooting enough elephant, lions and leopards to pay for his trip up there and back to Southern Rhodesia. He returned and spent about a month in Bulawayo where he had left his cart and mules, and then went off on a private venture in search of lions and leopards and he writes that he made expenses and 'a bit over'. Then spent a year hunting and prospecting and in December 1922, after prospecting around Belingwe he drove through to Mazunga. From there he went on to Nuanetsi where Mr Richard Kelly was managing the ranch.

On arrival at Nuanetsi, Yank found that a pride of 11 lions had been very troublesome and in two months had killed 166 head of cattle on the one section alone. He put out some impala meat as bait and managed to shoot two of the lions and then got two leopards on the Lundi River.

...his favourite dog, Nigger...

Yank thought there were no lions left, but *Mr Kelly manager seemed to no more lions about he told me to carry on and he would give me £15 per month and what I could make I excepted This is 1923 my luck seemd to change lions all directions.*

In a short time he bagged another 10 lions and three leopards and he kept at it until 23 August.

By this time the wheels of his spider were giving trouble, requiring new tyres and new axles, so Yank decided on a trip to Messina where he would have the necessary repairs done while he went on to Johannesburg with a load of lion skins which he had sewed up in sacking. He found a blacksmith in Messina and gave him the job of repairing the cart. While offloading the skins at the Station he suffered a most unfortunate injury which, it is feared, also contributed to his death just over a year later. Here is the story in Yank's own words:

> I had lion skines on cart 7 in a roal skines in roles 14 skines in pulling off skines one claw crached me in rist I pad no techen of it taken then to Ralway saton that day tran goes to Johannesburg livig 6 a.m. I got on train nuthin Rong with me 8 a.m. Crist my wrist went burning by the time I got to petersburg 6 p.m. I was near mad got in a motor car and went to Doctor green he put on hot foimetativ and got worse for 2½ months I carried it in a sling near lost my arm the Doctors wanted to cut arm off I woulden hear to that after arm got better I returned to Ranch Rhodesia.

This was after a spell in Johannesburg, but poor Yank never completely recovered the use of his arm, and he continued to hunt with his arm in a sling. In the first ten days after his return he killed six lions with the aid of traps.

As he finishes his story Yank writes that he had killed on Nuanetsi Ranch in 16 months *55 larg lions and 7 cubs lions and a number of leopards and wild dogs and they payed me 20/- per head for crockes. I from the time of the poisoned hand haven been well and up till this day my hand no strench in it.*

Owing to the deterioration in his health he returned to Bulawayo in February 1924. He was admitted into Gwelo Hospital later in the year suffering from Tuberculosis and died there from heart failure on 29 October 1924.

Yank is still remembered by a few of the older hands in the country, and Mr Power Jackson, the retired District Commissioner who is now living in Lingmell Road, Borrowdale, Salisbury, was with him in hospital in Gwelo at the end, and well remembers an African rubbing Yank's legs daily in an attempt to restore the circulation, but without avail.

Thus ended the career of one of the most picturesque characters Rhodesia has even known, and her most successful lion hunter. The legends about Yank Allen live on while he lies in the obscurity of the heap of stones over grave Number 469 in Gwelo cemetery, hardly an adequate epitaph for

a man who contributed so much to one of the major industries of present day Rhodesia.

An obscure grave in Gwelo cemetery

Outpost, October and November 1967

PART FOUR

Great Characters of the Lowveld, by George Style

Peter Forrestall
Thomas Whitfield-James
Thomas Murray MacDougall

PETER FORRESTALL

Peter Forrestall was the first man to bring law and order to the Victoria Lowveld and it can be said with justice that he was the founder of civilisation in the region. He was appointed Native Commissioner of the Chibi District in December 1896, the area then comprising the whole of the Nuanetsi District as well – a vast area to administer.

Peter was a French Canadian and came from Aulds Cove, Strait of Canso, Nova Scotia. He was educated in France and at an early age went to sea to serve behind the mast. He left his ship, presumably without his captain's permission, while it was docked in Cape Town about 1889, and made his way up country to enlist in the British South Africa Company's Police with the Regimental Number of 255.

In his *Men Who Made Rhodesia*, written by Colonel A.S. Hickman, MBE, the author has this to say about Forrestall:

> He had been a sailor and attested on 7 February 1890, serving in 'D' Troop. With a group of the Company's Police he was witness to a fight at Zimbabwe Ruins between two rival factions of Makalanga, About 70 held a kopje against the attack of 500, and after about a dozen had been killed the Police stopped the fight. According to No. 458, Trooper S. Kemp in *Black Frontiers*, he (Forrestall) was an American – a short, heavy-set fellow and very proud of his country. He is said to have played practical jokes on his comrades by bringing harmless snakes into their tents and causing alarm. 'This procedure became a little monotonous, and one night our tent went on guard. Two men faced the opening, flat on the ground. When Forrestall poked his head between the flaps to let out the yell, they caught him by the ankles and pulled him over backward. Now they in turn made use of pretence. Shouting that they had caught a native who was attempting to steal, they pummelled Forrestall unmercifully and tossed him into the brush beyond the camp. Thereafter the camp was surprisingly free of snakes. Believe it or not, Kemp was the equal of Baron Munchausen for his fabulous tales
>
> Forrestall was discharged from 'D' Troop on 6 February 1892, and was then employed in the Civil Service at Fort Victoria. He served as

a trooper in the Victoria Rangers in the Matabele War of 1893 and in 1894 became Native Commissioner of the Charter District. He was appointed Native Commissioner of the Victoria District in 1896 and of the Chibi District in December the same year.

In his capacity as Native Commissioner he was especially complimented by H. Wilson Fox, the Director of Transport and Supply, for valuable assistance in the supply of grain and cattle during the Mashona Rebellion of 1896-97. After leaving government service he owned a ranch at Chibi on which he ran 4,000 to 5,000 head of cattle, and became wealthy. He had a coloured daughter who qualified as a nurse in the United Kingdom, and married there, her husband going through her fortune of £15,000 to £20,000.

Forrestall was a fine game shot. He died about 1927, a bachelor. (Actually he died in 1921.)

When I knew Forrestall's daughter, she was married to Tom Agar who farmed in the Fort Victoria District. I visited them once or twice on patrol. A grand-daughter, Mrs Koekemoer of Bulawayo, has given me the information on Peter Forrestall's place of birth etc. Mrs Agar is also now living in Bulawayo and says that her father was called by the Africans *Ndambakuwa* – because he refused to fall off his horse. This would be an abbreviation of *Nda ramba kuwa* (I refuse to fall off). Forrestall was reputed to be quite a heavy drinker but no matter how intoxicated he became, he never fell off his mount. This was rather amazing as he had such a short, stocky and corpulent figure – as can be seen from the photograph (one of the very few of him available – and this one loaned to me by Mrs M. Brits).

Forrestall was to spend much time in his first few years at Chibi taking a census of all the kraals under their different chiefs and headmen and submitting these figures to the Chief Native Commissioner in Salisbury together with his recommendations for the boundaries of the Chibi and Matibi No. 1 and No. 2 Reserves. He writes as follows in a letter in the National Archives dated at Chibi on March 5, 1898: 'Reserve No. 2 appears very large but it must be remembered that a large portion of it is uninhabitable. I should judge that with the exception of the country on the banks of the Nuanetsi and Lundi, the country beyond a line drawn from the junction of the Tokwe and Lundi is practically uninhabitable and a large slice to the north of this line is also poor, being infested with tsetse fly up to where the old hunter's road is shown on the map.'

The reports are very full and beautifully written, Forrestall's handwriting being of stylish copperplate. Incidentally, his letters up to 1915 carry a message of frequent and bitter complaint of his inability to obtain a surveyor.

Peter Forrestall was the first man to moot the formation of the present Gona-re-Zhou Game Reserve. The suggestion was made in a letter to the Chief Native Commissioner dated 7 October 1900. Forrestall wrote:

> 'The lower and uninhabited portions along the Lundi and Nuanetsi rivers are very well stocked with game such as Giraffe, Eland, Zebra, Rhinoceroses, Hippo and all the smaller kinds of antelope, and although unfitted for cultivation, could be used as a Game Reserve.'

It is interesting to note his mention of the presence of rhino in those days for, as we know, they had become quite extinct in that area when the Game Reserve was eventually formed some years ago. Initially some 40-odd were resettled from the Zambezi Valley a few years ago and more followed later. The last report of the species being seen in the area was in the 1920s when Alec Page of Lydiate Farm, Norton, who was then working with Cold Storage Commission cattle, came across three in the hills south of the Lundi in Chief Chironga's country.

Forrestall was much respected by the Africans. They considered him both efficient and successful. It was said that if there was ever any delay in opening a hut door when he was on one of his patrols, he never hesitated to kick it open. The story is told of how on one occasion he went out to meet an impi of Matabele approaching Zimbabwe. He sat down on a chair in front of them and told them what he thought of them – much to the admiration of the warriors who went about their more peaceable business! Over the years Forrestall built up a very large herd of cattle in the Chibi – Nuanetsi area. This, incidentally, was a practice followed by many native commissioners and members-in-charge of police stations up until the 1920s. He was a generous man and, when his God-daughter, Edith Whitfield-James (whose famous pioneering father lived on Chitanga Ranch at Nuanetsi) celebrated her 21st birthday, he presented her with 25 cows.

The following year he was to leave Derrick Loades – the 10-year-old son of his popular Assistant Native Commissioner 'Nappy' Loades – a cow which turned out to be the best milker in the Loades herd.

Perhaps Forrestall could afford to be generous. Former Detective Sergeant Sandy Sandes, who served as a trooper in the Fort Victoria area in the early 1920s, writes:

> After the death of this man (Forrestall) an alleged cousin of his, Peter Martin, who was a Canadian, came to his farm and tried to claim the estate. As there was likely to be trouble I was sent to check up on his cattle as it was rumoured that he had literally hundreds and hundreds of cattle dotted about the Native Reserves. Forrestall, in fact, acted in the manner of local chiefs and collected his portion of any fine imposed. In some cases he had even charged a 'Hearing fee'. Consequently he had accumulated large herds of cattle and nobody knew exactly of what his alleged estate consisted. Even when I was on patrol in the Gona-re-Zhou area in 1923 and on leave there in 1928 the workers returning from the Rand seemed to expect me to extract my due when I examined their boxes. This, I was given to understand, was one of the personal revenue devices adopted by Forrestall. Although I had no personal proof, it was common talk that Forrestall used to return from the border after a long patrol with diamonds and other precious stones. At first I gathered the impression that he had found the diamonds and that's why his first wife had taken out a diamond-digger's licence for the area. We later came to the conclusion that the diamonds had been 'recovered' from workers who had filched them at Kimberley and were taking them back to their homes in Nyasaland and elsewhere!

When Bibra took over from Forrestall in 1919, the latter retired to his ranch Nyazugwe on the Tokwe. One morning in 1921 his personal servant heard a shot fired within the house and, on going to investigate, found his employer had apparently taken his own life. He was lying dead with the weapon at his side.

Chibi – 1916 Peter Forrestall on right

Peter Forrestall, with pioneer rancher Thomas Whitfield-James behind him

Note:

From information in the Deeds Office, Nyazungwe Ranch was granted to Peter Forrestall on 16 September 1914. The extent of the ranch was then 10,022 morgen, 233 sq. roods (metrication experts can do their best with a conversion!). It would appear that Forrestall had made plans for his retirement well in advance. A cousin of his, Peter Martin, who has been a fisherman of Gloucester, Massachusetts, USA, joined Forrestall at some time on the ranch on the Tokwe and it was here that I met the much bearded Martin on patrol in 1926. At the time he was running a fine pedigree herd of Sussex cattle.

In 1924 the ranch was sub-divided, half going to Peter Martin and half to Forrestall's daughter Lizzie, who had married Thomas Agar. On 15 April 1926, Peter Martin took over the whole ranch and on 5 December 1929, it was transferred to the Rhodesia Land, Cattle and Ranching Corporation Ltd., passing to the Nuanetsi Ranch Ltd. For £106,000 on 18 December 1938. – G.S.

Police Camp Chibi at the turn of the century

Outpost, November 1974

THOMAS WHITFIELD-JAMES

Thomas Whitfield-James was born 22 February 1869, somewhere in the County of Cheshire where his father was engaged in a business partnership with a man named Drinkwater. Thomas emigrated to South Africa in 1887 at the age of 18 but prior to this he had received a very sound education, indicating that his father was a man of some means. Apart from his normal schooling, he was given some tuition in surveying in England and was also sent to Leipzig in Germany for pianoforte studies. He became a brilliant player, giving much pleasure to his family, friends and visitors in later life.

Details of his early life in South Africa are unknown but towards the end of the century there is record of him practising surveying in Pretoria. From there he moved north to survey farms in the Waterberg district of the Northern Transvaal where he was allotted Elandsberg Farm which he worked for some time.

In 1896 Thomas married Sarah, a daughter of Robert Roxby who had emigrated to South Africa from Yorkshire where he had made a name – but apparently not much money – for himself as an artist. Roxby had been trying to unearth a fortune at the Kimberley diamond diggings before moving up to Sibasa in the Northern Transvaal and there is evidence that he was not unsuccessful. (Mrs Maggie Brits, one of the daughters of Whitfield-James, reports that her maternal grandfather had in his possession a large bottle of uncut diamonds which he hid. He wouldn't tell where they were hidden and no doubt they were eventually profitably disposed of.)

At Sibasa Roxby established himself as a hunter and trader. Ivory was at that time worth going after and, like the famous poacher, Cecil Barnard, Roxby was not averse to collecting tusks on the Rhodesian side of the Limpopo. On one occasion he hunted with Selous in the vicinity of Litope Spruit on what is now Liebig's Ranch. Presumably this was a rather more legal venture.

A year after the outbreak of the Boer War, in August, 1900, Thomas Whitfield-James decided to leave the Transvaal where he'd befriended many of the 'enemy' and, incidentally, promised one of the Boer generals that he would not take up arms against them. He trekked to Rhodesia by ox-wagon and it was an eventful journey. On reaching what was then known as Malala

Drift on the Limpopo he had just outspanned when he received word that a party of mounted Boers was approaching. Taking with him his wife and their three weeks-old baby, Edith, he found a hiding-place in the river-bed.

There they remained while the Boers rode up, inspected the wagon and having satisfied themselves, moved on. Whitfield-James promptly inspanned, crossed the drift in Rhodesia and later made his way up to the Lundi River.

Here he remained with his family starting a trading and cattle-buying business. As he became more familiar with his surroundings he was particularly struck with the view at Chitanga, ten miles south of the Lundi, which was where he set up home two years later.

Whitfield-James prospered. Eventually he was to own four stores in the area – at Gwaai, near the Lundi; his home-base at Chitanga; Madziwiri in the Chibi district and the last of the quartet, Pinduka Store, which was conveniently situated near the Nuanetsi police camp opened up by Trooper Brewer from Chibi in 1921. He visited Gwelo frequently in order to offer his cattle at the periodic sales.

At Chitanga Thomas and Sarah raised a large family but not without heartache. Of their ten children, one was to die at birth and several others succumbed to the ravages of malaria and blackwater fever over the years. Their father suffered from blackwater on no less than six occasions. Of the children the chief sufferer seems to have been Maggie and it is amazing that she is alive today to relate the trials of those early days. Deep concern for the health of Maggie and the other children is expressed by a devoted father in his diaries for 1908 and 1919. A conscientious diarist, Whitfield-James left the chronicles of a lifetime but sadly all had been eaten by white-ants but for these two years when they were discovered in an outbuilding by Angus Macdonald, the present occupier of Safari Ranch, where Whitfield-James' daughter, Maggie, lived after her father's death.

Open house was kept by the family who were extremely popular with the residents of the Lowveld. Visitors were frequent and when I was stationed at Nuanetsi in 1927 I was invited to spend the Christmas period with the family. I was just one of many guests as virtually all the residents of the Chibi and Nuanetsi areas had been similarly welcomed. Prominent in the gathering was the popular and hard-drinking chief stockman of Nuanetsi Ranch, Dan Swart, and other personalities from sections of the ranch were

Paddy Ryan who went on to become manager of Leopard Ranch near Lusaka during World War II; Vivian Taylor who was to become Magistrate at Malindi, Kenya, after the war; John Crawford, the Hargreaves brothers and many others now forgotten. Robinson, the heavy-drinking trader of the district, was present with his young wife, as was ex-Trooper Bill Fryer (*mbombomera* ... (he of the deep voice) who was similarly trading in the Chibi district. A grand time was had by all. After a sumptuous dinner on Christmas night we gathered around Whitfield-James at the piano to sing songs. None of us got to bed until the early hours of Boxing Day. What a memorable Christmas!

Up until about 1925 Whitfield-James kept a four-in-hand – four beautiful greys harnessed to a 'spider'. It was nothing for him to drive down to Johannesburg or up to Fort Victoria on business and to buy goods for his four stores. In addition to the greys he had a legendary mount, Bushwacker, on which he toured the immediate district and even went as far afield as Chibi. (There was no police camp or native commissioner's office at Nuanetsi until the first camp was built by the Australian member of the BSA Police, Ben Brewer, in 1921, as already mentioned.)

Whitfield-James was the exception to the rule among Nuanetsi residents in that he had little time for hunting. If he needed meat he would despatch his hunting-boy, Mahleka ('the laugher'), to bag a buck or some guinea-fowl. He himself seldom carried or even used a rifle. Actually it was illegal for an unescorted African to carry arms but this law was often broken by those living in remote parts of the country – with some justification.

One morning Whitfield-James rode out on Bushwacker with a customary billy-can for tea attached to his saddle but no rifle. Arriving at Muzanjiri Spruit, he dismounted, lit the pipe from which he was never parted, and attempted to lead Bushwacker to a pool to drink. The horse reared and refused to go near the water and it was only then that Thomas noticed a lioness with cubs lying on the far bank watching him intently. Whitfield-James departed hastily.

Lions could be heard grunting almost nightly at Chitanga in those days and took a heavy toll of the stock. Leopards, wild dogs and hyenas were almost as bad. On 14 May 1908, a diary entry reads:

Poor old Wolf taken in the night by wild wolf; feel very sorry; such a good old companion;

The predator would probably have been a leopard.

In his diary for 1919, Whitfield-James records frequent visits from Peter Forrestall, the Native Commissioner who administered the whole of the Chibi and Nuanetsi districts from his base at Chibi and who was then in his last year of office. Police visitors all the way from Chibi were Troopers Brewer (a frequent caller), de Villiers and Cooper. Campbell, who was carrying out a survey on Nuanetsi Ranch, dropped in frequently and obtained most of his supplies from Chitanga. A legendary figure who later assisted in the survey was the famous lion hunter, Yank Allen, who constructed beacons on the top of Nuanetsi's many kopjes.

There are some interesting entries in the 1919 diary concerning developments at Chitanga Ranch and which also show that Whitfield-James always had time for his family:

> 1 May 1919: Arrive Pinduka 10.30. Little David also rather bad; looks very enaemic (sic) poor little chap. Self still rotten but leave for Ranch H. Qtrs. at 3 p.m. Walsh discusses land for me and agrees for self to take whole lot between Muzanjire & Makwe as far as Tshikuli on Lundi & triangle piece on E. side of Lundi = 30,000 acres.

(David Whitfield-James, 'Little David' above, was to die from blackwater fever at the age of 31 when employed by Murray MacDougall on Triangle Ranch.)

> 2 May 1919: Walsh and P. Gilpin leave after breakfast. Campbell makes sketch of land for Chitanga Ranch. Get back to Pinduka at 2 p.m. David better but self feel still too rotten to leave.

(Presumably this is a reference to Richard Walsh who later became General Manager of the BSA Company's ranching operations. Captain P. Gilpin was the Nuanetsi Ranch manager.)

> 4 May 1919: Say goodbye to my little boy; may God take him under His care! Mashona does a good day's trade. Feeling better.

The loving father's concern for his family appears again and again in the diaries. Eleven years previously he had written:

> 10 Aug. 1908: Self somehow feeling very lonely and down in the dumps and cannot get my thoughts away from Sadie and the children. God grant that they may all be well.

Two days later there is another poignant entry:

13 Aug. 1908: *Chummy's birthday; would have been 13 years old if lived.*

Chummy was the eldest of the family. But Whitfield-James' humanity was not confined only to members of his family. Three days later he arrived home to be greeted with the news that Assar, his boss-boy, had been killed by a lion on that same fateful August 13. After hearing the circumstances of Assar's death, Whitfield-James wonders how he can convey his grief to his boss-boy's widow. But not all the entries convey such sadness. Five months before he had noted a father's pride and joy in his daughter's birthday:

26 March 1908: *My darling little Maggie's 4th birthday. God bless her! And may she live to see very many more, each happier than the last.*

Besides being faithful to his diaries, Whitfield-James was a great correspondent and spent many days writing letters. At other times he would be busy with carpentry, making windows and putting up shelves in the store. He was also a very keen photographer.

The education of the children was something of a problem in those early days and Edith, Maggie, Lucy and David were sent to Sibasa in the Transvaal where they boarded with the Rev. A.D. McDonald and received their schooling from him.

On 31 December 1920, a happy event took place at Chitanga when Edith, the eldest daughter, married a former policeman, Christopher George Johnston (known as *Mafenge* – he of the small waist – among the local Africans). Johnston had come up from King William's Town to join the BSA Police in August 1915, as he could not get on with his stepfather, Maclachlan, and served in the Force for nearly six years. The marriage service was conducted by the Rev. Hugo of the DRC Mission at Chibi. Among the many guests was Edith's godfather, Peter Forrestall, the Native Commissioner at Chibi. He had come over for the wedding having presented Edith with 25 cows for her birthday, on August 7.

The police camp at Nuanetsi had come into being that year and Whitfield-James had erected his Pinduka Store nearby. Johnny Johnston took over the management of the place for his father-in-law. One afternoon he picked up his rifle and went off in search of buck. Those who have been stationed at Nuanetsi will know how easy it is to get lost in the flat, thickly-wooded country around the camp, especially on an overcast day. And this is precisely what happened to Johnny. As night came on he decided to make a large fire and doss down with his African companion. When they woke up the next morning they discovered they were within two hundred yards of the store!

One evening in 1928 Whitfield-James called in at the Nuanetsi Police Camp with his daughters, Maggie and Lucy. He was in a state of great excitement and told us that he had been awarded the contract for cutting the road from the Nuanetsi turn-off on the old Fort Victoria–Messina road, down to the Limpopo where the Beit Bridge was then under construction. This was long before the days of the bulldozer and all the work had to be done with pick, shovel and axe – no easy matter over a total distance of 80 miles, 50 miles of which, according to Whitfield James, would be dead straight.

It could hardly have been a profitable venture for Whitfield-James as Maggie thinks he was paid no more than £15 a mile. But 1928 was a progressive year as development of communications went in that part of the world. Apart from the Beit Bridge construction, low-level bridges over the Bubye, Lundi, Nuanetsi and Tokwe rivers were started with a grant from the Beit Trust. The improvements did little to reduce the chronicles of mishap suffered by travellers along the road to the south…

In Salisbury at this time lived a certain married woman whom we shall call Mrs Jones. She had fallen passionately in love with a bachelor who was employed in Messina. Mr and Mrs Jones were the proud owners of a Model 'T' Ford and one day Mrs Jones informed her husband that she intended to drive down to Messina to spend a few days with a 'girlfriend'. Dressed to kill – including high-heeled shoes – she set off with her suitcase and a few provisions, accompanied by a piccanin employed in the house. She spent the first night in Fort Victoria where she was told that she could drive through to Messina down the new section of road that Whitfield-James was then cutting. In the early morning she set off, passing the road camp – which was some distance off the road – without seeing anyone who might have warned her of what lay ahead. Later she stopped for lunch and then continued her journey over the truly appalling road until, shortly before sunset, the car gave up the ghost with the radiator boiling madly and no more water available to top it up. Mrs Jones could also see in the dusk that her journey had ended in more ways than one. A short distance ahead the 'new road' ended abruptly.

Having given up hope of restarting the car, Mrs Jones decided that her best plan was to walk back up the road in the hope of finding the construction camp and obtaining help from Whitfield-James. With the piccanin carrying her suitcase and what little food they had, she set off and very soon found that in her high-heeled shoes it was very hard going. As darkness descended they called a halt, collected wood, made a fire and dossed down for the night. It is doubtful if they slept. Lions could be heard roaring in the distance with additional orchestration provided by hyenas. At dawn, after consuming what little food was left, they continued their trek, relieving their thirst with water found in spruits here and there. By nightfall they had still not reached the road camp and another miserable night was spent in the bush. At about noon on the third day Mrs Jones and her servant stumbled into the Whitfield-James camp in a state of near collapse.

Mrs Jones must have been really sold on her lover over the border. After a good night's rest, Whitfield-James sent her and the piccanin on to Messina by scotch-cart. Mrs Jones spent a few nights in the arms of her boyfriend and then took the train on the long circuitous route via Pretoria back to Salisbury. The car took the same route after having been towed to Messina by Whitfield-James. No doubt Mrs Jones thought her excursion worth all the trouble but for the rest of her life she must have suffered nightmares over her agonising walk in those high-heeled shoes.

In 1929 Whitfield-James was awarded the contract to cut a section of the new Victoria Falls road. At one point this road passed through a vlei where his vehicles were inevitably bogged down. He had a brainwave and cut small logs, the width of the tyre tracks, and laid them in the ruts. The idea solved the problem very successfully. Soon afterwards, the Chief Roads Engineer, Chandler, arrived to check on progress and caught sight of the log strips. He was most impressed and it was then, according to Whitfield-James, that the idea of Rhodesia's very original strip roads was born in Chandler's mind. After the experimental laying of a few miles of concrete strips along the Beatrice road, and later 40 miles of similar construction in other parts of the country, Chandler received official blessing in 1931 to begin laying tarmac strips on all the main roads.

The 1920s saw the heyday of rustling in the lowveld with the huge Nuanetsi Ranch being the greatest loser. Three section managers on Nuanetsi and a trader were the chief culprits and they tried to enlist

Whitfield-James' help. Predictably, he was far too honest and wise to allow himself to become involved. The affair is however worth a mention.

There were so many cattle on the Nuanetsi Ranch then that the rustling of as many as a couple of hundred at a time went almost unnoticed. Allan Tredgold, who managed the ranch recently, recalls that when he was there in 1923 the stock sheet recorded no less than 105,000 head of cattle. By 1927-28 this number had been only slightly reduced but the ranch was still carrying in excess of 100,000 head. No one seemed to know the exact figure and how could they, with hundreds of calves being born each year and hundreds of mature animals dying from disease, being taken by predators – and being rustled. The stolen beasts would be driven down the dry bed of the Lundi, across the Limpopo and then sold to an Afrikaner on the other side. Some of the cattle were said to have been similarly driven across the Portuguese border. Eventually the trader skipped the country in the nick of time and went to Uganda where he was employed on elephant control. But the three ranch hands were never caught and have since passed on to happier rustling grounds leaving behind some quite wealthy widows.

The Whitfield-James 'Four-in-hand'

The first Whitfield-James home at Chitanga and Thomas in the early days

Construction of Beit Bridge Whitfield-James in 1946

A great-grandfather of Whitfield-James had been an English bishop and no doubt this illustrious ancestor had a bearing on Thomas' very religious upbringing and the innate honesty which kept him out of the rustling game. Allan Tredgold writes of Whitfield-James:

> He was a great character, one of those who, in spite of a somewhat rough and ready life, always retained that old world dignity and courtesy – except of course when one mentioned the British South Africa Company.

The latter remark is a reference to a series of incidents that in 1928 resulted in Whitfield-James being evicted from Chitanga Ranch where he had lived happily with his family for 26 years. Whitfield-James had originally been allotted Chitanga by the BSA Company (as owners of the Nuanetsi Ranch of which Chitanga formed a part) in return for survey work he had done for the Company. As far back as 1923 there had been moves afoot to re-absorb Chitanga in the Nuanetsi Ranch. Then in October 1927, Dreyer had come up from the Cape to take over the management of Nuanetsi from Captain Gilpin. Whitfield-James saw the writing on the wall and redoubled his efforts to get title from the Government. But every time he went up to Salisbury to discuss the matter, he received the same answer – 'Go back to your farm, Whitfield-James, and we will send the title deeds down to you!'

Nothing happened of course. At the height of the eviction trouble ill-feeling between Whitfield-James and the new manager of Nuanetsi, Dreyer, came to a head when the latter reported to Corporal Richens of BSA Police Nuanetsi that Whitfield-James was using an unlicensed scotch cart on the main road. 'Richie' had no option but to take the offender to court where he was fined £7 with the option of a week in gaol. Whitfield-James was furious, refused to pay the fine and elected to go to gaol. In effect this meant nothing more than Whitfield-James being a guest of Corporal Richens for seven days. Richie was alone on the station at the time so was no doubt glad of Whitfield-James' company. One day, early in the period of imprisonment, Richie had to escort some African prisoners to Fort Victoria and so Whitfield-James was left in charge – a novel situation. When Richie returned in the evening he found out that, much to the annoyance of his European prisoner (and convenient deputy), the fine had been paid with Stan Morris, the Native Commissioner's clerk, and Vincent, one of the ranch assistants, forking out half each. A disgruntled Whitfield-James returned to Chitanga the next day, not a bit appreciative of the generosity of his friends.

The eviction process finally succeeded and although Whitfield-James was generously compensated financially, he never forgave the Company for turfing him out of his home. And it was all so unnecessary. At that time Nuanetsi Ranch was the biggest in the world, comprising no less than 2.3 million acres. Whitfield-James felt, with some justification, that his comparatively paltry 30,000 acres, like the rustled cattle, would not have been missed. Initially he refused point blank to move and all his goods and chattels were removed from the homestead and put out on the side of the road.

At this stage Whitfield-James had another of his brainwaves. He immediately pegged the very aptly-named Checkmate Mine close by and actually lived there with his family for a time. For mining purposes the Nuanetsi area came under the jurisdiction of the Mining Commissioner in Gwelo, Mr V.E. Gray. The latter was not prepared to act as an ally to Whitfield-James in the eviction matter however.

He wrote in an official report:
> I regret that I can find no record of the Checkmate Claims or of Mr Whitfield-James. The perusal of old mine outputs revealed nothing, but if he pegged the claims merely to forestall eviction then possibly he never actively mined the property.

This assumption has been proved correct. Mrs Maggie Brits, Thomas' daughter, confirms that there were no worthwhile minerals in the area. Her grandfather's bottle of diamonds would have come in handy at that stage!

In August 1929, Whitfield-James bought a 3,000 acre ranch on the Bubye. This he named Swanscoe Park (after Cheshire), and there he spent the rest of his life running a few hundred head of cattle (of which lions took a heavy toll) while Maggie ran a tea-room. One day in June 1946, Thomas Whitfield-James and his daughter, Maggie, drove to Bulawayo for the wedding of one of his granddaughters. After the celebration he caught a severe chill which developed into pneumonia. He died in Bulawayo hospital on 16 June at the age of 77. Maggie returned to Swanscoe Ranch and pluckily tried to carry on by herself for the next three years. One afternoon in 1949 Cornelius Jacobus Brits, a Marandellas farmer, called in for a cup of tea and fell in love with Maggie. They were married five years later and moved into Safari

Ranch, this being sold to Angus Macdonald and Oldrieve when Maggie's husband died in 1966.

Lucy, another of the Whitfield-James daughters, had married Jock Crane of Fort Victoria several years before and today the descendants of this grand old pioneer, Whitfield-James, one of the real characters of the lowveld, are scattered throughout Rhodesia.

Note: BSA Company eviction notice from Chitanga.

> One of the B. S. A. Company files in Archives tells much of the history of Nuanetsi Ranch and indicates that Whitfield-James was doomed to be evicted from Chitanga Ranch as early as the year 1923. He managed to put off the fateful day for five years. Here is some of the relevant correspondence between the Lands Department and Director of Land Settlement, Frank W. Inskipp:
>
> COPY 27/8/23
> D. L. S.
> APPLICATION FOR CHITANGA RANCH
> CHIBI DISTRICT: T. WHITFIELD JAMES
>
> 1. Please see Mr Whitfield-James' letter of 29th May last and your reply of the 11th ultimo, also the General Manager's letter to you of 8th June last.
> 2. If it is intended to re-include Chitanga Ranch as part of the Nuanetsi Ranch perhaps it would be advisable for Mr Surveyor Campbell to receive instructions at once to mend his diagram of the Nuanetsi Ranch accordingly.
> 3. Mr Whitfield-James has a trading site on the Chitanga Ranch for which he is paying a fee of £22/10 a year to this Department. In the event of Chitanga Ranch again forming part of the Nuanetsi Ranch this latter fee would be due to the Ranching Branch of the B. S. A. Co. say as from 1st October next
>
> The General Manager
> I agree with para. 2 above. The B. S. A. Co. cannot afford to lose control of the area in question even if they have eventually to lease it to Witfield-James.
> 28/8/23 (sgd.) F. W. Inskipp
>
> Four days later the following letter was written to the D. L. S. by the B. S. A. Co.:
>
> BRITISH SOUTH AFRICA COMPANY
> General Manager's Office.
> Salisbury.
> August 31st., 1923
> THE DIRECTOR OF LAND SETTLEMENT
> I am directed by the General Manager to request that you take steps forthwith to re-include the Chitanga Ranch as part of the Company's Nuanetsi Ranch. I return the papers herewith.
> (sgd.) C. W. Carnegie Brown
>
> On September 3, 1923, Frank Inskipp, Director of Land Settlement, wrote to the Surveyor-General informing him that the lease of Chitanga Ranch to Whitfield-James had fallen through, and asking him if he was in possession of the necessary data to re-include it in the Nuanetsi Ranch without any further survey.
> The following day the Surveyor-General, W. J. Atherstone, replied to the effect that the necessary data was on record in his department.
> Back in May, 1914, B. S. A. Company cattle were first established on the Nuanetsi Ranch, between the Lundi and the Limpopo, according to a reply to a cable from London — a reply sent by Richard Kelly who would have been the first ranch manager.
> The Deeds Office reveals that the original grant of the Nuanetsi Ranch to the B. S. A. Company was made by Sir John Chancellor on September 11, 1926, when they took over 1 256 073 morgen. A month later, on October 26, the Ranch was transferred to the Rhodesian Land, Cattle and Ranching Corporation Ltd. £400 000 W. O. P.
> Richard Walsh was General Manager of the B. S. A. Company's Rhodesdale Ranch in 1919 and was for a time General Manager of the Company's ranching operations with an office in Bulawayo. He would be the man referred to by Whitfield-James in his diary for 1919 who

Outpost November 1974 and June 1975

THOMAS MURRAY MacDOUGALL
MC, OBE

Towards the end of January 1926, Trooper Richens, the acting Corporal-in-Charge of Victoria Rural, decided that it was time I made the acquaintance of what was then known as No. 3 Patrol Area. This lay in an area bounded by the Mtilikwe river on the east, the Tokwe river on the west and the Lundi river on the south; with the Zaka district east of the Mtilikwe, the Chibi district west of the Tokwe and Nuanetsi south of the Lundi, 'Richie' handed me the patrol sheet and remarked: 'When you get to the spot on the Mtilikwe opposite to where MacDougall lives on Triangle Ranch, go across and see him. He's a good chap. Pay your respects and ask him if there is anything you can do for him. At the same time give him my regards.'

MacDougall's house was on the kopje Gangarabgwe, three to four miles from the river. When I reached the nearest point to it on the Mtilikwe I discovered that crossing was easier said than done. The river was running a banker – to my mind every bit as high as when it took away the centre portion of the Cedric Gibbs Bridge on 27 December 1973: and the bridge had been built at this identical spot. We experienced a heavy rainy season in 1926 and in my diary I recorded rain falling every single day or night for the whole of February. Neither of the sodden two pairs of boots I had with me ever had a chance to dry out and many were the nights when, having dossed down on my grass bed under a starry sky, the rain pelted down at two or three o'clock in the morning to send me running for the nearest hut.

While discussing with Native Constable Mondiwa the means of effecting a crossing of the river a Shangaan appeared and offered to paddle us across for a small fee. I gladly accepted the offer. After all, the BSA Police, like the Royal Canadian Mounted, 'always got their man'. Clutching my service .303 Lee-Enfield to my side, I very gingerly stepped into the wobbling dug-out, Mondiwa following and squatting behind me. There was a free-board of no more than six inches when we were seated and the Shangaan, sitting in the front, began paddling fiercely, weaving his way in and out of the tree tops. I had reached the ripe old age of 22 a few months before then, but now, 50 years later, I would most certainly not have emulated the RCMP and attempted the voyage. There was nothing to stop us hitting a submerged rock or tree, or perhaps even a hippo. But youth takes no account of risks.

The Shangaan, an expert with his paddle, eventually brought us to the eastern bank at least half-a-mile lower down and Mondiwa and I set off for MacDougall's residence. It was a very hot, humid afternoon, but I didn't pass my rifle to Mondiwa to carry as was normally the case but carried it over my shoulder. Lion and other vermin were extremely plentiful in the area and although we met none of these predators, we saw much game in the way of impala, zebra, kudu and sable antelope.

On our arrival at the foot of the kopje at about three o'clock, we found Mac, wearing khaki slacks and a blue linen shirt open at the neck, doing a blacksmith's job at a forge under a tree. He was hammering a piece of red-hot iron and his face was covered in perspiration. According to a neighbour, Basil Beverley of Faversham Ranch, a descendant of the Duke of Northumberland: 'Murray was a real expert in iron work and could weld iron as if done with an electric welder'.

Immediately Mac saw me, he dropped the iron and the four-pound hammer, took off his large veld-hat and wiped the perspiration from his face with a large bandanna handkerchief. 'Hullo, laddie, what can I do for you?' I introduced myself, passed on Richens' regards, and in turn asked him if there were anything I could do for him. 'No thank you, laddie,' was his reply. 'Come up to the house and have a cup of tea.'

We climbed the kopje and enjoyed our tea in his newly-built brick lounge. Meanwhile, I gave the questioning Mac what news I could have of the outside world. Much later Mondiwa and I re-crossed the Mtilikwe and continued our patrol. Many years afterwards I became a confidante of Mac's and learnt the real reason why there was nothing I could do to help him.

'No thank you, laddie!' Mac had replied when I asked him if there was anything I could do for him on the occasion I visited him in February 1926. I was to meet Mac many times after the last war and once he confided in me as to why my assistance had not been necessary. First of all it should be mentioned that Mac had the greatest affection and respect for the Shangaans and the feeling was reciprocated. At the same time he was completely isolated from civilisation. In the 1920s and 30s, the nearest police station was at Zaka, about 70 miles away by road – where the road existed! Roads were virtually non-existent and the building of the low-level bridges, sponsored by the Beit Trust, commenced only in 1928. If Mac had a visit from a police patrol at Zaka more than once in twelve months he was lucky, as in the rainy season, with the flooded rivers, a patrol seldom got through to Triangle.

Now any reasonable person will realise how necessary it was for Mac, if he were to continue to live on Triangle, to devise some means of maintaining law and order, and protecting his property. Failing this, there is no doubt that eventually he would have been robbed of all his cattle and other possessions.

In consultation with Shangaan grey-heads of the area, who were in full agreement and realised Mac's predicament, he formed with them a 'Council of Justice' – call it what you like. There would be about six or eight in the Council and the accused in the case – most often one of theft – would be brought before them for trial. There was really only one form of punishment, and that was lashes from a hippo-hide sjambok, wielded by Boss-boy Tom Dunuza, the number to be given being decided by the Council with the maximum being 25.

Mac never interfered with the decision and never was there a complaint made to the police, as the accused in each case knew that he had been fairly punished.

The latter fact was borne out by Lieutenant-Colonel Rowley who, soon after he took command of the police in the Victoria district in October 1934, had occasion to inspect Zaka Police Camp. He found that Trooper Bowbrick had recently reported that, on a visit to Triangle, he had learnt that Mac was in the habit of taking the law into his own hands and administering corporal punishment. Bowbrick had protested and Mac had explained…

'Triangle Ranch is a considerable distance from the police station at Zaka, there is no telephone and police patrols to the locality are so infrequent that it is not practicable to report offenses to the police for investigation and trial before the Native Commissioner at Zaka as this procedure takes too long. Furthermore it is necessary to maintain discipline and order in this remote locality, and so I have for some time been administering moderate corporal punishment to offenders on the spot.'

A month or so after his inspection at Zaka, Colonel Rowley was invited to a sundowner at the house of the Barclays Bank Manager in Fort Victoria, Jerry Cranswick, and who should he find there but old Mac, wearing as usual an open neck shirt and with his hunting knife, as usual, in his belt. On being introduced, Rowley exclaimed, 'You are just the man I want to see!' Whereupon Mac, pointing his index finger at Rowley, exclaimed in turn, 'Yes! And you are just the man I want to see. What do you mean by sending down one of your police to warn me about chastising natives?'

Mac then explained his position at Triangle, while Rowley explained the legal implications of Mac's actions if the victims complained. At the same time Rowley promised to step-up the number of patrols from Zaka. 'This seemed to pacify him,' writes Rowley, 'and we soon made friends and enjoyed the drinks provided by our mutual hosts.'

No one who has not lived isolated in the wilds for many years can appreciate the frustration and dismay suffered by ranchers when they are continually, year after year, and day by day subjected to poaching and stock theft. Nor can they appreciate the bitterness aroused when, after very considerable trouble, as culprits are not so easily caught, the accused are brought to trial and the sentences given are so inadequate that they are no deterrent to would-be offenders. The poaching and perhaps stock theft continues.

A policeman learns much after he has left the force, and one day Mac was to tell me of an incident that happened one morning on Triangle. He had risen early, as was his custom, to take an early morning ride around the estate in the cool of the day. Mac always rode with a rifle slung over his shoulder owing to the prevalence of lions and other predators in those days.

Now Mac had lost a great number of cattle from stock theft over the preceding years and was getting really desperate. All of a sudden, as he topped a rise, he spotted two Shangaans ahead in the bush cutting up one of his cows. When they saw the horse and Mac approaching they turned and ran. Hastily vaulting from the saddle and aiming at the middle of their backs, he shot them both. He then returned to the homestead for breakfast, and while enjoying his bacon and eggs, he told the cook to call up boss-boy Tom.

'Tom, down near the large Baobab tree on the side of the road near the Cheche river there is a dead cow. Have it cut up and ration the boys with it.'

No mention was made of the two corpses lying by now stark and cold not very far from the carcass of the cow. And nothing was ever said to Mac about them. However, just ten years later, when stock theft had again become rife, Tom approached Mac one morning after a slaughtered beast had been found, and placing his hand on Mac's shoulder, said: 'Boss Mac! It's time you shot another!'

No! There was nothing I could do for Mac.'

Thomas Murray MacDougall was born at Achnasheach on Loch Awe, Argyllshire, in the Scottish Highlands, on 4 March 1881. He was the son of Coll and Kathleen MacDougall and, as was family tradition, a porridge spoon was duly carved by the chief cowman from a cow's horn. Undoubtedly the porridge consumed with this spoon by the young MacDougall played a very large part in the development of the big, strapping man he was to become. Coll was at this time the wealthy owner of two farms and also had large banking interests. But he did not believe in coddling his children and young Murray, as he was called, had to walk the six miles to school, his father remarking that as the children of the shepherds and cow herds had to walk, his children must do the same.

In 1894 ill-fortune came to the MacDougall family when the Bank failed. Coll was forced to sell his two farms and send his children out to work. Mac joined the ship-building firm of Cammell-Laird and what little he learned of engineering and mechanics in the short time he was there, was to stand him in good stead in later life. One day, about a year later, Mac wandered down to the docks as was his wont and saw a cattle-boat being loaded. He was tempted to travel and on an impulse signed on as a hand on the boat which was leaving for Brazil and on around the coast to British Guiana. Here, at the age of 14, he decided he had had enough of the sea and moved to a sugar plantation, about 50 miles inland on the Demerara river, where he obtained a job as an overseer.

Mac worked on the plantation for two years for £6 per month and his keep. Once again a cow's horn was to play a part in feeding him. One was blown three times a day to let the numerous feral pigs know that molasses had been laid out for them in troughs, and one or two animals would be shot for rations. Pork appeared on the menu three times a day, and after leaving Demerara Mac was so sick of pork that he never touched it again.

For a short period of five months over the years 1897-98 Mac, who was now approaching 17 years of age, served in President's Castro's army in the adjoining state of Venezuela.

After seven years Mac again succumbed to the itch to move on. He took a boat for South Africa where he landed in February 1902. He was now, at 21, a lanky but strong and very mature young man. He attested in the South African Constabulary soon after his arrival in Cape Town with hopes of participating in the Boer War which had broken out in 1899. However, three months after his arrival, peace was signed at Vereeniging on 31 May 1902. Mac was too late to see any action. Two years later he had taken his discharge, acquired a wagon and team of mules, and for the next couple of years was transport riding in Swaziland, Natal and the Eastern Transvaal.

After seeing service in the Natal Rebellion of 1906 for which he was awarded the campaign medal, Mac decided to have a look at the country north of the Limpopo. He left Pilgrim's Rest on horseback leading a change of mount, the unridden horse acting as pack-animal for his few possessions. He depended on his rifle to shoot game, not only for the pot, but also with which to trade meal and other food with the Africans. In August 1906 he first set foot on what later became Triangle Ranch where he was fascinated by the vast herds of game of all varieties in the lowveld. Greatly impressed with the land in the Triangle area, Mac rode back to the Transvaal determined to return some day. Meanwhile he continued with his transport riding and at Pilgrim's Rest obtained a contract to cart supplies for the hydro-electric scheme on the Blyde river.

Towards the end of 1908 Mac again trekked north with his wagons and mule teams. This time he was accompanied by six other Europeans, a coloured man and Tom Dunuza, a Swazi picannin who had worked for him at Carolina and who was destined to become his boss-boy and right-hand man at Triangle.

For the next four years Mac made Salisbury his headquarters, transporting supplies, mining equipment and building materials to the gold mines in the Mazoe valley and surrounding districts. He became famous throughout Mashonaland for his mule teams and made a name for himself when he drove a fully-laden wagon up the very steep hill to the Bernheim gold mine at Mazoe, a feat considered impossible in those days. This mine had first been registered on 13 December 1890 by Collin Cole for the Rothchild Syndicate.

In 1912 the Africans in the Fort Victoria lowveld were suffering from a very serious famine. Mac was engaged by the government to deliver grain to the stricken areas – no easy task as there were no real roads in the lowveld in those days and it was necessary to cut tracks to the Sabi and other areas. Shortly after returning to Salisbury he applied to the Lands Department for 300,000 acres between the Mtilikwe and Lundi rivers. Initially this application was shelved, as the territory was unfamiliar to the Lands Department and no surveying had been done in the lowveld. And then, just prior to the outbreak of the Great War in 1914, Mac was informed that he might occupy the land which would be surveyed in due course.

When Mac realised that the Great War, which had broken out on 4 August 1914, was not going to be over in a few months as so many had predicted, nothing could prevent his enlistment. After disposing of the few possessions he had on Triangle, he sailed for England. Initially he enlisted in the 1st King Edward's Horse in which he served from 21 April 1915 until 5 March 1916, going abroad with the Expeditionary Force. On the latter date, Mac was seconded to the 1st/18th London Regiment, in which he served with distinction until 11 December 1918, just a month after the Armistice, when he was discharged with the rank of captain. His war record was a chronicle of praise and achievement.

Mac's vast pre-war experience with mule transport had become known and, in consequence, he was appointed Transport Officer to his battalion. The outstanding job of work he did for both the Battalion and the Brigade resulting in his receiving two Mentions-in-Despatches, the first on 7 June 1916 and the second on 9 April 1918. He was awarded the Military Cross on 17 June 1917, the citation reading:

> Lt. Thomas Murray MacDougall, London R. – for conspicuous gallantry and devotion to duty when bringing up a train of pack mules with supplies to his battalion. With exceptional skill and fine judgement he sent his convoy singly through a heavy barrage, afterwards reassembling them and delivering his supplies without

casualties. This occurred in complete darkness and his example of personal courage and decision was invaluable to his men.

BATTLE OF MESSINES, June 7th 1917.

Three other commendations were received by Mac from his Commanding Officer, Lt-Col. Parry, in which his gallantry, powers of discipline and organisation and his knowledge of animals and transport were praised, as well as his understanding of the management of men.

Mac had certainly proved himself to be an outstanding soldier of indomitable courage, but once he was discharged in December 1918, he wasted no time in taking the first available ship back to Cape Town. The Spanish 'flu was raging throughout the world at the time and Mac was the only person not to contract the disease. Thus his services were much in demand. His ability and versatility came to the fore when he served as Purser, Assistant-Engineer and in several other capacities on board. In Cape Town, as in other parts of Africa and the world in general, people were dying from the 'flu like flies.

When Mac's boat docked he found that volunteers were being called for to help control the epidemic in every way. So once again he offered his services. And once again his transport capabilities were made use of when he was assigned the job of carting bodies from District Six. Mac did make one stipulation which was apparently honoured. It was that he be given a case of whisky to keep the germs at bay. Whether or not the whisky helped, Mac was extremely lucky to escape the 'flu.

In the meantime, his one thought was to return to Rhodesia and his lowveld property. As soon as the 'flu was under control he entrained for Salisbury, only to find that his land had been granted to someone else. Mac was furious and immediately returned to England and to the BSA Company's offices in London where, thumping the table, he told the officials in charge what he thought of them in no uncertain manner. After all, he had been fighting for King and Country for the best part of four years and saw no reason why, as a result, he should lose his land to someone who had sat at home during hostilities. The Company immediately reconsidered the matter and the land was restored to Mac.

It was in 1919 that he first bought cattle in Salisbury and Fort Victoria and had them driven to the ranch, accompanied by a couple of wagons. He himself escorted them on horseback. Having forded the Mtilikwe, he pitched camp under a large baobab tree near the Cheche river. He straight away sank a well to be assured of a clean water supply throughout the year, hauling the earth and stone, and finally the water, to the surface with a rough mopani-pole windlass and a bucket and reims. He then made Kimberley bricks (sun-dried bricks) on the banks of the river, carting them to the top of Mac's Hill (*Gangarabgwe Kopje*), and erecting his first homestead, thatching it with reeds. The hill commanded a splendid view of the surrounding country, while the air was cooler than on the plains below.

Mac, in the meantime, continued with his development of the ranch and built a dipping tank on the banks of the Mtilikwe. A toilet was badly needed on Mac's Hill and, on its precipitous edge and overlooking the plain below, he now built himself what was to become the most famous long-drop PK in Rhodesia. It faced north and, as it looked out into space, Mac decided that a door was superfluous and none was fitted. He regularly placed salt licks on the plain below (which later was to become the first Triangle airstrip) to attract the game – impala, zebra, kudu, etc. Mac much enjoyed watching the parade of wild life through the doorless opening as the sun was rising. However, Mac's visitors were not so simply satisfied. Mr Keen, who erected the first mill on Triangle, in a letter to the doctor's wife, Mrs 'Minto' Strover, who built up the original Murray MacDougall museum on Triangle, wrote in 1966:

> Mac used to love lady visitors – they had huts to sleep in with hard riempie beds. Mac just roared with laughter with all the moans and stiffness and grouses next morning, and about the path to the toilet which had no door!

Isolated in the bush as Mac was, having only the Shangaans as neighbours, he at once realised the necessity of branding his cattle and looked around for a suitable brand. The Brands Register showed that Hendrick Cornelius van Niekerk, who had received a Pioneer Grant of land in the Victoria district which he called Niekerk's Rust, had on 4 September 1895 registered a brand in the shape of a triangle with the letter 'N' inserted inside the triangle. By 1919, van Niekerk had given up the brand, and Mac made application for it minus the 'N'. It was granted to him. As a result he decided to call his land Triangle Ranch.

The wheels of officialdom moved slowly in those days and it was not until

8 August 1922 that the brand was officially transferred to MacDougall and Spraggon, the latter being a temporary partner, and on 1 July 1938 to Triangle Sugar Estates.

Mac was a keen hunter and on more than one occasion accompanied Cecil Barnard, the notorious elephant poacher, known to the Shangaans as *Bvikenya*, on his illegal expeditions. The BSA Police had never been able to catch Barnard until one night in the early 20s when two troopers, accompanied by a 'Black Watch', crossed the Limpopo and, without an extradition warrant, arrested him in a hut on the other side. They escorted him to Fort Victoria for trial. No evidence of poaching elephant could be produced, but Barnard was fined £5 for shooting a hippo. Barnard had no money and Mac, who had accompanied him to Fort Victoria, paid the fine.

On one occasion Mac went off hunting and exploring on horseback with nothing more than his rifle, a blanket and a little food. In the evening he arrived at a waterhole where he decided to spend the night. He was saddling up the next morning when an African arrived to say that the European for whom he worked was lying very ill at another waterhole about ten miles distant. The African explained that he had left the evening before to seek Mac's aid, but had been tree'd for most of the night by lions. By the time Mac arrived at the other waterhole he found that the man had died of blackwater fever. All that the carriers were able to tell him was that the deceased was an Englishman from the Transvaal. There was nothing at all in the camp with which to identify the deceased. Mac described him as being about 35 years of age, short and thickset. Had the African not been besieged by lions it is possible that Mac could have travelled through the night and saved his life, but, as it was, all he could do was give him a decent burial, leaving an unknown grave at a waterhole named by the Shangaans Lepilamunu. There was nothing in the camp of any consequence other than a .256 Mannlicher rifle which Mac took home. No firearm permits were issued in those days so the man could not be traced through the rifle.

The post-war depression brought the price of cattle down to less than $4.00 per head. In the Tribal Trust Lands in the early 1930s the biggest and fattest ox fetched only $2.00, the best cow $1.50 and a good heifer 75c. There was certainly no profit in ranching and Mac had to look to another source of livelihood. For a time he grew tobacco on the banks of the Mtilikwe, selling the leaf to the Shangaans. He also started breeding pigs but certainly not for his own consumption. In 1931 there occurred the first outbreak of Foot and Mouth Disease, and this was a further set-back to the cattle industry. Mac was unable to move either cattle or pigs to Fort Victoria and all he could do was render down the pig-fat and sell the lard in town. As a further source of revenue he erected a store at Marubeni, at the Sabi–Lundi junction, and later erected another at his kopje, moving this to the mill when the latter was eventually built.

As early as 1922 Mac had decided to turn his attention to the growing of sugar, realising that both the soil and the climate were ideal for this purpose. The snag, however, was the low rainfall, which averaged only 18-20 inches a year. Mac realised that it would be necessary to bring water from the Mtilikwe river for irrigation. He began to look around for a possible weir site. This he found at a place called Jatala, a rocky outcrop crossing the river. He then took levels to see if, after building a weir, leading water onto the land by a furrow was feasible. He came against a colossal snag, one which would have immediately daunted a lesser man in that outlandish part of the world. To bring water onto the land meant that the furrow would have to pass through two adjacent kopjes, necessitating the excavation of a tunnel 1 400 feet long.

In 1923 Mac appealed to the government for help and received only discouragement. That year an engineer made a six-day trip by mule-cart from Fort Victoria to study the proposition and do some surveying. Mac took him up to the weir and tunnel site, and after one look at the solid granite kopjes through which the tunnels would have to pass, the engineer told Mac that he was a crank and that the scheme was an impossible one. Having given his verdict he inspanned his mules and returned to Fort Victoria.

This discouragement made Mac more determined than ever to see the venture through. He built the Jatala weir that year, and commenced the Herculean task of tunnelling through the kopjes with the aid of dynamite and jack-hammers. He was helped by an Irishman, Mick Shanahan, who was a good miner and bush-engineer. Mick was a heavy drinker when he got the chance, but as Mac said later:

> We were flat broke. I didn't have a drink for about six years. We were living on buck meat, mealie-meal and the vegetable garden. We couldn't afford pumps, so when the river rose in summer and flooded

the tunnel, we couldn't work on it at all. It was 26 months of work over seven years.

Johnny Renders, a descendant of the German, Adam Renders, one of the first Europeans to see the Zimbabwe Ruins in 1867 and who showed them to Karl Mauch on 5 September 1871, was placed in charge of the labour force.

Mac constantly ran short of money during the seven years of tunnelling and would periodically take himself off transport riding in order to replenish the coffers. Meanwhile life on the ranch went on. When game was shot for meat, no part of the carcass was wasted. Even the bones were crushed into bonemeal for the cattle. Buffalo hides were made into reims, and antelope skins cured. Tanning was done in a cement tank below Mac's Hill with the aid of bark from mopani trees and thus leather was produced. Mac set up a pit-saw where mahogany and leadwood were cut into panels and beams for use in his red-brick lounge erected in 1925. The same wood was used in the furniture he designed.

Supplies had to be fetched from Fort Victoria by ox-wagon and routed over a bush-track, passable only in the dry season when the rivers were low enough to cross. During the rains, horseback was the only means of transport. However, no obstacle seemed unsurmountable to this remarkable man. If some essential commodity were needed and unobtainable, Mac would set to and make it in his workshop. The two tunnels were finally completed in July 1931 and a canal, eight miles long and dug with pick and shovel, led the water on to the land from Jatala weir. The weir and tunnels are now a National Monument, the Historical Monuments Commission have erected a bronze plaque at the weir which carries the inscription:

> From this weir built in 1923, Thomas Murray McDougall led water from the Mtilikwe River through two tunnels hewn by hand over seven years for a distance of 1,400 feet through solid rock and thence to his lands through a canal eight miles long. This historic enterprise was the first development in the Lowveld's great irrigation project.

Now that the tunnels were completed Mac was a happy man and his abstemious six years came to an end. His neighbour, Basil Beverley, writes:

> A cask of whisky, about 20 gallons, was sent out to Murray from Oban in Scotland every year. In the evenings when I was there, Murray had three whiskies; Geordie Muir (the book-keeper) was

Thomas Murray MacDougall
Tom in London, World War One

The Trek to Rhodesia in 1908 Tom and Marjorie, Glendale

The original homestead on Triangle Ranch

The new homestead on Mac's Hill

The legendary 'Long-Drop'

The view from the Throne

allowed two. I was allowed one but Colin, his nephew was allowed none! At table Murray was very particular as to how he placed his guests, both Colin and Geordie being banished to the bottom while I was mostly placed on Murray's left. Now and then, when he was particularly pleased with me, I was placed on his right! Murray always whistled most doleful Scotch Laments and when I used to dance with Marjorie (his sister) to music she brought out, he was most disapproving.

(Mac's nephew was Colin Sproull, who, as a young man, came out from England and worked for him during some of the early years of Triangle's history. Mac was said to have treated him somewhat harshly. Colin joined up at the outbreak of World War Two, and serving with distinction, became a Tank Commander. Mac's sister, Marjorie, a spinster, used to come out and spend the summer months on Triangle. She returned to England to be with her sister during the war and they were both killed in a bomb raid.)

With the major task over, Marjorie now treated her brother to a holiday overseas. As far as the rest of the family was concerned, one of their brothers had joined the Royal Canadian Mounted Police and was never heard of again; another had become a sugar-planter in Peru. On the holiday Mac returned to Scotland and is thought to have also visited the sugar-planter and been spurred on to further efforts in this direction.

On his return he started extensive irrigation and grew sub-tropical crops such as mangoes, paw-paws, bananas, maize, tobacco, cotton, vegetables and wheat. He was very successful with Madagascar butter beans, which brought him £10 a bag on the London market. He experimented with Tung-oil trees, but without great success. A sample of Mac's wheat was sent to London through the Agricultural Department and an enthusiastic report on the quality was received. He thereupon ordered a combine harvester from Massey-Harris but a little later sent them a telegram which simply said: *Cancel harvester STOP Locusts have done it for you.*

Locusts were certainly a curse in the country in the 1930s. Huge swarms would sometimes blacken out the sun, while trains were held up by swarms of 'voetgangers' – the young, walking locusts – which caused the engine wheels to slip as they were crushed on the line. The locust invasion prompted Mac to forget wheat and concentrate his efforts on sugar-cane, as

Tom MacDougall in his locust-ravaged wheatfield

The view from Mac's Hill looking towards Zaka

Mill under construction

Siphon head under construction

Tunnel entrance
Another stage in Mill construction

this would not be ruined, as had his wheat, by the locusts and the birds (*Quelea*).

In 1934 he asked for a permit to import a truckload of cane from Natal with which to start a seed-bed, but for some reason best known to the authorities – probably a fear of importing some disease – the permit was refused. Once again, Mac had received no encouragement from government. Eventually he was granted a permit to import just three sticks or setts of cane a yard long. The indomitable Mac drove his 3-ton lorry down to the Mount Edgecombe Experimental Station in Natal to fetch the three sticks – and in addition brought up a stack of cane neatly tied up under the lorry!

The initial seed-bed of cane was soon flourishing and it was obvious that conditions on Triangle were ideal for the production of sugar and that a mill would be required. A Mr John Murray, who was a consulting engineer in Durban, had visited Triangle, realised the sugar potential, and in 1936 took Mac and his sister, Marjorie (out from Yorkshire for the winter months as usual) down to Natal. There he introduced Mac to all the large sugar concerns, principally Reynolds Bros. and the Crookes Bros. A tour was made of the mills and various parts bought here and there for the construction of the Triangle mill.

All this machinery was railed to Beit Bridge from where it had to be transported by lorry and ox-wagon to Triangle. Two lorries were driven by Colin Sproull and Tom Dunusa for this purpose. In addition the latter used a wagon when and where necessary. It took two years to move all the parts to Triangle and for part of one rainy season many sections had to be off-loaded and hung in trees (in order to move the transport), until the road, if such it could be called, was dry and passable. The 59 miles of road, running from Ngundu Halt to Triangle, was cut at this time for the purpose of transporting the machinery. By August 1938 all the mill parts were at the mill-site, having been transported over 1,200 miles from their source and the last 180 by lorry and wagon. Mr Ken Keen of Natal was engaged as Chief Engineer, with the responsibility of erecting the mill. It was a stupendous task even with Mac assisting and generally in charge of the whole operation. Keen had both engineering and process experience.

During the time that the mill was under construction Mac was very worried because so few people were convinced that sugar could be produced in Rhodesia. Keen wrote, in 1966, the following in a letter to Mrs Strover:

> I squeezed some juice out of a few sticks of cane and boiled it outside over an open fire and concentrated it into sugar by stirring with a piece of wood. I then got his cream separator, drilled holes in a syrup tin and lined it with butter muslin, then separated the crystals from the molasses. I filled two Herald tobacco tins with very fine sugar which Mac took to Salisbury. He was very friendly with Mr Frank Harris, who was Minister of Agriculture at the time. They had a meeting with certain government people and from that Mac got his first loan from the government.

As usual, money was in short supply, and in 1938 Mac formed a small company, 'Triangle Sugar Estates Limited', with a capital of £10,000. The Chairman was Mr W. Moubray, while Mac was the Managing Director, the other two directors being the late D.M. Milne then manager of Meikle's Store in Fort Victoria, and the late W. Paley, a forwarding agent in Fort Victoria.

On 12 September 1939 the official opening of Mac's mill took place, with his sister Marjorie performing the ceremony by turning on the steam which set the big fly-wheel in motion. To the wheel Miss MacDougall had tied a bunch of white heather brought from Scotland. The Scottish Standard was hoisted in triumph. *The Rhodesia Herald* for 15 September 1939 reported the starting of the mill by Miss MacDougall...

> ... in the presence of a large number of spectators. The Minister of Agriculture and the Minister of Finance had intended to be present but were prevented by the international situation (war had been declared on the 3rd of the month – 'N') and the Government was represented by Mr van Broembson, Civil Commissioner at Fort Victoria.

Mac now stepped up the area under cane from 45 to 300 acres. Initially only a crusher and two mills were used and 96 tons of raw sugar were produced. Towards the end of the month Mac took by lorry 10 tons of the first milled sugar over to the refinery in Bulawayo where he proudly handed it over to his great friend, Stanley Cooke, the manager.

Still more money was needed for all the development. In 1940 Mac and Moubray again visited Natal, this time in search of finance. George Crookes and one of his companies took up the unissued shares in the Triangle Company.

In 1944 Mac realised that the full development of the estate was something beyond his financial resources. He sold his company to the Southern Rhodesian Government who created a Sugar Industry Board which was promulgated on 22 December 1944 and run under the chairmanship of an old friend and adviser, Mr Cecil Robertson, the Director of Irrigation. The Board then built the Esquilingwe weir, a few miles above Jatala, to augment the water supply.

Mac stayed on at Triangle until 1945, when he went overseas and joined a fishing fleet in Stornaway in the Hebrides. In 1947 the ever resourceful man got himself a lift back to Salisbury on a freight flight which took 13 days from London.

In the National Archives there is only one report of the Sugar Industry Board, and that is the ninth annual report for the year ended 31 December 1953. In conclusion the Board writes that it …

> … feels that it has fulfilled its function of proving the potentialities of the Estate for the production of cane under irrigation in the lowveld, having overcome many initial difficulties, and therefore it is desirable at this stage to encourage private enterprise to take an interest in the venture as this would be likely to result in economies in operating and administrative costs.

By 1954 the Sugar Board was running at a great loss and the government was prepared to close operations down. Only 1,189 acres had been planted to cane by this time. Mac happened to be in Parliament when the matter was being debated and he had a hurried conversation with Mr Ray (now Sir Ray) Stockil, then Member of Parliament for Fort Victoria. As a result Ray Stockil persuaded the government to persevere with the scheme until such time as it could be sold to private enterprise. At this time the Sugar Board approached Hulett and Sons to take over, but as the latter were fully committed in Natal, the offer was turned down.

However, before the end of 1954, a sugar syndicate consisting of a number of Natal planters, approached the Rhodesian Government and purchased Triangle. The operative part of the estate, about 12,600 acres, plus the mill and other assets, including cattle, were sold to the syndicate which leased the remainder of the land. This syndicate agreed to place over

80 settlers on the land and the first three to take up 400-acre farms were Brigadier Peter Hingeston and Nainby Starling – both of whom had come up from Natal to organise the take-over – and Ritz Eastwood, an accountant from Salisbury.

In 1956 the Natal Syndicate decided to sell out and negotiations took place between Hulett's and the Rhodesian Government resulting in Triangle becoming a wholly-owned subsidiary of Hulett's. They however refused to introduce the settler scheme. The government then agreed to build the 35-square-mile Kyle Dam and the 40-mile-long Kyle canal, subject to Triangle contributing a sum of £300,000 towards the construction costs. The Kyle Dam, with a capacity of over 255,000 million gallons, was opened by Sir Edgar Whitehead on 11 May 1961 and Mac's initial small sugar venture on Triangle then expanded beyond all bounds. Hulett's installed the biggest over head irrigation scheme in the world at an initial cost of £175,000 and by 1967 Triangle was producing 160,000 tons of sugar from 30,000 acres of cane.

Fantastic development followed. The four-and-a-half-square-mile Bangala Dam was built on the Mtilikwe below Kyle, Esquilingwe weir was enlarged, and Triangle constructed a road to Mbizi Station, the nearest railhead at a cost of £25,000. In October 1962 the control of Triangle Sugar Estates changed again and this time passed to a consortium of Natal Sugar Companies. The tempo of development and expansion was even further increased. In September 1964 the first train steamed into the new railhead at Triangle Station and the new Triangle mill erected shortly before. Sir Humphrey Gibbs, then Governor, drove the engine as the train left Mbizi Siding.

In the meantime, soon after his return from overseas in 1947, Mac had bought Glendale Farm, ten miles south of Fort Victoria. Here he ran a few hundred head of cattle with frequent visits to his first love, the lowveld. On 29 December 1949 he married Miss Marjorie Cooke who had been receptionist at the Land Bank, Salisbury. On many occasions a very old friend of Mac's, Brigadier 'Scrubbs' Hartshorn, accompanied Mac and Marjorie on hunting trips, when they would hunt the buffalo and other game from horseback.

In 1957 the MacDougalls sold the farm and went on a long trip to Australia and New Zealand, spending five months in each country. They trekked around in a Volkswagen pick-up with a canvas canopy, and much enjoyed seeing the cattle and the sugar in Australia. Mac even spent some time 'logging' in a timber camp – just for the experience, but no mean feat for a man of 76!

Back from Australia in 1958, Mac availed himself of a longstanding promise made by his friend, Alfred Gifford, a Cattle Inspector, back in 1931. When he had then been discussing with Gifford the possibility of dam-sites on the Mtilikwe to augment the water supply he had just brought on to the land through the two tunnels, Gifford had offered to show Mac a very promising proposition and had promptly driven Mac to the site at which the Kyle Dam would be built more than a quarter-century later. Mac was most impressed. Later, when the two men were sitting smoking on the verandah of Gifford's homestead on his Oatlands Farm which over-looked the dam site, Gifford remarked: 'Of course a dam will never be built there!' Mac replied, 'I bet it will!' 'Well, if it is, I'll give you 250 acres around the kopje, on which you can build yourself a house!' retorted Gifford.

By the time the dam was completed in 1959, Gifford had passed on, but the son occupying the farm at the time honoured his father's promise. That year the MacDougalls built their last home, which they called 'Dunollie' (the castle of that name having been the seat of the head of the clan) on the kopje mentioned from which they had a good view of the lake. Here they spent many happy years boating and fishing.

In 1962 Mac was awarded the OBE in the New Year's Honour List and, wearing his sheath-knife from which he was never parted, he received the decoration from the Governor, Sir Humphrey Gibbs. To quote from Mrs Strover's brochure written on Mac's life for the Triangle Murray MacDougall museum:

> Mac's love of Triangle and the whole of the lowveld had never waned and he took a keen interest in all the developments that were taking place. On 2 April 1964 the Triangle Company arranged for him to be flown over the area in the company's plane, and one can imagine the wonder and pride which stirred his heart as he and Marjorie gazed down at the sparkling waters of the great Kyle canal, snaking its way for 42 miles from Esquilingwe weir through acres of emerald sugarcane to the dark green, orderly fields of citrus at Hippo Valley, while smoke billowed into the sky from the sugarmills. Murray

MacDougall's dream of a great sugar industry was a dream no more. The branch railway-line to Chiredzi from Mbizi was on its way and soon the sugar from Triangle and Hippo Valley would be transported by rail to the refineries.

In May 1964, Mac suffered a stroke and, though convinced to the end that he would recover, he died in St Anne's Hospital on 30 May 1964. Thus ended the life of this outstanding character.

A few weeks before his death Mac had received a special invitation from Cedric Gibbs ('Gibbo' to his host of friends), a former sereant-major in the BSA Police and then business-manager of Triangle, inviting him to the opening of the new mill by the then very new Prime Minister, Ian Douglas Smith. In his letter Gibbo mentioned that Mac need not wear a tie, knowing that Mac hated dressing up. Owing to his death, and at the special request of Ross Armstrong, Chairman of the Board, Mac's seat of honour was left unoccupied during the opening.

Later, in a simple ceremony, Mac's ashes were laid to rest under a large rock under the marula tree in front of his house on the hill. This last duty was performed by his great friend and hunting companion, Brigadier 'Scrubbs' Hartshorn.

Outpost, February and March 1977

www.ingramcontent.com/pod-product-compliance
Lightning Source LLC
Chambersburg PA
CBHW050141170426
43197CB00011B/1914